More praise for *Thrivers*

"*Thrivers* is a call to action. Our children are hurting, and *Thrivers* shows you the cost—not only in accurately describing the challenges our children face but also showing how to make it better. I urge any person who cares about children and the health of our communities to read *Thrivers* and apply the wisdom and common sense advice you will find in its pages to every aspect of your life."
    —Rosalind Wiseman, author of *Queen Bees and Wannabes, Masterminds & Wingmen* and *Owning Up*

"*Thrivers* brilliantly weaves together research and stories that grab your heart as they teach you how to be the parent you hope to be—a stunning master class in parenting, from pre-K through adulthood."
    —Catherine Steiner-Adair, Ed.D., author of *The Big Disconnect: Protecting Childhood and Family Relationships in the Digital Age*

"*Thrivers* can be summed up in one word, POWERFUL. In a world that is in crisis, with a generation that is emotionally crumbling, Borba gives us hope as well as the tools to help give our children and teens the moral courage they need to flourish in an unpredictable life. We must turn our strivers into thrivers! A mandatory read for every person who cares about raising kind, compassionate, and successful children."
    —Sue Scheff, author of *Shame Nation: The Global Epidemic of Online Hate*

"Michele Borba is the coach, mentor, and motivator that today's parents crave. This brilliant guide—full of heart and backed by research—redefines success and shows us how to raise happier, healthier kids who will become champions of the things that last and matter."
    —Kari Kampakis, author of *Love Her Well: 10 Ways to Find Joy and Connection with Your Teenage Daughter*

"*Thrivers* offers both science-based information and respectful, practical, and effective tools. Full of activities and ideas to cultivate the skills and mindset kids need to thrive, Borba encourages parents to use everyday moments to respond in ways that build relational and neural connections to promote optimal development, independence, and success. More than ever, our children need us to parent in ways that promote growth and resilience in the face of adversity, and *Thrivers* can serve as an essential guide."
    —Dr. Tina Payne Bryson, *New York Times* bestselling co-author of *The Whole-Brain Child*, *No-Drama Discipline*, *The Yes Brain*, and *The Power of Showing Up*, and author of *The Bottom Line for Baby*

"There's a huge gap between what we, as parents, say we want for our children (to be good people) and what our kids say we want for them (achievement). This book is the absolutely perfect book to help us close that gap, to help our children thrive and be all they can be!"
    —Ellen Galinsky, author of *Mind in the Making: The Seven Life Essential Skills Every Child Needs*

RECENT BOOKS BY MICHELE BORBA, ED.D.

*UnSelfie: Why Empathetic Kids Succeed in
Our All-About-Me World*

*End Peer Cruelty, Build Empathy: The Proven 6Rs of Bullying
Prevention That Create Inclusive, Safe, and Caring Schools*

*The Big Book of Parenting Solutions: 101 Answers to Your
Everyday Challenges and Wildest Worries*

*Don't Give Me That Attitude!: 24 Rude, Selfish, Insensitive
Things Kids Do and How to Stop Them*

*Building Moral Intelligence: The Seven Essential Virtues That
Teach Kids to Do the Right Thing*

*No More Misbehavin': 38 Difficult Behaviors and
How to Stop Them*

*Nobody Likes Me, Everybody Hates Me: The Top 25 Friendship
Problems and How to Solve Them*

*12 Simple Secrets Real Moms Know: Getting Back to Basics
and Raising Happy Kids*

*Parents Do Make a Difference: How to Raise Kids with Solid
Character, Strong Minds, and Caring Hearts*

Thrivers

The Surprising Reasons Why
Some Kids Struggle and
Others Shine

Michele Borba, Ed.D.

G. P. PUTNAM'S SONS
NEW YORK

PUTNAM
— EST. 1838 —

G. P. PUTNAM'S SONS
Publishers Since 1838
An imprint of Penguin Random House LLC
penguinrandomhouse.com

ISBN 9780593085271
eBook ISBN 9780593085288

Printed in the United States of America
1 3 5 7 9 10 8 6 4 2

Book design by Ellen Cipriano

Note to the reader:

All quotes in this book are from actual phone or face-to-face interviews with teens, parents, and educators. Stories are based on cases of children, teens, and their families and educators whom I have known and worked with over the past several years. A few stories are composite cases of children I have treated or interviewed. All names and some identifying characteristics have been changed to protect the privacy of the individuals involved. All examples from schools and counseling centers are gathered from my actual observations. The exceptions are children and teens interviewed for newspapers or written about in books as examples of children displaying the seven Character Strengths of Thrivers. The three-part organizational format in *Thrivers* of "Heart, Mind, and Will" is based on the ancient work of the Greek philosophers and Aristotle, who wrote, "Educating the mind without educating the heart is no education at all." I agree wholeheartedly.

With love to Charlie,
who adores baseball, basketball hoops,
football, balloons, and Daniel Tiger.

And to our new Hazel: We can't wait to discover
who you are and what you love!
May you both thrive!

CONTENTS

Introduction: Running on Empty: We're Raising a
Generation of Strivers, Not Thrivers   1

PART ONE—NURTURING HEART

Chapter 1 Self-Confidence
Thrivers focus on "who," not "what."   27

Chapter 2 Empathy
Thrivers think "we," not "me."   65

PART TWO—DEVELOPING MIND

Chapter 3 Self-Control
Thrivers can think straight and put the brakes
on impulses.   103

Chapter 4 Integrity
Thrivers have a strong moral code and stick to it.   137

Chapter 5 Curiosity
Thrivers are out-of-the-box thinkers.   162

PART THREE—CULTIVATING WILL

Chapter 6 Perseverance

Thrivers finish what they start and don't
need gold stars.   197

Chapter 7 Optimism

Thrivers find the silver lining.   224

Epilogue   259

ACKNOWLEDGMENTS   265

NOTES   269

INDEX   289

BOOK DISCUSSION GUIDE   299

HOW TO CONTACT DR. MICHELE BORBA   305

"Character is destiny."

—Heraclitus, 535–475 BC,
Athens, Greece

Thrivers

Introduction

Running on Empty:
We're Raising a Generation of Strivers, Not Thrivers

"It's like we're being produced to be test takers.
We're missing the pieces on how to be people."

—*Aaron, twelve, Los Angeles*

OUR KIDS ARE IN TROUBLE.

That simple, terrifying fact was brought home to me when I reached sixteen-year-old Eva via phone at seven o'clock on a Sunday evening. She sounded stressed, and I asked if there was a better time to chat.

"No, my schedule is always jammed," she said, "and I'd love to talk about what it's like to be a teen these days."

Eva hardly looks like a kid most of us would worry about. She lives in an affluent area near Newport Beach, California, and attends a posh private school. She realizes that she's privileged. Her dream is to be accepted into a top-tier college with a Division 1 women's swim team; UCLA and University of Texas are her first picks.

So Eva wakes up at 4:00 a.m. each weekday for her 5:00 a.m. private swim practice, and then heads to school. She's an honor student with a 4.3 grade point average and takes four AP classes plus French III and physics honors. After school there are two more hours of swim practice with her team; once a week is school newspaper and student government. She's home at 6:30 p.m., has a quick family meal, and then has three to four hours of homework and thirty minutes of SAT test-taking practice.

"I got a 1450 last time and need to improve by at least a hundred points to have any chance of getting into my dream colleges," she explained. She finally heads to bed at midnight.

I was weary just listening. Eva averages five hours of sleep a night (eight to ten hours are recommended, but only 15 percent of teens come close), so she is sleep-deprived.

"What do you do for fun?" I asked.

"I'm wiped out most of the time so I try to connect with friends on social media." She laughed. "I know I'm fortunate to attend a great school and my parents love me, but I worry about disappointing them if I don't get into Stanford—that's where they want me to go." And the teen admitted that she was not alone.

"All my friends are stressed and overwhelmed. We're just burned out."

Welcome to the "running on empty" generation. Eva's age cohort (called Generation Z if born from the mid-1990s on) is smart and dearly loved. They are more inclusive and open-minded.[1] ("We're the first generation to have dolls that can be boys, girls, neither, or both," Eva pointed out. "That's got to be good, right?") They're well educated with high aspirations for college and their future.

But they're also less happy and more stressed, lonely, depressed, and suicidal when compared with any previous generation—and those descriptions were identified *prior* to COVID-19 and all the resulting anxiety it produced.

Every few months I called to check in with Eva until one day I was surprised that her mother answered. From the sound of her voice, I knew something was wrong. Through her sobs she explained that her daughter was in the hospital suffering from severe depression.

"I didn't realize how sad and overwhelmed she felt," the mom sobbed. "I thought I'd given her everything she needed to be happy and successful, but I was so wrong. I missed helping her enjoy herself."

I hear so many similar heart-wrenching stories from parents, but always when they realize that their kids are not faring well. Why are these kids struggling so hard, when they seem to have so much? Why does this generation strive but fail to thrive? I decided to dig deeper.

THE GENERATION OF STRIVERS

"We are college and career ready, but sure aren't 'human' ready."
—*Erin, sixteen, Greer, South Carolina*

A few days later, I was halfway across the country, at a middle-class middle school in Boston. The security guard escorted me to the library where twelve middle school students were waiting to share their views on what it's like to be a kid today. All were chosen by the counselor based on my criteria: diverse, articulate students with a "pulse on the social scene." This was my twenty-fifth student focus group, so I had an idea of what to expect, but I was still interested in seeing what they were going to tell me. This is a unique generation that has faced a pandemic, school shootings, terrorism, and natural disasters along with intense pressure to succeed like no other past cohort.

"Tell me about your generation," I inquired.

I looked out at the group of students in front of me. I saw what I always see: a bunch of kids who were thoughtful, sincere, and frankly amazed that someone wanted to hear their opinions.

A blond twelve-year-old named Amelia was first to share. "We're definitely the most stressed generation, and it's only getting worse." The group agreed. (I've yet to hear a kid disagree.)

"Do your parents know how stressed you are?" Every kid shook their head.

"We hide our anxiety," a brown-haired boy wearing a Nike shirt explained. "It doesn't work telling our parents because they don't understand what it's like to be a kid."

Then I asked these eleven-, twelve-, and thirteen-year-olds to describe their age group. Listening to their comments was when I knew it was time to alter our parenting course.

"Every friend I know says they feel stressed."

"We're lonely because we're so immersed in social media and losing face-to-face connection."

"Our generation always focuses on trying to make everything picture-perfect, so we're drained."

"We're constantly compared to each other so never feel good enough."

"We're afraid of failing because our grades mean too much so we're always stressed."

"Our lives are crammed, but we're social beings with no time for friends and lonely."

"We are forced to grow up too quickly and need more time to be kids and have friends."

"We lack passion because everything is pushed on us so we don't know who we are."

"Our generation has had lockdown drills since kindergarten. They get to you after a while. And then we were sheltered in place because of that coronavirus thing. It's scary."

"We may look good on the outside, but we're not so good inside. We're kind of lost."

Every student group I interview—regardless of zip code—shares similar descriptions. These are greatly loved kids: warm, bright, with endless opportunities. Their parents think they have it all together, and that they are setting up their kids for future success. So why are they so much unhappier than kids in the past? Why are they struggling? Leave it to a kid to give the best answer.

An unfinished wooden puzzle lay on the next table. The box cover showed children from different countries playing together in the world, but pieces were missing. A red-haired boy named Aiden kept staring at it and finally said, "That puzzle is us: we're trying to fit into the world but can't because we're missing pieces."

"Which pieces are you missing?" I asked.

"The pieces on how to be people, like how to get along, handle mistakes, cope with stress, that kind of stuff—pieces that build your character and make you human. But we're being raised to just be products, so we all feel empty."

And suddenly the mystery of why this generation feels so unhappy, overwhelmed, stressed, and lonely made perfect sense. We told them that if they strive for more—more likes, better grades, greater accolades—they'd be happy. But these young Strivers aren't happy . . . and what's more, they're not thriving. They are stunted, anxious, and unhappy. We have raised a generation of kids who have more of everything, but we've forgotten to give them the thing they need most to succeed: the mental and moral qualities that make them human.

Character is what builds inner strength, genuineness, and wholeness and helps turn kids who strive for the next gold ring into young adults who thrive in a fast-paced, ever-changing world. When kids are missing character strengths like optimism, curiosity, empathy, and perseverance their development is incomplete. They often don't succeed outside the very narrowly defined parameters of school and class-rooms. They're not ready for the uncertain world that awaits them—a world that's even more unpredictable with every passing year. In short, they turn out like beautifully wrapped packages but are missing the gifts inside.

It is *not* too late to fill in the missing pieces in our kids' development, but it requires switching our myopic obsession with scores, grades, and big fat résumés to a farsighted view of what they will need to lead meaningful lives. At present, our smart, loved, stellar test takers are failing to launch and handle life. The character void in their development undermines their human abilities and reduces their potential to thrive. Character is the missing piece.

But here's the good news: It's not too late. Character is not innate—you're not born with it. Character Strengths can be taught.

In fact, they *must* be taught.

This book shows parents, teachers, and other educators how to instill those missing character pieces to produce strong, resilient kids with the complete package of strong heart, mind, and will. A kid who has character is what I call a Thriver—a person who is ready and able to take on the twenty-first century. But first, let me tell you why this situation really is so dire—and why all of us need to pay attention.

WHY WE SHOULD WORRY

"There's an amazing amount of depression and anxiety. Seventy percent of my friends are in therapy; forty percent are on medication. We're hurting but nobody does anything until another kid is suicidal."

—*Ava, fifteen, Green Bay, Wisconsin*

I've been an educational consultant for over four decades and worked with hundreds of parents, teachers, and children from poverty to privilege across the United States and around the world. I've seen child trends come and go, but I've never been more concerned about kids than now. The urgency in writing this book was triggered by an email from a distraught mom seeking help for her suburban community:

> "We have forty dead kids in two-and-a-half years to suicide within a twenty-mile radius. Most are white, affluent, high-achieving males who did not use drugs but hung themselves. Most look like your kids and mine. The last seven have been females—two with guns."

The following week a high school guidance counselor contacted me with a similar plea:

> "Our community is in crisis as we live in a suicide belt and are extremely short on therapists. We don't know the cause, but something is terribly wrong with our kids."

Each week educators voiced similar worries.

> "Something about kids has changed."
> "They seem overwhelmed and anxious."
> "They're suffering."

They were concerned about younger students as well.

> "Our third graders can't focus as well and are quicker to anger."
> "First graders have trouble coping."
> "Five-year-olds worry about failing."

A speaking engagement in Palo Alto, California, twenty minutes from where I grew up, put the child scene into crisis mode. Parent volunteers started a Track Watch program after a high number of teens killed themselves on the train tracks.[2] The ten-year suicide rate at their two high-achieving high schools is four to five times the national average. But the mental health epidemic is not confined to the Bay Area. Over the past decade, reports from coast to coast show teens and young adults to be more depressed and suffering higher levels of psychological distress than their predecessors.[3] Visit your local high school bathroom and you'll find suicide hotline numbers posted for students.

Teens confirm that they are burned out and worry about their well-being and for their peers. Sara, a bright, red-haired Austin, Texas, fifteen-year-old, summed up what I often hear. "The worst place I can be is in my head, but I don't know anyone who feels good about who they are. No matter how hard you work, you never feel good enough."

Jack, a Pittsburgh teen who said he was just accepted to Yale, still felt empty. "High school is nonstop studying, test taking, filling out applications, and worrying. I never could come up for air."

Josh, a musically gifted Wisconsin junior with a 4.3 grade point average, said, "Our days are so jammed with school, SAT prep, studying, and activities that I can never do things to recharge, like being with friends and music. We're all burned out." Burned out, and their lives are just beginning.

I wish I could tell these kids one important thing.

Grades don't matter.

Okay, maybe that's a little hyperbolic. Grades do matter, of course. They can open the door to a scholarship, college or university acceptance, and employment.

But what I mean when I say "grades don't matter" is that they aren't the gold-plated indicator of success they might have been even a generation ago—even as the race for those grades is more fraught than ever before. Today's college admissions process has become all-consuming, frantic, and frankly terrifying, but once teens receive those coveted acceptance letters, there's still no relief. Anxiety, loneliness, and feelings of emptiness continue, and in all too many cases increase. *The New York Times* reported that in 1985, 18 percent of college freshmen said they "felt overwhelmed by all I had to do." By 2018 that number had surged to 41 percent. One in four college students was diagnosed with or treated for a mental health disorder in the prior year; one-fifth of all students surveyed have contemplated suicide,[4] and colleges are deeply concerned.

We've raised a generation of children who are really great at reaching for that brass ring. They're achieving, studying, and working hard. They're also full of anxiety and putting enormous pressure on themselves. They're Strivers. No matter what they do and how hard they push, they never feel "good enough." And when challenges arise, they often quit because they lack the inner reserve and preparedness that provide inner strength to endure.

I delivered a keynote to 2,500 university counselors last year, and they confirmed there is a mental health epidemic. A Princeton counselor told me, "The students are incredibly smart, but lonely. Something is missing." A Harvard counselor added, "It's as though they're soulless." A Stanford psychologist summed up what everyone felt: "They're empty, and that's a very sad commentary for America." Indeed.

One-third of college students drop out at the end of their freshman year. The United States now has the highest college dropout rate in the industrial world.[5] "Stress, inability to deal with expectations, and helicoptering parenting" are cited as leading causes.[6]

Maybe what we should be telling kids is not that grades don't matter . . . but that they're not the *only* thing that matters. Teaching them otherwise is a huge injustice to children.

TURNING STRIVERS INTO THRIVERS

> "We're growing up in a highly competitive, academically
> rigorous environment that breeds stress and constantly
> compares us with each other. It feels like we're being raised to be
> scores, not kids. We're just burned out."
>
> —*Gabi, seventeen, Chicago*

Helping children learn to thrive has been my life's work. I began my career teaching at-risk youth in Northern California. Most of my students lived in poverty, suffered abuse, or were challenged by learning, emotional, or physical disabilities, and I always wondered what I could do to help them succeed. I worked on my doctorate in educational psychology and counseling and studied resilience and learned an important lesson: *Thrivers are made not born.* Children clearly need safe, loving, and structured childhoods, but they also need autonomy, competence, and agency to flourish. Thriving is comprised of acquired skills. I developed ways to teach these skills to my students and discovered that they improved not only their academic performance but also their behavior, confidence, and optimism.

Over the next years I trained the strategies to educators, psychologists, and counselors at schools, education departments, trauma centers, foster care organizations, universities, and eighteen army bases, and then to hundreds of parents in forty-eight states and sixteen countries. (I'll never forget a dad in Cairo who thanked me. "I always thought parenting was like being a member of a food chain where you basically kept your kid nourished and protected. I didn't know I could actually help him become a more successful, capable human being.") I recognized that thriving delays were no longer confined to low-income or special-needs populations. Today kids from poverty to privilege are failing to thrive, but those growing up in affluent communities are especially prone to acute stress, loneliness, depression, and feelings of emptiness.

Suniya Luthar, a professor of psychology at Arizona State University, discovered that American teens from upper-middle-class families are more likely to have higher rates of depression, anxiety, and substance abuse than any other socioeconomic group of young people.[7] "Privileged young are much more vulnerable than in previous generations," Luthar says. "The evidence points to one cause: the pressure for high octane achievement."[8] Kids are finding it impossible to keep up with our unrealistic expectations of success, and adults must accept blame.

The root of the burnout problem and our children's dismal mental health is our obsession with developing kids' cognitive abilities because we assume that those skills and subjects that boost academic performance are the holy grail for success. Parenting is now an all-consuming effort to fine-tune children's intellectual growth. The more we cram into kids' brains, the smarter they get—or so we think—and so our child-raising roles turned from "parent" (a *noun*) to "parenting" (a *verb*). From the time our kids are toddlers, we plot their education with the intensity of an army planning a battle and fret over every move. The coveted prize is college acceptance, and the more prestigious the institution the better. Everything is an opportunity for raising kids' IQ and stimulating cognitive development, because we believe doing so improves their grades, scores, rank, and degrees. And how we worry!

Sherman Oaks, California, moms shared their fears if a top-tier preschool didn't accept their *two-year-olds*. "My baby's educational career will basically be over," one said. A Boca Raton counselor told me that a dad took his kid out of school to view Harvard. "You have to start early," the parent explained. *The child was five.*

Gus Knitt, the school superintendent of a small Wisconsin community, told me that the previous three Pardeeville High valedictorians said their high school memories were of studying and test taking. (Educators are now altering school days to free up student time for deeper learning, working on projects, and connecting with one another.) Everywhere I go, parents and educators tell me that their kids are burning out. Carefree days of unstructured play in the sandbox, cloud glazing, and kite flying are replaced by adult-led cramming, tutoring, and flash card sessions. And along the way, we spoiled childhood and left our kids feeling depleted.

Thrivers feel "We've got this": they meet the world on their own terms because they know they can control their own destiny. And so they keep trying despite challenges and are more likely to rebound from those challenges and overcome adversity with confidence. Strivers may have similar hopes and dreams but lack inner strength and an "I can do it" mind-set, so when confronted by obstacles they often fall short of success. But what makes kids become Thrivers or Strivers? We now know that answer, and it comes from science.

Over fifty years ago, Emmy Werner, a psychologist at the University of California, Davis, began a groundbreaking four-decade investigation of hundreds of children living on the Hawaiian island of Kauai. Nearly a third of the children were born into poverty or faced problems including family discord, parental mental illness, and family histories of substance abuse. Werner hoped to examine the impact of stressful life events on children's development from birth to the age of forty.

Two-thirds of the group developed serious problems like behavior issues, substance abuse, and mental health problems. But would any thrive? The findings surprised even Werner: one out of three of these children defied odds and grew into "competent, confident, and caring" adults and thrived in school and life *despite* adversity.[9] Other pioneering psychologists studied children experiencing homelessness, abuse, terrorism, war, and poverty, and were also amazed to discover that a remarkable number overcame trauma.[10] In fact, many "had surprising good outcomes in spite of serious threats to adaptation or development."[11] Some appeared even "stress-resistant."[12] They were Thrivers. But why?

Werner dug deeper and paid the closest attention to the *other* third: the kids in the high-risk group who defied and overcame the odds *in spite of* their hardships. She discovered that despite enormously different types of trauma, many resilient children shared two unmistakable strengths: strong bonds with at least one supportive adult and a set of learned traits that served as protective factors in their childhoods to help them to meet the world on *their own* terms.[13] The kids weren't necessarily gifted, and they didn't have particularly impressive test scores, but they "used whatever skills they had effectively," Werner commented. And perhaps most important: "they relied on themselves—not others—to solve their problems so that they, and not their circumstances, affected their achievements."[14]

The surprising reason why some kids struggle while others shine isn't due to genes, grade point averages, IQ points, particular sports, instruments, school types, or stress management classes but to a reliance on a few Character Strengths that they learned along the way to steer their own lives in a positive direction. Those traits and a caring adult champion serve to shield stress so children can keep on with their dreams with calm confidence, overcome adversity, and ultimately triumph. Best yet, the traits can be fostered and derive from common resources and practices that we can instill in our kids.

Applying the science of resilience can help *all* kids thrive; it just requires switching our mind-set. Instead of using interventions and a "fix the kid" mentality, we teach children protective factors so they can maintain strength in uncertain, challenging times and become their personal best.

This book is based on an idea that children are stressed, lonely, overwhelmed, and depleted because we are using a misguided, outdated child development formula that fails to foster traits that help them flourish mentally, morally, and emotionally. Sometimes termed "noncognitive skills," "personality traits," or "virtues,"[15] I call them Character Strengths. Though often trivialized as "soft and fluffy," character qualities, science says, are equally important to academic success and peak performance and core to resilience and mental well-being.

Character Strengths can and must be taught to our children. Doing so will stop the burnout epidemic, serve as protection against toxic stress and adversity, and help kids see themselves as more than scores but as human beings who strive to become their personal best—in short, Thrivers.

THE SEVEN ESSENTIAL CHARACTER STRENGTHS OF THRIVERS

"It's too late to fix things for my friends, but we need to find a quick solution before it's too late for younger kids. They're going to be worse off because they're already getting pushed too much, too soon."

—*Sophia, fourteen, Dallas*

For the past decade I've combed research on traits most highly correlated to optimizing children's thriving abilities and identified seven
Character Strengths: self-confidence, empathy, self-control, integrity,
curiosity, perseverance, and optimism. Instilling the seven boosts mental toughness, social competence, self-awareness, moral strength, and
emotional agility. But learning these strengths also reduces anxiety
and increases resilience, so kids *can* cope with adversity, solve problems, bounce back, develop healthy relationships, and boost confidence—
everything they need to lead meaningful *and* successful lives.

The selection of each of the seven Character Strengths was based
on six benchmarks. Each one is:

1. Proven by leading research to increase children's resilience.
2. Deemed "essential" for the twenty-first century and world
   readiness by the Occupational Information Network, Pew
   Research, the Fourth Industrial Revolution, and World
   Economic Forum.
3. Recognized as a universal strength that boosts moral or
   performance character.
4. Shown to optimize learning performance and academic
   achievement.
5. Teachable and not fixed or based on personality, IQ, or
   income.
6. Shown to increase mental health and well-being.

What's more, the kids I interviewed verified that the seven traits would
help reduce their feelings of emptiness. "Those are the traits that would
help us be our best in school *and* life," said a San Jose middle schooler.
We have work to do: each of the seven traits is also declining in American youth.

Part one shows you how to help your child develop strengths to nurture a caring heart.

- **Self-Confidence,** so he recognizes his strengths, accepts his weaknesses, and can apply that knowledge to help him find the best path to life success.
- **Empathy,** so he can recognize and understand the feelings and needs of himself and others and develop healthy relationships.

Part two is all about helping your child develop qualities of a strong mind.

- **Self-Control** will help your child learn to think straight, manage strong, unhealthy emotions, and reduce personal distress so he can cope with whatever comes his way.
- **Integrity,** so he will adopt ethical values that help him develop a solid moral code and guide his life and relations with others.
- **Curiosity** will help your child be open to possibilities, acquire new information, make discoveries, and stir creativity so he is inspired to follow his dreams.

Part three provides ways to help your child cultivate a determined will.

- **Perseverance** emboldens him to keep on when everything else makes it easier to give up, and realize that he can handle mistakes and learn from failure to triumph with his goals.
- **Optimism** will give him the tools to handle challenges with

a more positive outlook, thwart depression, be more hopeful about his world and believe that life is meaningful.

Though each strength can be taught to children from sandbox to prom, most kids have never been schooled in the teachings of character so they face a huge life disadvantage. *Thrivers* provides those crucial missing lessons so kids will thrive.

THE MULTIPLIER EFFECT

"We're burning out from working extremely hard with almost impossible goals. Then we're not sleeping, being with friends or see light at the end of the tunnel so we feel empty."
—*Ramon, fifteen, Beverly Hills, California*

Each Character Strength improves a child's thriving potential as well as academic performance, but is always more powerful when combined with another strength because they create a Multiplier Effect. In fact, one reason Thrivers are more adept at navigating life is because they use several strengths together.

Self-Confidence + Curiosity increases self-knowledge and
builds self-assuredness and creativity.
Self-Control + Perseverance boosts the chance of reaching a
goal and achieving success.
Empathy + Curiosity helps find common ground and strengthens relationships.
Self-Control + Integrity puts the brakes on temptations to help
you do what's right.

Optimism + Perseverance + Curiosity deepens learning, boosts
conviction, and optimizes flow.

Integrity + Curiosity + Empathy enhances purpose and can
start a social movement.

Pairing *any* Character Strength with another is a more certain
road to success; put three traits together and you multiply odds of increasing potential and peak performance. But there is also a "depletion
factor": as Character Strengths *diminish* from children's developmental repertoire, their odds of success reduce and they are more likely to
feel overwhelmed, burnt out and depleted. That is what is happening to
kids now.

Add heavy, prolonged doses of unhealthy stress to any trait and
you get burnout. Maya, a sixteen-year-old teen from Palo Alto explained it perfectly: "A lot of burnout is from working extremely hard
and still not seeing any payoff. No matter how hard you work there's
still no guarantee you'll get into college so you wonder, 'What's the
point?' So you feel purposeless."

All our energy has gone into stretching kids' cognitive abilities and
neglecting their human side—the source of energy, joy, inspiration,
and meaning. The good news: focusing on character can flip that equation and teach your kids how to find happiness, calm, and wonder in
the world.

HOW TO USE THIS BOOK

"Whatever I do is never enough. I always have
to do more and more to satisfy my parents."
—*Caden, fourteen, Houston*

The epidemic of unhappy Strivers is real, but it can be cured. This book provides solutions to get us back on track so we raise strong, caring, resilient, thriving kids. Each chapter is filled with evidence-backed strategies and skills you can easily teach your child from preschool through high school. I'll also share the latest scientific findings from top neuroscientists, psychologists, Olympic athletes, MIT scholars, as well as Navy SEALs. And throughout, I'll provide stories of real children who faced enormous obstacles like racism, attention deficits, abuse, and physical challenges but thrived because their parents helped them develop these strengths. You'll also find lists of books for varying ages and dozens of easy ways to boost the strength as part of your everyday routines.

The ultimate goal is to help your child adopt each Character Strength as a lifelong habit to optimize his potential and thrive. Each trait is also composed of three abilities and a few teachable skills that reduce burnout, increase success, and nurture self-sufficiency. So focus on one ability a month and practice it with your child—or even better, as a family—a few minutes a day until he can use it without reminders. When you no longer coax, prompt, or remind, it means your child has internalized the lesson and can use it without you anywhere, anytime.

Over the years I've observed brilliant lessons about character and realized that the best teachers never used worksheets or lectures but "wove them into" their lessons. I'll never forget a Fresno teacher. He read the fable "*The Three Little Pigs*" and then divided his fifth graders into groups to discuss what they learned about character from the pigs.

"The first two pigs were lazy so the Big Bad Wolf quickly blew down their straw and stick houses," a dark-haired boy noticed.

"Yep, they needed perseverance like the third pig," a redheaded girl added.

"But the third little pig also was optimistic and used his creativity to figure what foundation would stand up to the wolf," said a freckled kid.

"Don't forget the third pig's integrity and empathy," a blond-haired boy chimed in. His comment surprised his group members.

"Empathy?" they asked.

"Yep, empathy," he said. "That third pig knew his brothers had poor self-control and wouldn't take time to build strong houses. When their houses blew down he didn't leave them in the cold, he gave them refuge in his."

"Wow," another girl commented, "that third pig sure had a lot of good Character Strengths." And all her teammates nodded in agreement.

I looked at the teacher and we smiled. No fancy tutors, flash cards, or lectures were used to help students understand the importance of the Character Strengths; just retelling an old fable heard countless times.

Essential Character Strengths that help kids thrive can be taught to our children, but best lessons are always natural and included in their daily lives. One chat or book read about a Character Strength is never effective. Instead, find meaningful ways to nurture the seven Thriver traits: point them out, model, discuss, and prioritize them until your children adopt them as an indelible part of their makeup.

To thrive in a technologically driven, fear-based, rapidly changing twenty-first-century world, kids need more than grades, scores, and trophies; they need strength of heart, mind, and will. The seven essential Character Strengths build strong inner foundations so kids can handle life's inevitable huffs and puffs, lead successful, fulfilled lives, and *never run on empty*. Developing those traits may well be the greatest gift you can give your children because they will have protective factors to face inevitable hardships and be more likely to live meaningful lives without you.

ASSESSING YOUR CHILD'S CHARACTER STRENGTHS

Answering the statements below will help you determine your child's Character Strengths that help her thrive. There are no right or wrong answers. This is only for you to see where your child is right now and help you determine which traits are his strengths and which to encourage. To evaluate your child's strengths, write the number you think best represents your child's current level on the line following each statement.

5 = Always, 4 = Frequently, 3 = Sometimes, 2 = Rarely, 1 = Never

MY CHILD . . .

1. Can easily and accurately describe her special strengths and positive qualities _____

2. Is proud and confident in her abilities; enjoys being herself _____

3. Focuses mostly on her strengths instead of weaknesses and past failures _____

4. Speaks mostly positively about herself, rarely negatively _____

5. Has a few developed hobbies and interests that encourage natural strengths _____

6. Shows sensitivity toward the needs and feelings of others _____

7. Recognizes when someone is distressed and responds appropriately. _____

8. Shows a willingness to understand someone else's point of view _____

9. Displays concern and wants to help when someone is treated unfairly or unkindly _____

10. Tears up or is upset when someone else is suffering _____

11. Is honest, admits mistakes, and accepts blame for incorrect actions _____

12. Can identify his wrong behavior and turn a wrong action into a right one _____

13. Feels guilt about his wrong or improper actions _____

14. Rarely needs admonishments/reminders as to how to act right _____

15. Can be trusted to do the right thing and keep his word even when no one is looking _____

16. Able to manage her own impulses and urges without adult help _____

17. Easily calms down and bounces back when excited, frustrated, or angry _____

18. Can identify his unhealthy emotions and stress signs prior to their escalating _____

19. Has the ability to wait for something; can cope with behavioral impulses _____

20. Can remain focused on age-appropriate tasks without adult prompts _____

21. Asks copious why-type questions that don't always have yes/no answers _____

22. Enjoys finding new ways to use conventional things or solving problems _____

23. Loves learning new things that drive her interest _____

24. Intrigued or easy to motivate about trying something new, different, or surprising _____

25. Willing to be wrong and try a different, unconventional way _____

26. Willingly tries new tasks with little concern about
failing or making a mistake _____

27. Recognizes that the way to improve is by working
harder _____

28. Does not become upset when something is difficult;
rarely quits but keeps trying _____

29. Willing to try again if not successful with a task _____

30. Doesn't equate a mistake as a personal failure but a
learning opportunity _____

31. Expresses gratitude, is appreciative, and takes stock
of the good things around her _____

32. Uses positive self-talk to express hope and reinforce
good outcomes and attitudes _____

33. Doesn't blame but forgives; knows something she
can do to make things better _____

34. Can find the silver lining in a hardship or challenge _____

35. Equates setbacks and failures as temporary, not
permanent _____

Then add up the scores for each Character Strength: questions 1–5 = Self-Confidence; 6–10 = Empathy; 11–15 = Integrity; 16–20 = Self-Control; 21–25 = Curiosity; 26–30 = Perseverance; 31–35 = Optimism. Determine your child's highest and lowest character traits. The top traits are your child's natural strengths that build confidence and help him thrive, so continue nurturing them to ensure that your child recognizes them in himself. Go to the book sections that address the one or two traits receiving the lowest scores so you can enhance your child's potential to thrive.

PART ONE

Nuturing Heart

"Finding out who we are as a person would be one
of the greatest ways to reduce burnout. Once you find
yourself and your place in the world, you'll feel so much
better about yourself and your life."

—*Alex, seventeen, Santa Clara, California*

CHAPTER 1

Self-Confidence

Thrivers focus on "who," not "what."

F IVE DAYS AFTER THE END of World War II, the peasant women
in the Italian town of Reggio Emilia began building a preschool by
gathering bricks from bombed-out buildings. The ravages of war made
them realize that education must go beyond subjects and also teach
skills like how to collaborate, think critically, and help kids believe in
themselves. The school would become an investment in their children's
future, and the women named it *Scuola del Popolo*, or "School of the
People."[1]

Loris Malaguzzi, a young teacher, heard the news and rushed to
watch the women. They asked Malaguzzi to be the teacher who would
give their children a better chance in life. He agreed. Malaguzzi believed that all children are capable, curious, and full of potential, and
so their learning must be child-initiated.[2] He wanted children to be
actively engaged in projects where they could learn their strengths and
solve problems on their own. But knowing their "who" was essential.
Malaguzzi named his educational approach Reggio Emilia, in honor of
the town. In 1991, *Newsweek* named the school as one of the "ten best

pre-schools in the world."[3] Reggio Emilia education is now revered worldwide and prompted a rethinking of what children need to thrive.

In March of 2019 I observed the early-learning program at the American Community School (ACS) in Beirut, Lebanon, which experienced more recent explosions. Their School of the People is home to students from sixty different nationalities and based on the Reggio Emilia philosophy. Like the peasant women, the staff also believe that children's real confidence grows from the inside out, not from gold stars, false accolades, and helicoptering. "Our goal is to recognize children's unique strengths and then respond so each child feels successful," their principal, Sawsan Yaseen, told me. "Success breeds success."

I spent the afternoon viewing classrooms and saw engaged kids, heard excitement, and noticed smiles on every face. I watched four- and five-year-olds collaborate, discover, create, and direct their own learning, and never once caught an adult swooping in to rescue. Coddling was strictly off-limits. If blocks fell, the teacher calmly asked, "What can you do to fix it?" and the child brainstormed alternatives. If a project ripped, the teacher said, "Think of a solution." Kids bounced back and tried because they recognized their strengths and accepted their weaknesses. In most classrooms, students followed their teachers' instructions based on a set curriculum; the ACS staff followed their children's lead. They still taught core educational objectives, but also helped kids understand and believe in themselves.

Typical schools send report cards and grades to note students' abilities and limitations. The Beirut school described each child's learning progress as well as personal strengths. Imagine receiving this ACS teacher's report about your child:

"Ella is a strong-willed child able to express her needs and feelings with ease. She has no problem setting boundaries. 'You have to ask me if you can touch my cheek, and if I say okay, you can touch my face,' she told a peer. Her advanced verbal skills show during group discussions where she is always eager to share her views. Ella is a valuable member of our classroom community and continues to blossom on a daily basis."

Several ACS parents told me how much they appreciated receiving those descriptive accounts. "The reports help me understand who my child is so I can parent more effectively," one mom told me.

Another said, "The system helps me focus on my child's strengths and less on his weaknesses."

And from a dad: "Stressing my kids, assets made a major difference on my child's confidence." The ACS reports helped parents understand their children's strengths.

"We want our children to grow into who they are, not who we want them to be," Sawsan Yaseen told me.

Over seven decades ago the women of Reggio Emilia had the same hope for their children, and it must become ours as well. Helping kids "grow into *who* they are" is the first step to unleashing kids' potential so they can become the best version of themselves. It all begins with the Character Strength of self-confidence, which serves as your child's customized road map to peak performance.

WHAT IS SELF-CONFIDENCE?

A three-year-old: "I can zip it all by myself!"

A six-year old: "I know my loud talking turned people off so I went quieter!"

A tween: "I knew I could ace the test if I used my memory!"

A teen: "My kick was perfect because I told myself to focus and gave it my all!"

Four very different kids who share one commonality: a healthy, authentic sense of self. These children understand their strengths, accept their weaknesses, and can apply that self-knowledge to help them succeed. An accurate understanding of self gives kids a sturdy foundation for life as well as recognizing weaker areas that need improvement—and it all starts with self-confidence. This first crucial Character Strength is the quiet understanding of "who I am" that nurtures inner assuredness and appreciation of one's unique qualities, strengths, talents, and interests. Self-confidence blossoms as skills, capabilities, character traits, and self-awareness grow. It is also the foundational strength upon which all the rest are built—to be a Thriver, a child must first develop a positive sense of identity.

- **Self-confidence leads to better academic performance**. While a Thriver isn't focused exclusively on grades, the good news is that cultivating this trait does correlate with doing better in the classroom. Kids with a strong understanding and sense of self are happier and more engaged at school, more likely to stick with harder tasks and bounce back from failures so their learning increases. This first Character Strength creates smoother transitions for kids from kindergarten to elementary school and elementary to middle school, and produces higher levels of academic achievement in high school and college.[4]
- **Self-confidence leads to more resilience.** It helps kids navigate life, stay the course, and rebound from setbacks as well as provide sorely needed inner resources to help kids manage stress and adversity.[5]

- **Self-confidence leads to a greater sense of well-being.** A child with a stronger sense of self [6] tries harder, has greater self-assurance and creativity,[7] stronger relationships, more effective communication abilities, sounder decision-making abilities,[8] and overall more positive mental health.[9]

- **Self-confidence leads to more happiness**. Martin Seligman, former president of the American Psychological Association, points out: "Authentic happiness comes from identifying and cultivating your most fundamental strengths and using them every day in work, love, play and parenting."[10] Kids are just plain happier when they honor who they are and then perform in areas that nurture their strengths.

All this seems like common sense. But study after study shows that kids are lacking this crucial first trait: understanding who they are, recognizing their strengths, and having the self-confidence to go where their talents and interests lie. Benjamin Bloom's famous study of immensely talented young people who became world-class experts (Olympic swimmers, world-class tennis players, exceptional research mathematicians, neurologists, pianists, sculptors) found a stark commonality. Parents identified and nurtured their young child's interest or talent in a fun, supportive way. Within a few years the child saw himself as a "pianist" or "swimmer" or "sculptor" and respected his talent. Self-assuredness bloomed and the child became the driver to perfect his skill.[11] Countless studies confirm the power of self-confidence as the fuel to ignite a child's motivation to succeed. But the trait also provides children with meaning and purpose.

A thirteen-year-old Long Island, New York, girl told me that her days were filled with sports, music lessons, tutoring, and constant homework battles. "I know I'm smart and my parents love me but I didn't feel good about me. My music teacher told my parents that my strength was violin but I was losing my talent because I didn't have time for it. The best day of my life was when my dad said I could drop a couple activities so I had time to practice violin. I've never been happier because I'm doing what I love. I even like myself."

The story is common. We want our kids to be good at *everything*, and so we've turned parenting into a triathlon of endless activities for our kids or offer a very narrow menu of what we *want* our kids to excel at, say, tennis, piano, or golf. And we tell them they're good at *everything* to boost their self-esteem. But our efforts aren't doing them any favors: we're pulling them away from their special gifts that could help them enjoy their own company, respect themselves, give meaning to their lives and feel masterful so they persist. And so kids lose awareness of their authentic interests and unique talents and depression rates have never been higher.

It turns out many kids suffer from flimsy, inaccurate views of themselves and so they feel empty and depleted. Healthy change starts by unleashing ourselves from preset agendas for our children, and then respecting them for who they are—not who we want them to become. We have work to do.

WHY SELF-CONFIDENCE
CAN BE SO HARD TO TEACH

"We always strive to be someone else and
aren't comfortable enough being ourselves."
—*Sky, twelve, Seattle*

There's a book I often point parents to when we talk about instilling assuredness in younger children: Paula Fox's *Stone-Faced Boy,* the poignant tale of an awkward boy who doesn't fit in, rarely smiles, and hides his feelings behind a straight face. Gus disguises his emotions for so long that it is as though he shuts an imaginary door, closing others out as well as his belief in himself. His siblings call him Stone Face, and the name sticks.

Only Great-Aunt Hattie understands that Gus desperately needs to recognize and respect his strengths, and hands him a small geode. "If you crack it open, you'll see the power within." The boy doesn't grasp Hattie's message until one dark, snowy night when his sister's dog goes missing. Despite his fears, Gus ventures out alone to try to rescue the dog. And when he feels the rock in his pocket, he understands! Like a geode, his powers also lie within and he doesn't have to rely on others. Gus realizes that he has gifts: a good mind, problem-solving abilities, and optimism but just needs to use them. And when he finds his sister's dog all by himself, for the first time in a long while, the stone-faced boy smiles. He's found his strengths and knows he can handle whatever comes his way. Gus finally respects himself.

Though geodes appear ordinary on the outside, inside are hollow pockets that can harden into beautiful crystals . . . but they only sprout in environments suitable for growth. The same premise applies to kids: without proper nourishment, self-confidence also fails to develop and leaves children feeling empty. Here are a few reasons why many children's inner growth is stunted.

Self-Confidence Is Not Self-Esteem

Most parents view self-esteem as the flight path to happiness and success, so we constantly tell kids: "Believe in yourself," "You're special," and "You can be *anything* you want." We give trophies for showing up and gold stars for breathing (or just about). We smooth over every bump, solve any problem, and never, *ever* let them fail. But our well-intended efforts are reaping dismal returns. Today's kids are more depressed than any previous generation, while their narcissism ("I'm better than you") has increased more than their self-esteem.[12]

Here's what the research really shows: there is little evidence that boosting self-esteem increases academic success or even authentic happiness.[13] Yup. All those participation trophies were for nothing. Several large reviews of school-based programs conclude that trying to boost self-esteem "had *no* discernible effect on students' grades or achievement."[14, 15] Studies *do* show, however, that children who attribute their grades to their *own* efforts and strengths are more successful than kids who think they have no control over academic outcomes.[16] Once kids recognize what they do well, they're motivated to use those strengths again and again. Each success boosts self-conviction a bit more, but the *kid* is always the doer and director of his own triumphs or failures.

Real self-confidence is an outcome of doing well, facing obstacles, creating solutions, and snapping back *on your own*. Fixing their problems, doing their tasks, or making things easier for them only makes kids think: "They don't believe I can." Kids who have self-assuredness know they can fail but also rebound, and that's why we must unleash ourselves from hovering, snowplowing, and rescuing. Thrivers are always self-directed.

We Live in a Superficial, Appearance-Focused Culture

Status, wealth, brands, and appearance don't factor into acquiring a healthy sense of self—no surprise there. And yet that's the outside world our children are growing up in. Today's buy-buy-buy, celebrity-driven society is also causing kids' emptiness and making their interior qualities seem irrelevant. One in four nine- to sixteen-year-olds considers their appearance to be one of their main worries in life.[17]

Social media platforms also increase kids' concerns about their online images and decrease self-worth as they compare themselves with others. Fourteen-year-old girls, who spend far more time on social media than boys, are much more likely to display signs of depression linked to their interaction on platforms such as Instagram, WhatsApp, and Facebook.[18] Focusing on *"what* I look like, wear, or weigh" eclipses *"who* I am" and contributes to fragile, inaccurate selfhoods by sending a superficial message: "Your identity is what you have—not who you are."

Too much comparison is bad; we know that. But here's why: it's harder for kids to answer "What kind of person am I?" when status, wealth, brands, and appearance are deemed omnipotent. Placing strong priorities on money and things is associated with a variety of problems, including weaker self-esteem as well as depression, anxiety, and emptiness.[19] And that's not just coming from fellow students. It's coming from home as well.

Parents Are Missing Their Child's Real Strengths

Research is clear: given the right conditions, almost any child can rise higher, shine brighter, and succeed. But not by forcing your will upon your kids.

Case in point: Amy Chua's blockbuster *Battle Hymn of the Tiger Mother* aimed to convince us that her Chinese parenting philosophy produces more successful kids by pushing them to excel regardless of their passions. Chua demanded that her young daughters play only piano or violin, put severe restrictions on extracurricular activities, and banned them from playdates, sleepovers, or being in school plays so they could practice (and practice) for endless hours.[20] Many Western parents joined the Tiger parenting bandwagon in hopes their kids would become prodigies and wizards. But they missed the key point:

kids who thrive have parents who cultivate their child's talents *because those talents are part of who their child naturally is,* not because those talents support the parents' interests and longings.

A sure path to failure is setting out to raise a great talent. You probably won't, because you'll push too hard and with it goes the kid's passion for the field. A decade-long study that followed Tiger parents verified that the approach did *not* produce superior children. Tiger cubs had lower grades, were more depressed and alienated from their parents—and felt empty inside.[21] That's the opposite of a Thriver.

The End of the Well-Rounded Kid

Raising the "well-rounded, whole child" is gone; today's goal is growing a superkid. Character qualities are deemed "nonessential" and put on the back burner, and any strength not marked on a report card is undervalued: stellar grades are the holy grail. Talents are instead selected for what might give a "success edge" and not based on kids' natural gifts or personal passions. (Heaven forbid!) The pressures of living in a résumé-collecting world are enormous. No wonder kids say they feel overwhelmed, empty, and "never good enough."

Studies suggest that academically gifted youth[22] (especially affluent teens attending high-achieving schools) are most likely to abuse substances, both as teens and adults.[23] Children know we want them to excel, desperately don't want to let us down, but their anxieties and mental health needs are skyrocketing. And what they tell me is heart-wrenching:

"I'm just never going to make it to Harvard, but how do I tell my parents?"

"I don't think I'll ever be 'good enough' for my Dad."

"I wish my parents knew the real me, but I don't think they want to."

HOW TO TEACH KIDS SELF-CONFIDENCE

Kids are far more than test scores, and they have to be recognized for the unique people they are. To do so, we must unleash ourselves from *our* mandates and dreams, and follow *their* passions and gifts. That's easier said than done . . . especially when we love our children so much, want only the best for them, and assume that our efforts will help them find success and happiness. But if we want our children to thrive, then we must alter our parenting.

It starts by looking inward at ourselves, and then turning our lens to our children. In the next sections, we'll look at three key questions you'll need to answer in order to instill a sense of healthy confidence in your child. Who do you think *your* kid is? Who does *your child* think she is? And—crucially—who does *she* want to become?

Who Do You Think Your Child Is?

Wait, aren't we supposed to be following our kids' lead on who they are and who they want to become? Yes—and we will. But you have been studying your child since he or she was born. You know what they're good at. You know what they're drawn to. You've got something to add to this conversation!

But sometimes our ideas about this are stuck in the past (she hasn't loved drawing since first grade!), and sometimes we can overlook qualities that are staring us right in the face. That's why starting off with a clear-eyed look at who our child is—today—can often help us begin these conversations about the future with our kids. I call these strengths our child's Core Assets. After all, it's only when we have an accurate picture of our sons and daughters that we can nurture their strengths and help them compensate for their weaknesses. That doesn't mean it's simple; kids' strengths are easy to overlook, and one mom admitted her parental shortcomings. Here's what she told me.

"My middle son loved to tell stories. His grandpa recognized Kevin's linguistic strengths when he was three. Dad would come to our house carrying an empty cigar box and tell Kevin it was a 'story catcher.' 'Open the lid and let a story come out,' he would tell him. And my son's make-believe tales just flew out of that box. My father urged me to keep encouraging Kevin's talent. 'He'll use that ability someday.' It took me a few years to realize the strength of my son's verbal abilities, but Dad was right all along. Kevin now works on films, and still tells stories."

The fact is, identifying our children's Core Assets can be one of our most important parenting tasks. It helps us honor our children for who they are, not who we want them to be. Showing our respect for who they are is the greatest way to help kids respect themselves. It also unleashes competence, peak performance, and thriving abilities and reduces emptiness and burnout, but it starts by discovering who our magnificent kids are and then using those findings to help them develop accurate views of their assets and limitations.

So, what are your child's Core Assets? Simply put, they are her strongest positive qualities, character traits, and signature talents that can help her thrive. They are what make her who she is. These Core Assets can be personality features such as friendliness, being a good listener, or being a smart collaborator. They can be character traits like empathy, grit, and kindness. Or they can be talents and gifts like music, acting, and original thinking. Most important: Core Assets are those that you actually recognize in your child—not strengths you hope he possesses or those you see in yourself. Our children are not our clones but rather their own wonderful selves that we must respect.

How do you know if your child possesses a Core Asset? The acronym TALENT describes six common characteristics of Core Assets when exhibited in an individual. Core Assets feature a child's:

⇒T = **Tenacity.** The child shows determination and perseverance to succeed at the task involving his asset.

⇒A = **Attention.** The child is easily absorbed in the task and focuses longer than when compared to other strength areas or Core Assets.

⇒L = **Learning.** The child learns quicker and easier when using the Core Asset.

⇒E = **Eagerness.** The child is motivated and energized to be an active participant in the task, and doesn't need adult prodding or rewards.

⇒N = **Need.** The child is possessive about the Core Asset: "It's *my* thing." The asset is a confidence booster, relaxer, or fulfiller of a positive need.

⇒T = **Tone.** The child sounds excited, proud, or joyous when talking about the asset.

Was identifying your child's talent easy or difficult? Many parents report amazement that they'd overlooked some of their children's strengths or admitted that they spent more time trying to nurture their kids' weaknesses. Discovering a child's strengths can sometimes catch you off guard. That's what happened to a dad from Fairfax, Virginia, who uncovered his son's hidden talent by chance. Here's what he shared:

"I have two sons, and they're as different as night and day. My older son is a computer wizard, my younger is fascinated with wolves. I know, it's not the most common kid pastime, but he reads everything he can about wolves, and always wants to know more. Yellowstone Na-

CORE ASSETS SURVEY

 Each child is born with a unique constellation of positive qualities, traits, and Character Strengths that can be developed to increase the odds of thriving in a winner-take-all world. Those that are a child's strongest qualities I call Core Assets, which enhance the seven essential Character Strengths. While dozens of strengths exist, these were selected because they help unleash children's potential to thrive, can be developed, have a positive outcome on well-being, and will help them better the world. Mark only those that are present and authentically define your child.

CHARACTER STRENGTHS			
SELF-CONFIDENCE AND SELF-RESPECT	**EMPATHY AND RELATIONAL SKILLS**		**INTEGRITY AND MORAL STRENGTH**
☐ Authentic	☐ Affectionate	☐ Humble	☐ Admits mistakes; tries to make amends
☐ Autonomous	☐ Altruistic/caring	☐ Includer	☐ Courageous
☐ Confident	☐ Collaborator/team player	☐ Kind	☐ Dependable
☐ Grounded	☐ Communicator	☐ Likeable	☐ Does right without reward
☐ Insightful	☐ Considerate	☐ Loving/compassionate	☐ Ethical
☐ Independent	☐ Courteous	☐ Perspective taker/understanding	☐ Faithful
☐ Individualistic	☐ Empathetic	☐ Peacemaker/restorer	☐ Good judgment
☐ Passionate	☐ Fair	☐ Relates well with others	☐ Honest/truthful
☐ Sense of purpose	☐ Friendly	☐ Sensitive	☐ Just/fair
☐ Self-advocates	☐ Generous	☐ Service/contributor	☐ Leader: sticks up for what is right
☐ Self-assurance	☐ Gentle	☐ Shares/takes turns	☐ Peacemaker
☐ Strong beliefs	☐ Good listener	☐ Understands and expresses feelings	☐ Responsible/reliable
☐ Strong self-understanding	☐ Helpful		☐ Sportsmanlike

CHARACTER STRENGTHS			
SELF-CONFIDENCE AND SELF-RESPECT	EMPATHY AND RELATIONAL SKILLS		INTEGRITY AND MORAL STRENGTH
			☐ Strong moral character
			☐ Trustworthy
			☐ Wisdom
SELF-CONTROL AND ADAPTABILITY	CURIOSITY AND CREATIVITY	PERSEVERANCE AND GRIT	OPTIMISM AND HOPE
☐ Adaptable	☐ Brave/courageous	☐ Attentive	☐ Forgiver
☐ Coping abilities	☐ Creative	☐ Determined	☐ Fun/joyful
☐ Delays gratification	☐ Creative movement	☐ Disciplined	☐ Gratitude
☐ Focused	☐ Generates options	☐ Entrepreneur	☐ Good-natured
☐ Flexible	☐ Healthy risk taker	☐ Experiences flow state	☐ Hopeful
☐ Patient	☐ Imaginative	☐ Follows through	☐ Humorous
☐ Prudent	☐ Inquisitive	☐ Fortitude	☐ Open
☐ Self-discipline	☐ Insightful	☐ Goal setter	☐ Optimistic
☐ Self-regulates	☐ Innovator/developer	☐ Growth mind-set	☐ Positive attitude
☐ Temperance	☐ Loves learning	☐ Hardworking	☐ Resilient
	☐ Nonconformist	☐ Initiator	☐ Spiritual
	☐ Open-minded	☐ Perseveres	☐ Zest
	☐ Problem solver		

UNIQUE STRENGTHS AND CORE ASSETS	
LINGUISTIC STRENGTHS	
☐ Reading	☐ Poetry
☐ Vocabulary	☐ Debate
☐ Speaking	☐ Storytelling/joke telling
☐ Remembers facts	

UNIQUE STRENGTHS AND CORE ASSETS

LOGICAL/THINKING STRENGTHS

☐ Abstract thinking	☐ Organized
☐ Common sense	☐ Intelligent
☐ Computer skills	☐ Problem solver
☐ Deciphers codes	☐ Quick thinker and learner
☐ Deeper thinking	☐ Knowledgeable about topic
☐ Keen memory	☐ Science
☐ Math and numbers	☐ Thinking games

BODILY KINESTHETIC/PHYSICAL ABILITIES

☐ Acting/role-playing	☐ Endurance
☐ Athletic	☐ Graceful
☐ Balance/dexterity	☐ Gymnastics
☐ Coordination	☐ Running
☐ Dancing	☐ Specific sport
☐ Dramatics	☐ Physical strength

MUSICAL STRENGTHS

☐ Instrument	☐ Recalls tunes
☐ Singing pitch	☐ Reads/composes music
☐ Rhythm	☐ Responds to music

NATURE STRENGTHS

☐ Observer	☐ Science collections
☐ Loves animals	☐ Hiking

VISUAL STRENGTHS	
☐ Artistic	☐ Photography
☐ Drawing/painting	☐ Recall for details
☐ Map skills/directionality	☐ Visualizes

LIST CHILD'S ADDITIONAL POSITIVE QUALITIES, CHARACTER STRENGTHS, CORE ASSETS, AND TALENTS
☐
☐
☐
☐
☐
☐
☐
☐
☐
☐
☐
☐
☐
☐
☐

The list was culled from various sources including Personal Values Card Sort,[24] Values in Action Institute,[25] Gallup's CliftonStrengths,[26] and Thomas Lickona's Ten Essential Virtues.[27] These qualities also exist across a large range of nations as well as in remote tribes and indigenous cultures.[28]

tional Park is considered one of the best places to view wolves, so I planned a father-son weekend trip and arranged for my son to meet with the head wolf biologist. And that's where I heard my twelve-year-old review the Yellowstone Wolf Project's annual report (which I didn't know existed), discuss why the wolf was removed from the endangered species list, and politely correct the ranger as to the number of wolf subspecies. I was shocked: I never realized my child's interest in wolves was so deep. Turns out he even dreams about wolves! I have a whole new appreciation for who my son is. Now I know the road he wants to take, and I'm helping him get there. I wonder what would have happened if I didn't take that trip."

As you finalize your overview of who your child is and what their Core Assets are, ask yourself the following questions:

- Suppose you ran into a friend who has never met your son or daughter and asks: "Tell me about your child." What would you tell them? And if your friend asked your child, "Tell me about yourself?" How would your child answer?
- What positive, enduring traits do you want to remember most about your child for the rest of your life? These are usually strengths children use in relationships (like friendliness, appreciation, courtesy, loving), and others you value in your child as well.
- What does your child love or choose to do most in free time? Watch her play to see what she gravitates toward. If she has a social media account, check her virtual persona for how she portrays herself. Ask those who know your child well, such as grandparents, siblings, teachers, coaches, friends and their parents, when she appears most eager, engaged, or happy?
- What are your child's weaknesses or challenges? What traits

or behaviors stand in the way of success or could hinder her reputation?

Self-confidence grows when kids know who they are and can apply their special gifts. Our role is to respect our kids for who they are, and then unleash their assets so they can develop to their fullest potential. If we are to succeed, we must let our kids lead us.

Who Do Your Children Think They Are?

Eleven- to thirteen-year-olds are great to interview because they have such an interesting take on life. So I was eager to chat with six San Diego kids at their favorite restaurant, and they couldn't wait to share what it's like to be a tween. All attended a high-performing middle school and were selected by their counselor (with parental blessings) to join me, despite their jam-packed schedules.

These kids were super achievers: "honor roll lifers," award winners in numerous categories (debate, science fair, sports), student leaders, and in accelerated classes. They spilled their views on everything from Snapchat ("love it"), cafeteria food ("disgusting"), and an upcoming robotics competition ("nerve-racking"), all while checking their smartphones. And they shared feeling "enormous pressure" to keep their grades high, test scores stellar, and athletic performances strong. Ivy League was their dream.

"So, what do you do in your free time?" I asked, and the table suddenly turned quiet.

"What do you mean by 'free time'?"

"You know, activities that aren't school related. Things you enjoy doing alone," I said.

"Play video games."

"Text friends."

"Watch YouTube."

"Download movies."

"But what do you do that isn't plugged in? What about hobbies like drawing, reading, or swimming?" They all looked at me in absolute disbelief.

"When would we have time for hobbies?" said one (while answering yet another text).

"Do some kids really do things they like to do?" asked another.

Childhood has dramatically changed. Hobbies, unstructured "alone" time, and even reading for pleasure have been replaced by plugged-in, adult-structured, or school-related activities. Without time to enjoy their own company, how do kids discover who they are? And since resilient individuals often rely on hobbies, what protective buffer will these kids use to thrive? So I asked, "How would you describe yourself? You know, 'Who are *you*?'" Answers came quickly.

"Good student."

"Soccer player."

"Student council president."

"Tennis player."

"Chess club member."

"Debater."

Their self-labels continued, but not one kid described a strength beyond school or sports. Sorely missing were personal qualities that build confidence, bring joy, and help kids find meaning in their lives. That's a striking similarity with every kid group I've interviewed.

As we said goodbye, two eighth graders hung back. "I don't think we really know who we are beyond school," one said.

The other nodded, and added, "Could you tell parents to help kids figure out our 'who' part?"

I promised that I would.

If you've just completed the Character Strengths/Core Assets exercise above, you're starting to see your child in all their complex, multi-layered glory. But it's not enough for *us* to realize how wonderful they are. We need to get *them* to understand what makes them unique and special—and to value and nurture it in themselves. Here are ways to help kids develop a stronger sense of "who."

1. **Acknowledge your child's Core Assets.** Identify a few core strengths that you want your child to recognize about himself right now. Make sure they are legitimate and already present, and then acknowledge them frequently. Be specific so your child knows exactly what he did to deserve recognition. "You're *patient*: you always wait until it's your turn and never get flustered." "You're *tenacious:* you hang in there and never give up!" "You're *kind*. I noticed how you asked that older woman if she needed help." Kids need to recognize their gifts before they want to put in any effort to improve.

2. **Use "earshot" praise.** Let your child overhear your praise by affirming her strength to someone while "eavesdropping" (without knowing that you want her to). You tell your spouse: "Wait until you see Kisha's drawings! You'll be so impressed with her artistic ability." Your child overhears, and it magnifies your praise.

3. **Use nouns, not verbs.** Ever wonder if our praise is valuable? Adam Grant describes an experiment with three- to six-year-olds that offers important clues.[29] In one test, the quality "helping" was referred to as a verb: "Some kids choose to *help*." In the other test, "helping" was referenced as a noun: "Some kids choose to be *helpers*." Children invited to be "helpers" were

far more likely to actually help than kids who heard the verb "to help." Researchers concluded that using a noun descriptor may motivate kids to use their strength more frequently *because they want to pursue a positive identity*. So use a noun to amplify your child's strength. Instead of: "You're good at painting," say: "You're a *painter*." Instead of: "You're great at playing soccer," say: "You're a soccer *player*." Instead of: "You like to write," say: "You're a *writer!*" Continue praising the strength when deserved, until your child identifies it in himself. "Look, I'm an artist!" can be magic to our ears.

4. **Carve time.** "I wish you could tell my parents that I'm a one-sport kid," an eleven-year-old girl from Daytona Beach, Florida, told me. "Four sports are too much. I love tennis but will never get good at it if I also have to do swimming, soccer, and track." Many kids say there just isn't enough time to spend on an interest they love if it isn't considered "necessary" for school or sports success. We all want to help our children prioritize the skills we think will help them succeed in the world . . . but by redirecting their time we can inadvertently be quelling their true interests and passions. In fact, studies show that the average American kid gives up their talent because they don't have enough time to practice their gift.[30] Check your kid's schedule: Is there *one* activity that can be cut that could free up thirty to sixty minutes a week for the strength? Can chores be taken care of more efficiently? Is that one extra tutor really necessary? Can time playing video games, texting, or TV be reduced? Let's help kids find time to cultivate their natural gifts while ensuring it's the gift they love!

5. **Make practice fun!** The way to improve a strength is through practice. But studies found that practice sessions should be fun and enjoyable. Tailor expectations so the practice is at or

above the child's skills.[31] And remember: be a cheerleader, not the doer.

6. **Praise effort, not talent.** An ultimate goal is for children to realize that their strengths can be improved through effort and practice. That means that the child has developed a strength mind-set—the belief that if she works on her strengths they will improve and help her become her best. That simple belief can guide your child to success and happiness. Each time your child puts out effort to practice the strength, emphasize her *effort*, not talent. For instance: "Your art is improving because you put in so much effort." "Your practice is making a difference on your kicking skills!" "Your singing is better because you work hard."

7. **Don't stress weaknesses.** Studies find that we fixate far more on our kids' deficits instead of their assets. In fact, 77 percent of us think that our child's lowest grade always deserves the *most* time and attention.[32] Yet strengths are the areas where kids have the most potential for greatness. And kids rely on their strengths-not weaknesses-to bounce back from adversity. A dad told me that he put a memo on his screen saver: "Stress the strength!" and it worked! Find a way to remind yourself to focus more on your child's strengths.

Who Does Your Child Want to Become?

Alana is a gifted teen attending a private, accelerated high school in Tampa, Florida. Her parents are well educated, affluent, and have selected law school for their daughter's future. She knew I was a writer, and becoming a writer was her dream, and so she asked to speak to me.

"Have you seen the writer mugs at the Chipotle restaurant?" she asked. I admitted that I was clueless. "The mugs have great quotes from famous writers, but few are by women. That really bothers me. I want to contact the company so they change it." Then she paused and asked, "Should I?"

She'd obviously given a lot of thought to the issue so I asked, "What's stopping you?"

"My dad says it's not a high enough aspiration on my 'goal chain.' He wants me to focus on law school, but I want to be a writer," she said. "But I'm just drifting from who I am."

"Drifting from who I am" is a theme I often hear. Teens list their countless activities but say almost all are selected by parents. They feel enormous pressure to get into the "right" colleges but worry that it's countering their passions. And so they worry and feel empty, like these teens from a prestigious Houston school.

"I only do what my parents want me to, but I don't know what to do with my life."

"I'm in AP math because my parents want me to be an engineer, but I hate math!"

"I guess my activities make me look good on résumés, but I don't know who 'me' is."

With best intentions, parents are driving kids down a one-way path toward fancy degrees but failing to check which route is best for them. For too many, it's a dead end to happiness.

Case in point: many of today's graduates are failing to launch. Forty percent of young adults—a seventy-five-year-record high—live with parents or relatives.[33] Serious psychological distress, including feelings of anxiety and hopelessness, jumped 71 percent among eighteen- to twenty-five-year-olds from 2008 to 2017; depression surged 69 percent among sixteen- to seventeen-year-olds.[34] Beware: a crisis like the pandemic exacerbates preexisting stress and mental health issues. We may be overlooking one solution: helping kids find their purpose or identifying something that really matters to them—and then doing something about it.

Kids who feel that their life has meaning are apt to have stronger self-awareness, do better in school, are more resilient, and are mentally healthier. But Stanford psychologist William Damon warns: "only about 20 percent of teens have a strong sense of purpose."[35] Damon also believes that the biggest problem for youth today is meaninglessness.[36] A lack of purpose is causing too many to drift, feel stressed, and struggle to thrive instead of shine.

Today's academic frenzy, which focuses exclusively on grades and scores, also pulls kids away from their passions. Research by University of Chicago psychologist Mihaly Csikszentmihalyi finds that we're happiest when in a state of flow: those peak moments when we're fully absorbed in an activity[37] that uses our strengths. But Damon's work shows that almost 80 percent of today's youth are *not* engaged in activities driven by their purpose. Instead, they are leashed into adult-driven subjects, clubs, or activities whose sole objective is to secure that scholarship or admission acceptance.

Knowing their purpose steers children closer to the path that brings deeper joy and pride, and aligns them with something bigger than themselves. Kids who perform meaningful tasks and see their positive results don't need our cheerleading or trophies, and they can finally stop wondering, "Am I good enough?" Purpose-driven activities also have a "Mutiplier Effect" because they can increase kids' self-confidence, empathy, integrity, self-control, curiosity, perseverance, and optimism: the same seven Character Strengths that unleash potential and help kids thrive. And purpose-driven activities increase healthy identity and authentic self-assuredness and decrease emptiness.

1. **Find the spark.** "I do service at a food bank because my parents think it will look good on my résumé," a Greensboro,

North Carolina, teen told me. "I wish they'd let me choose what I care about, but they never ask." Start by discovering the interests that excite your child. What gives her pride? What does he want to share with others? When does she take more risks, and more willing to experience failure? What does she get up earlier to do? Share stories about different types of issues and notice what makes her sit up straighter. Conference with the teacher or ask adults who see your child in different settings. Offer different experiences (tour an art museum, enroll in a chess club, read up on astronomy, provide art supplies, sign her up for a sport) to help you zero in on your kid's passion, but once you find it, encourage and support it.

2. **Watch your footwork.** To find a kid's purpose, you can't write his script or do the work. Unleashing Character Strengths requires slowly stepping back until kids pull us in the direction they want to go. Kids are more likely to thrive when they are in control. Where is your typical footwork pattern when engaged with your child?

⇒**In front** so you *pull* your kid toward your goals and dreams

⇒**To the side** so you *support* your child, but only when needed

⇒**Behind** so your *child pulls you* in the direction that ignites her passion

If you're pulling, chances are your child is thinking, "This isn't my interest, but what Mom and Dad want." Find what your child is drawn to, offer support, and then slowly move your footwork until he pulls you in the direction that energizes or gives his life meaning. The goal is to assume the role of counselor and cheerleader for your child, not manager or director.

3. **Ask "why?"** William Damon says asking kids "why" helps gauge the level of their interest. So hold frequent, reflective chats with your kids. "*Why* do you want to play hockey?" "*Why* is photography important in your life?" "*Why* are you doing that community service?" (If it is to "look good on a résumé," ask: "Is that a good reason? Is there a better one?") "*Why* do you want to go to that college?" Let kids ask you "why" so you can share your own purpose.

4. **Offer variety.** Letting kids experience different activities can help identify what they care about as well as help you see what gives them joy. Susan Cain, author of *Quiet,* points out that the choice doesn't have to come from a grand passion. "A big liking can become a deep source of meaning."[38] So expand your child's horizons by encouraging new interests: blogging, guitar playing, horseback riding, bird-watching, or quilting. Plan vacations that are more experiential, like building homes with Habitat for Humanity, playing soccer in a shelter, painting with kids at the pediatric unit. Share news about issues near or far: bullying, the environment, endangered species. Try various family service projects: volunteering at the Special Olympics, planting vegetables to give to a soup kitchen. Tune in to what fuels your child's passion, and then encourage it.

5. **Identify potential mentors.** Studies find that purposeful youth often seek people outside their home to help them find their purpose. Look for adults in your community, business, religious affiliation, or school to introduce to your kid and support her dreams. If your child is concerned about climate change, seek a climatologist at a university; bullying: find a school counselor; domestic abuse: connect with a social worker

at a women's shelter. Adults who share your child's interest can also help them develop a plan to pursue their quest.

6. **Build an entrepreneurial spirit.** My friend Linda's eighth grader dreamed of becoming a doctor, so she asked her pediatrician if her daughter could watch him—from a viewing box—perform surgery. She's now a surgeon. Early business experiences can help kids at any age identify a passion. Try taking your child to work one day. Ask an adult to share their work passion. Encourage her to volunteer or get a summer job. In July 1986, 57 percent of sixteen- to nineteen-year-olds were employed; in July 2017 only 36 percent worked.[39] Those are lost opportunities for kids to discover vocations that might become their passion.

Above all, let your child know that his life matters and that he can make a difference in the world.

HOW SELF-CONFIDENCE CAN BE YOUR CHILD'S SUPERPOWER

Every parent hopes that their children are happy and successful, but the truth is some have a much harder time. I've taught students with severe emotional, physical, and academic challenges, but I've discovered that those most likely to overcome those challenges usually have a parent who focuses on their strengths—respecting and cherishing what makes their child unique and special so that the child can see themselves through that same lens. Countless stories confirm that parenting secret, like this one.

Jim was born without a right hand, and wore a metal hook to compensate. Schoolmates called him Captain Hook, and he considered himself as "the kid with the deformity." He ached to be just another kid on the playground or point guard who could dribble with either hand. "But I wasn't and couldn't ever be," he recalled.[40]

Despite immense challenges, Jim learned to believe in himself. In fact, he grew up to be a Major League Baseball pitcher, threw a no-hitter, and became a legend on the pitcher's mound. Jim Abbott credits his parents for helping him thrive.

His dad was determined not to let his son's challenges define him. Like every other neighborhood kid, Jim fished, rode a bike, flew a kite, and, eventually, played ball. Anytime Jim felt sorry for himself or had an "I can't do it" attitude, his father would ask, "So, what are you going to do about it?"

"He let me fail with the faith that it would teach me to succeed," Jim said.

Dad knew that rescuing wouldn't help; his son had to find his own strengths before he could believe in himself. That meant he needed to fall, in order to stand.

His parents' strategy was powerful. "They believed there were many ways to navigate our worlds," Abbott said, "and that because my way was different, didn't mean it wasn't as efficient."[41]

His parents also knew they had to find a different path to help their son find his strengths, and they discovered it in an unexpected place: his arm. Though missing a hand, Abbott found a way to place his glove pocket down atop his right arm, and then practice constantly during childhood until he could pitch. Throwing became their son's Core Asset that helped him learn to trust himself, thrive, and eventually become a peak performer.

"When my confidence ebbed or I found myself giving the hitter or situation more than I should, I would step off the rubber and find that focal point, imagining the word 'TRUST' written confidently in sturdy block letters across the golden ball. It was a reminder to myself to return to my strengths, to what I do best."[42]

Hundreds of children with physical challenges have asked Jim for advice. "Believe in who you are, believe in who you can be, believe in becoming more," he tells them.[43] And that's the same message we must teach our kids.

The odds of becoming a superstar are remote, but finding their gifts can help every kid weather adversity, build character, and become their personal best. The path to self-confidence starts by knowing your strengths and then developing them into Core Assets. The process requires grown-ups to unleash from protecting, managing, and rescuing. That's how we help all kids thrive and shine.

AGE-BY-AGE IDEAS TO INSTILL SELF-CONFIDENCE

Over the years I've read countless articles about resilience, but a six-year-old taught me one of best ways to help children thrive. Michael (not his real name) was sweet, loving, and plain adorable with big brown eyes and curly dark hair. He was diagnosed with severe learning disabilities in kindergarten and placed in my special education classroom—and already his seeds of self-doubt were sprouting. He was struggling to read, and the more he struggled the more he withdrew. Whenever we tried a new class activity, Michael's refrain was: "I can't do it. Kids will think I'm stupid." Helping him recognize his strengths and positive qualities was crucial, but he was so afraid of failing that it was proving impossible to reach him and connect. My mission was to find a way to help him shine. But how?

And then one day the class was doing an art project, and he momentarily dropped his armor. His pencil flew, and lo and behold: Michael could draw! During that one lesson, he was joyful and forgot his learning difficulties—all because he was doing something that he was truly gifted at. My pathway to help Michael develop self-confidence was for him to focus on his artistic strengths rather than his learning weaknesses. I met with Michael's parents and we formed a plan. They took him to art museums and found an after-school art class (which he loved). I had our class do art projects more frequently and even invited an artistic parent to work with him one-on-one some Wednesdays.

Slowly we all noticed a change: Michael was happier, more positive, less hesitant, and when he was drawing he was full of the confidence he lacked at other times. He even let me pin his drawings on the bulletin board for all to see. His self-confidence was beginning to bloom. The turning point was when other students told him he was a "great artist." That was the day he started to smile, stopped saying, "I can't do it," struggled less—and, soon, his reading improved along alongside his blossoming artistic ability.

Through the years, I kept an eye on Michael and made sure that each teacher was aware of his drawing skills. I heard he won a county art competition in middle school. I eventually lost track of Michael, until one day many years later when I received a letter from him. He told me that he'd finished high school and really found his groove in college, where he'd graduated as an art major. Now, he was working for a well-known movie studio as an animator, and he wanted to thank me for one small act that I'd almost forgotten about: simply putting up his drawings on the bulletin board.

"That was the day I stopped worrying if kids would think I was stupid," he said. I reread that letter and cried. Michael helped me realize that instead of always trying to "fix" kids' weaknesses, we should spend time nurturing their strengths and building up their self-confidence so that they have the drive to go on and accomplish amazing things.

Discovering our children's unique strengths and talents is one of our most important parenting tasks. Victor and Mildred Goertzel[44] studied the childhoods of seven hundred immensely gifted and talented individuals in our century, (Eleanor Roosevelt, Winston Churchill, Mother Teresa, Thomas Edison, and Albert Schweitzer were among them) and were startled to discover that three-fourths had tremendous handicaps in their lives, including troubled childhoods, emotionally fragile or alcoholic parents, or serious learning problems. What helped them compensate for their challenges and become so successful? From an early age, each individual had a "significant someone" who helped him recognized a hidden talent he possessed and encouraged its development to help them thrive. Here are ways to help children recognize their own unique strengths so they too can shine.

Symbols designate recommended age suitability for each activity: Y = Young children, toddlers, and preschoolers; S = School age; T = Tweens and older; A = All ages

- **Define "strength."** Begin by defining what a strength is. When kids hear the word they usually think of muscles and weight lifting, but explain to your child that "strengths are also your unique talents and qualities that make you powerful inside." Ilona Boniwell, a European leader in positive psychology, explains strengths to older kids like this: "On a sheet of paper write anything with your normal writing hand. Now write the same thing with your non-writing hand. Strengths are things you perform that you're good at and find easier to do. They also give you energy and you use them often. Once you know your strengths, you'll be able to use them again and again to help you learn faster." Try the fun approach with your older kid. **S, T**

- **Strength hand talks.** Hold "strength talks" as a fun way to remind younger kids of their positive qualities. Clasp your child's hand in yours and let each of his fingers be a reminder of a Core Asset. Just make sure that you are only acknowledging legitimate strengths. For instance: "You have many strengths. You're a great listener," (hold his thumb); "A hard worker," (pointer finger); "Kind to friends," (middle); "Artistic," (ring); "Trustworthy, I can count on your to do what you say," (pinkie). Beware: I did this as a bedtime ritual with my sons and wrote a special strength on each finger. One night I used a permanent marker instead of watercolor. Their teachers laughed, and reminded me for months afterward. My boys kept requesting the talks but politely suggested that I use a nonpermanent pen. And I did. **Y**

- **Ask "what."** Asking *why* helps kids develop purpose, but a study by J. Gregory Hixon and William Swann found that *what*-type questions are more likely to improve self-awareness. Undergraduates asked to reflect on "*What* kind of person are you?" were more open to new information about themselves and how they might act on those insights. Students asked to think about "*Why* are you that kind of person?" spent more energy rationalizing and denying what they'd learned and were even sidetracked with negative thoughts.[45] Hixon and Swann concluded: "Thinking about why may be no better than not thinking about one's self at all." So instead of "*Why* do you like tennis?" ask: "*What* aspect of the game do you enjoy?" Instead of "*Why* do you not like school?" ask: "*What* part of class do you look forward to?" Instead of "*Why* do you want to learn saxophone?" ask: "*What* would you enjoy from learning to play it?" **S, T**

- **Capture strength images.** Take photos of your child displaying her special strengths. If she is athletic, the image might be of her shooting a basket; artistic: drawing pictures; kindness: sitting with her arm around a friend. Put the photos around your home or encourage an older child to post one as her screen saver to serve as visual references of her Core Assets. **A**

- **Ongoing strength portfolio.** Recording students' growth in academic areas is not new, but many schools now challenge kids to create an ongoing portrait of "who they are" that displays positive qualities. I visited several New Zealand schools and saw students depicting their strengths using photos, essays, and videos beginning in kindergarten. The portfolios were then passed on to the next teachers so they understood their students' Core Assets. Consider keeping an ongoing strength portfolio of each child. **A**

- **Strength mobiles.** Construct a mobile from an old clothes hanger and yarn. Your child can draw pictures of each strength on paper and hang them with yarn lengths from the wire. Suspend the finished mobile in a visible spot and add to it as strengths are discovered. **Y, S.**

- **Asset collages.** Instead of a mobile, help your child create a collage on poster board by pasting pictures, photos, or words that show her assets. A mother told me that her daughter struggled with low self-confidence, and so she started a strength collage for her. Each time the mom recognized a core strength she pasted a word or picture depiction on a poster board. Her daughter hid the collage for years, but the mom was pleasantly surprised to see her take it to college. "She thanked me for helping her believe in herself," the mom said. "I'm so glad I never stopped trying to help her find her strengths." **A**

- **Family strength chats.** We're quick to inquire about our kids' grades and academic successes, but we often overlook discussing their strength gains. Set aside time to hold family strength chats. "What subject did you like most?" "What activity did you enjoy most?" "What did you look forward to doing in class?" "What was your proudest (easiest, hardest) moment?" "What did you learn about yourself?" "What did you improve?" "What activity do you hope to do again?" You can also write questions on index cards stored in a basket to use at mealtime. Answers can help you keep track of your child's interests and passions. **S, T**

- **Brag boards.** Set aside a space where family members can post and share their talents and skills. Pin up articles, photographs, and news clippings of role models depicting strengths to encourage members to keep developing their own strengths. For instance: Tiger Woods, perseverance; Malala Yousafzai, moral identity; Jim Abbott, resilience. **S, T**

- **Read about strength building.** For younger children: *True You: Authentic Strengths for Kids* by Fatima Doman; *Red: A Crayon's Story* by Michael Hall; *It's Okay to Be Different* by Todd Parr. For older kids: *The Self-Esteem Workbook for Teens* by Lisa M. Schab; *The 7 Habits of Highly Effective Teens* by Sean Covey; *The 6 Most Important Decisions You'll Ever Make* by Sean Covey. **A**

- **Victory logs.** Fold a few sheets of paper in half and staple them between a construction paper cover and you have a victory log! Provide one for each family member as a place to record their strength discoveries and victories. Younger kids can add drawings. A Sacramento dad told me he started a family strength journal. Each member adds strength findings and then discusses them at regular, monthly meetings. Best yet, siblings now point findings out to each other. "You're getting really good at drawing. You should think about taking a class!" **Y, S**

- **Offer hobbies.** The right hobby can help kids learn to set goals, manage time, make decisions, even relax, but it can also nurture a strength and help them thrive. Studies of resilient children found that their hobbies "became a solace when things feel apart in their lives."[46] Begin by offering a range of experiences—rocketry, photography, coin collecting, woodworking, art, stargazing—and see what fascinates *your* kid. A dad told me that his family takes on a different monthly hobby (like learning about castles, calligraphy, and bug collecting) to gauge his kids' interests. The goal isn't to force an interest on a child but to find something that they care deeply about. Once you discover even a shred of curiosity, encourage it: provide basic materials to get started, show your child how to begin, engage with your child, and then watch if the appeal blooms. If so, move away from managing until your child takes ownership and can call it "my hobby." **A**

TOP FIVE TAKEAWAYS

1. Kids who understand, value, and apply their Core Assets are happier, and more resilient.
2. It's only when we have an accurate picture of our sons and daughters that we can nurture their strengths and help them compensate for their weaknesses.
3. Real confidence is an outcome of doing well, but the child is always the doer and director of his own triumphs.
4. Knowing your purpose steers kids closer to the path that brings deeper joy and pride, and aligns them with something bigger than themselves.
5. While we can't eliminate hardships, we can minimize potential negative effects by helping kids develop and apply their core strengths.

ONE LAST LESSON

Sometimes lessons come from unexpected places: mine came while touring the Shatila refugee camp in Lebanon. Buildings were pitted with bullet holes, the water was unsafe, violence and drugs were commonplace, electrical wires dangled dangerously: hopelessness permeated. The camp is called "home" by hundreds of children, and it is estimated that one-fourth will develop deep psychological problems. I worried how they could possibly overcome such chaos.

Then my guide directed me into a dark alley and up a flight of stairs. I turned on my flashlight and saw brightly painted Arabic letters covering a cement wall. They spelled "Freedom and Life," and were painted by the children to signify what lay behind the door. I walked in and found a kid chess club: their oasis of hope.

Mahmoud Hashem, a kindhearted man from the camp, knows that kids need to feel safe, feel connected, and believe in themselves, and so he created the club. The small room had twelve tables, each with a plastic chess set, and for a few hours after school the kids left their worries behind and experienced "Freedom and Life."

I asked the children why they liked chess, and they rattled off answers.

"Chess helps me think harder."

"I discovered that I'm good at math and can think ahead!"

"I learned I can do something hard and I'm good at it."

"I found out that I love chess . . . I'll always love chess."

Mr. Hashem's after-school club was helping the children find a way to overcome chaos, find their strengths, and develop a strong belief in themselves. "Every kid needs a cool place like this . . . a place to learn who you are," a boy told me quietly. Such truth.

Every child, from poverty to privilege, must find their strengths and have opportunities to display them. Those who have learned that lesson—like the Reggio Emilia women, Great-Aunt Hattie, a dad at Yellowstone, Kevin's grandpa, ACS educators, and Mr. Hashem at the refugee camp—stop at nothing to ensure that their children gain it.

All kids have challenges, some more difficult than others, that help them learn their inner strengths and what can minimize hardships. Self-confidence is the first Character Strength to steer kids toward becoming their personal best and piloting their own destinies. Unleashing it in our children is crucial, and never more so than in a competitive, winner-take-all world in which kids are desperate to feel fulfilled.

CHAPTER 2

Empathy

Thrivers think "we," not "me."

EACH YEAR, TAMPA FIFTH GRADERS in Barbie Monty's class at Carrollwood Day School engage in a student-driven learning project. The choice of what topic to study is entirely in the hands of the students themselves—they begin their project by reading, watching news, discussing ideas, and then coming together to choose the issue they will all be focusing on and learning about for the rest of the year. Last year, the ten- and eleven-year-olds in Monty's class chose empathy, because they realized it was crucial for their lives.

They also realized they weren't seeing enough of it in their world.

Over the school year, Mrs. Monty's students researched articles, formulated questions, and wrote businesses asking for resources to support their study. I met the class when they emailed me requesting a Skype session—my previous book, *UnSelfie*, was all about teaching empathy, and I've studied its benefits for years. I spent an hour explaining empathy and ways to instill it, and at first, I felt great about the information I'd imparted.

But as they started asking me questions, I realized these students weren't reassured at all. Instead, they were deeply concerned.

"You said that empathy has gone down forty percent in thirty years," one boy pointed out. "Don't you think adults should worry?" They may have been young, but they understood why this Character Strength mattered.

They read stories about empathetic children and (as their teacher told me) "realized that no one is too young to make a difference." They were moved by reading about Trevor Ferrell, who was watching a television report about Philadelphia street people when he was eleven and begged his parents to drive him downtown so he could see if it was true. "When he gave a homeless man his pillow the man's gratitude transformed Trevor," one boy said. "Two years later, he organized a 250-person operation to give food and blankets to the homeless."

They also loved learning about Christian Bucks, who arranged a playground Buddy Bench when he was in the second grade so a lonely classmate could sit and signal peers that he needed a friend. And they adored six-year-old, Dylan Siegel's effort to help his friend with an incurable liver disorder by writing the book *Chocolate Bar*, which raised more than a million dollars for treatments.

Commitment to a Character Strength grows when children understand its value. One student explained, "Those kids showed empathy in action." They were learning the key lesson: the optimum goal is not talking about character, but doing it.

The students' concluding task was teaching their discoveries to others. So the fifth graders created children's stories, interactive games, and activities to teach younger students, and purchased games with questions that encouraged students to stand in others' shoes. Finally, they shared their empathy lessons at an assembly for parents and their student body.

I asked students what the empathy project taught them, and their answers gave me hope. "I'm more empathetic because it made me recognize how other people feel." "I learned to consider what's going on in other people's lives to understand them better." "It changed me; I'll never look at someone the same way."

Most adults underestimate empathy; not these eleven-year-olds. But their passion for the Character Strength was due to how Barbie Monty taught it. Her empathy lessons were not a one-time assignment, long lectures, or worksheets, but instead offered meaningful, active, child-directed experiences. And the actual evidence that our lessons have gelled is when kids use them *without* us. Mrs. Monty's proof came when a mom shared her daughter's transformation because of the project.

"A homeless man was outside our store and Rachel wanted to buy him lunch. We did, and she gave the meal to a very thankful man. Rachel was so pleased that she made him happy: she literally beamed! She explained, 'That was empathy in action, Mom.' I knew something inside my daughter changed. I wanted to thank you."

Empathy in action is always the end goal. It's at the heart of the Thriver mind-set. But why is this strength—which we know is a crucial one for not just happier kids but also more successful ones—in such short supply these days?

WHAT IS EMPATHY?

Most people describe empathy as the heartfelt moment when you "feel another's pain," but this essential Character Strength has three distinct types. I call them the Empathy ABCs.

A = Affective Empathy, when we share another's feelings and
    feel their emotions

B = Behavioral Empathy, when empathic concern rallies us to
    act with compassion

C = Cognitive Empathy, when we understand another's
    thoughts or step into their shoes

Each empathy type helps children care about each other and helps bring out their humanity in the best possible way. The Empathy ABCs are also our best parenting tools to respond to our children.

Your child tells you that her "friends" excluded her at lunch and she ate alone. She hunches over, starts to cry and within seconds you catch her feelings and cry with her. You share your child's pain. **Affective Empathy** (the "A" in the empathy triad) is the emotional part of empathy that moves us to "feel with" another, and it evolves early in children. I remember crying when I learned that my mom was ill, and my toddler crawled up in my lap, patted my face, mirrored my pain, and cried with me. Those are unique human moments when we are deeply connected with another and for a short while, "we become one," Stanford psychologist Jamil Zaki points out: "Our brains even respond to each other's pain and pleasure as though we were experiencing those states ourselves."[1] But there are two other empathy types that can also be nurtured.

Your seven-year-old watches the news about a tornado and sees a child standing outside his house, which is now rubble. "Oh wow, Mom," he says with such sorrow. "I know how I'd feel if I lost everything." Your teen runs to the mailbox and finds that long-awaited envelope with the symbol of the university he's dreamed of going to all these years. You anxiously watch as he tears it open and suddenly you're in his thoughts. "Will they want me?" "Was all the work worth it?" "What if they turn me down?" You are stepping into your child's shoes, understanding his view and taking his perspective. This is **Cognitive Empathy** (often termed, "perspective taking"). It's more sophisticated than affective empathy and takes longer for children to develop, but it is a powerful tool for understanding and relating to others and for reducing conflict.

The third type is what I call B = **Behavioral Empathy** (sometimes called "empathic concern"): when you *see, hear,* or *feel* someone's pain so that you want to *do* something to help. Rachel, the student from Mrs. Monty's class, called it "empathy in action." She saw the homeless man, read his body language and facial expressions as "I'm lonely and hungry," and her empathic urges were ignited. Rachel had to help, so she asked her mom to buy the man food. Behavioral empathy (empathy in action) brings out our best selves, makes our world more humane, and gives children tremendous advantages.

Empathy is anything but soft and fluffy: it affects our kids' future health, wealth, authentic happiness, and relationship satisfaction, and it fosters resilience to overcome setbacks.[2] It also reduces stress and boosts trust, creativity, connection, kindness, prosocial behaviors, and moral courage,[3] and is an effective antidote to bullying, aggression, prejudice, and racism.[4] Empathy is also a positive predictor of children's reading and math test scores and critical thinking skills,[5] prepares them for the global world, and gives a job market boost. It's the reason *Forbes* urges companies to adopt empathy and perspective-taking principles, the *Harvard Business Review* named the strength as one of the "essential ingredients for leadership success and excellent performance,"[6] and the Association of American Medical Colleges identified it as an "essential learning objective."[7] And that's why we should worry: empathy is decreasing in our kids.

Researchers have collected the empathy levels of thousands of

American college students[8] and then compared their scores to the same age groups but in different birth cohorts. In thirty years, the empathy of young Americans has dropped more than 40 percent, and in the same period narcissism increased 58 percent.[9] But their mental health is plummeting as well: one-third of American college students say they frequently feel anxious; one in eight are frequently depressed.[10] In fact, eighteen- to twenty-two-year-olds are now *more disconnected, lonely, and isolated than any other generation.*[11] Those findings came prior to a long period of social isolation during a pandemic where kids were alienated from peers. Relationships are key to thriving.

So let's connect the dots: as empathy drops, stress and burnout mount. And that's what teens say is happening. From a fifteen-year-old: "I'm burned out from always 'doing'; I don't have time to just 'be.'" From a fourteen-year-old: "My constant pace makes me feel I'm running on empty." From a twelve-year-old: "I wish I had more time for friends, but we just text." Trying to raise "successful" kids without empathy shrinks resilience and boosts loneliness and emptiness, so kids feel depleted. The Character Strength of empathy is unraveling and our kids are suffering.

WHY EMPATHY CAN BE SO HARD TO TEACH

"It's not one thing, but a few things combined
that are hurting us. But adults better do something:
it's like we have no fuel left inside."
—*Layla, thirteen, Washington, D.C.*

I've had the privilege of speaking about empathy, character, and resilience to over one million parents and teachers on five continents. Over the years I've learned to anticipate one question from every group anywhere in the world: "Is empathy really teachable?" Most parents and educators assume that kids' empathy is locked in an uncrackable genetic code and are surprised that the trait of humanness can be cultivated. They also assume that their daughters will be more empathetic than their sons; if their kids don't sob through the ending of *Charlotte's Web* they're not empathetic and after a certain age (like teenage), it's too late to nurture empathy. But science counters all those parenting beliefs.

Empathy can be cultivated and at any age, kids show different types of empathy (affective, cognitive, or empathic concern), and genetics plays a much smaller role. One study found that only 10 percent of differences between people's abilities to empathize are due to genes.[12, 13] (Which means that parenting and experiences are key in determining children's abilities to feel with others.) Whether boys are lower than girls in empathy is hotly debated, but we can't deny the impact of nurture. That "boys don't cry" message is still embedded into our culture from an early age. And it is never too late to nurture this Character Strength. In fact, the most empathetic are women in their late fifties and sixties. Empathy researcher Sara Konrath explains, "it's not so surprising that middle-aged women have high empathy after years and years of practice."[14] That's because empathy is like a muscle—the more you use it, the stronger it gets.

Yes, empathy *is* teachable, but several toxic factors in our culture are decreasing children's abilities to feel *with* others. Here are three reasons this crucial Character Strength is diminishing and why our children's feelings of emptiness are increasing.

Our Hyper-competitive World Boosts "Me Versus You"

Competition is a verified empathy reducer,[15] and our children are growing up in a society driven by high stakes testing that pits kid against kid.[16]

"How do you build relationships if friends are your competition?" Grayson, fourteen, asked me plaintively one day. It's a sentiment I hear over and over again—especially among high school students, but also in middle school and even in kids as young as elementary age. The "me versus you" mentality is starting early—and it's increasingly toxic for young people and their mental health.

But isn't a competitive spirit actually good for our kids? I'm not so sure. Research shows that an "I'm better than you" mentality increases self-centeredness, boosts loneliness, atrophies altruism muscles, and creates emptiness. And more than eighty studies refute the "competition is crucial for success" claim.

"Children who learn cooperatively—compared with those who learn competitively or independently—learn better, feel better about themselves, and get along better with each other," writes Alfie Kohn, author of *No Contest: The Case Against Competition*.[17]

Comparisons also diminish empathy. Schools now post grades online (often during school), allowing parents to check their kids' grades and scores. Teens tell me that electronic grading "surveillance" systems just add *more* stress, *more* competition, *more* burnout, and beg us to *stop* our constant checking and comparing.

"I take my first period test and by third period my mom is texting to ask if my friends scored better," said Sara, sixteen, from Austin, Texas.

"My teacher posts grades third period. I know my mom is checking so I can't think the rest of the day," said Isabella, fifteen, from Orlando, Florida.

"My dad compares my grades to what my friends get, but I really can't do any better," said Jerome, sixteen, from Boston.

Kids crave our approval and need peer support. But when *everything* becomes a winner-take-all contest, relationships tank and emptiness increases, and kids lose.

Technology Reduces Human Connection

"My generation is really nihilistic. One of my friends even has a
shirt that says: 'World's greatest nihilist.' I think it's because
all the mass amount of social media and news at such a young
age caused depersonalization. We really need to see goodness."
—*Mary Catherine, seventeen, Boca Raton, Florida*

The gateway to empathy *and* thriving is human connection, but technology is drastically altering children's social lives and increasing emptiness. Ninety-five percent of teens own a digital device, 70 percent of teens use social media multiple times a day, 38 percent use it multiple times an hour, and over half even admit that devices "often distract me when I should be paying attention to the people I'm with."[18] Just seven years ago, almost half of teens preferred to talk in person; today their favorite way to communicate with friends is texting.[19] While we used to discourage digital use, the need for distance learning during the pandemic has only increased their reliance on virtual exchanges instead of the face-to-face interactions kids crave.

Psychology professor Jean Twenge states that four large studies show "happiness and mental health are highest at a half-hour to two hours of extracurricular digital media use a day; well-being then steadily decreases. Teens who spend the most time online being the worst off."[20] Social distancing could decrease kids' mental health and happiness even more.

The kids agree: "We live big parts of our lives on our phones and don't have genuine connections with other people. It's probably why we're stressed," says Kara, twelve, from Atlanta. "We need real-people connections," says Jared, sixteen, from Chicago. "Sheltering in place and distance learning just makes us lonelier."

It's not that parents and educators aren't concerned, but we're often stumped about how to set digital limits for kids. Some parents are hiring "screen consultants" (and paying up to $250 per hour) to learn how to wean their offspring from technology and fill the digital void in their lives. And just what are those pricey consultants suggesting parents say? Try these: "Is there a ball somewhere? Throw it!" "Kick the ball!"[21]

Save your money and just say no to excessive and early digital use, and watch your kids' empathy and happiness levels increase.

Too Much Praise Can Backfire

If there's a common thread in our parenting club it's that we love our kids dearly. We don't feel we've done our job if we don't let our kids *constantly* know that they're special, loved, and oh so valued. Some so-called parenting "experts" advise parents to give ten positive statements to counter any negative comment. (One mom even told me she posted a "10" on her wall to remind herself to adhere to the "sacred ratio.") But all our best intentions are backfiring.

> "My generation is more self-centered and everyone thinks they're better," says Sophia, twelve, from Napa, California. "Some of it is because we're so used to being praised and rewarded for everything."

College-age kids are now the most entitled, self-absorbed generation on record (defined as "having a very positive, inflated view of the self"). Narcissists are interested in getting only what *they* can for *themselves* and always feel *superior* to others, and narcissism rates among college students increased almost 60 percent in thirty years.[22] Make no mistake: self-absorption erodes empathy, reduces prosocial behavior, builds false confidence, and boosts emptiness, and there's no gene for self-centeredness. We have only ourselves to blame. Narcissism does not evolve because a child is unloved but from being repeatedly reminded: "You're special, entitled, worthy, and *better.*" Let your kids know they're *loved and cherished* but not *better, superior, or worthier* than another.[23]

And please, praise your kid for more than their grades and scores! We're so quick to inquire "What did you get?" and not so much for "What caring deed did you do?" Focusing exclusively on achievement without acknowledging character sends the message: "Grades trump kindness." A Harvard study even found that 81 percent of kids believe their parents value achievement and happiness over caring (despite 96 percent of parents reporting that above all they do want their kids to be caring).[24] Well, the kids aren't hearing that message, and desperately want to be valued for being who they are. A Deerfield teen broke my heart: "I wish my mom would acknowledge me when I'm good and nice. I want to be loved for being more than just a score!"

HOW TO TEACH KIDS EMPATHY

Remember those ABCs of empathy we talked about earlier? The good news is that we can use those tools to put empathy into action in our kids' lives by teaching them how to recognize and feel others' emotions (emotional literacy), asking them to put themselves in someone else's shoes (perspective taking), and actually putting empathy into action in our daily lives (empathic concern). These three teachable abilities actually build empathy. And when you combine that strength with the others we discuss in this book—self-confidence, integrity, self-control, curiosity, perseverance, and optimism—the Multiplier Effect kicks in and we optimize chances of raising Thrivers who are not just happier but who are contributing to something beyond just themselves.

Learn How to Recognize Others' Emotions

Before kids can feel with others or step into someone's shoes, they must be able to interpret nonverbal cues in facial expressions, gestures, posture, and voice tone. "She looks stressed." "He sounds frustrated." "They seem angry." The gift of reading feelings is called "emotional literacy." Kids who can recognize emotions are more likely to act on their empathetic urges so they help, console, and care. ("I'll give her a hug" or "I'll ask how he feels" or "I'll see if they need help.")

This first ability is actually easy to teach and can ignite empathy. I learned so from students.

For ten years I taught special education to children from poverty to privilege. My students were six to twelve years of age with emotional, learning, and behavioral issues. I knew they had challenges, and I saw that they often disguised their feelings to mask their pain. To reach them I had to understand their emotional states, so one day I made a long cardboard "Feeling Thermometer." I drew six feeling faces—happy, sad, stressed, scared, frustrated, and angry—from bottom to top, printed each student's name and my own (why not?) on a clothespin, and clipped them to my creation. "It's our feeling thermometer," I explained. "Just leave your clip next to how you feel so we can take care of each other."

The kids were at first leery but slowly began sharing their feelings with their clips. I'd check the thermometer to see who was having a bad day and try to help. One day I found my students gathered around a classmate.

"Ethan looks sad, so we're trying to cheer him up," they explained. A simple cardboard gimmick helped them understand their feelings ("I feel sad a lot," one said) as well as their classmates'. And once they learned to read emotions, my students changed. Their anxieties lessened, caring improved, and relationships bloomed—all because of a cardboard feeling thermometer. It's the reason identifying feelings is a gateway to empathic concern.

Years later, I was meeting with a group of plugged-in Chicago teens at a posh private school. The teens were having difficulty "reading" each other, so their counselor brought her Bernese Mountain Dog to help. Much of human communication is nonverbal: facial expressions, body language, gestures. Research shows that dogs help kids read nonverbal emotional cues (like happy, disturbed, sad, afraid, angry). Those four-legged creatures also help our lonely generation feel safe, connected, and even heal from trauma. It's why you see photos of rescue dogs greeting students who experienced a school shooting or shared grief like a pandemic.

As I watched teens talk to the dog a boy near me whispered, "Sad, isn't it? We need a dog to learn to relate." I agreed. Kids need an emotional vocabulary to learn social competence, and they learn them best face-to-face. But there are some concrete things parents can do to help with this, starting when their children are young.

- **Label emotions.** Begin by just intentionally naming emotions in context to help your child develop an emotion vocabulary: "You're happy!" "Looks like you're frustrated." "You seem upset." The process is called "emotion coaching," and parents who use it with their kids are happier, more resilient, and better adjusted.[25] Talk feelings more!
- **Ask questions:** "How did that make you feel?" "Are you anxious [tense, worried, sad]?" "You seem scared. Am I right?"

Help your child recognize that *all* feelings are normal. How we choose to express them is what can get us in trouble.

- **Share feelings.** Kids need opportunities to express feelings in a safe way. Share your emotions: "I didn't sleep much so I'm irritable." "I'm frustrated with this book." "I'm worried about Grandma." Ask questions requiring a response: "How do you feel?" "Are you stressed?" "On a scale of one to ten, how anxious are you?" Once kids are comfortable sharing their feelings, switch pronouns to *he, she,* or *they.* "How does he (*she, they*) feel?" The small word tweak helps kids consider others' needs and concerns.

- **Notice others.** Point out people's faces and body language at the mall, library, or playground: "How do you think that man feels? Have you ever felt like that?" Turn your feelings watch into a game: "Let's guess how she feels." "Look at her body language." Turn the TV sound off and predict how the actors feel from what you see: "How does he feel?" "Why do you think he feels that way?"

Set Digital Limits and Encourage Face-to-Face Connection

I walked across a Seattle high school while hundreds of students headed to class. Most were texting, but to the rare unplugged ones, I smiled and said hello. Not *one* response from *any* kid during the whole passing period. I finally pulled a teen aside and asked, "Why doesn't anyone say hello here?"

Her response: "We don't feel comfortable talking to others anymore. We're always looking down."

Today's digital kids are losing face-to-face connection, and each text, swipe, and tap on a screen reduces children's abilities to "read" each other's emotions. (Kids *do not* learn feelings from emojis.) Technology is one reason today's kids are the loneliest and least empathetic generation with the highest mental problems on record. Research is clear: people who spend *less* time looking at screens and *more* time having face-to-face social interactions are less likely to be depressed or suicidal.[26]

"Just listening to each other would help," Charlotte, fourteen, told me, "but we're so hooked into devices that we're losing the ability to connect." Her friend Harper agreed. "We're always texting and can't read each other. Even when we hang around with friends, we're on our phones." And then came the pandemic. For our children's sake, let's help them connect in RLT (translation: in "Real Life Time").

- **Set clear digital limits.** Eight- to twelve-year-olds now average just under five hours of screen media a day; teens view about seven and a half hours daily (not including use of screens at school or the rapidly growing use of computers for homework and distance learning).[27] This week, add up how often each family member is plugged in and decide the total minutes of data use allowed and specific times, context, and places your family is digital-free. Mealtimes, family gatherings, homework, and bed are often "family sacred, unplugged times." Have everyone sign a technology contract to cite as a reference, and *stick to it, including adults*!
- **Get on board with other parents.** Find like-minded parents and enforce one digital rule together: "When kids arrive to play, phones go in a box and stay until they leave." A college fraternity set a decree: "When together, all phones go on the table and the first to touch their cell pays for everyone's meal." (They regained face-to-face connection quickly!)

- **Create family connections.** Put digital devices out of sight or in a drawer at family gathering times and revive face-to-face conversations. An Iowa mom puts a basket of talking starters on index cards on the table. Then family members take turns pulling a talking card. Topics are endless: "What was the best/hardest/most fun part of your day and why?" "If you had a superpower what would it be?" "If you could travel anywhere, where would it be?" Do invite your kids to add talking starter ideas. If schedules prevent dining together, start evening "Meet and Greets" where everyone gathers nightly at a set time—like eight o'clock—to connect.

- **Use FaceTime.** Use the cloud-sharing feature on your phone, then routinely take family photos to send and receive to other members near and far. Encourage your kids to use FaceTime so you are speaking face-to-face *in real life time.* ("Watch Grandma's face so you'll know she's tired and it's time to say goodbye." "Listen to Aunt Betty's tone and you'll know when she's in pain.")

- **Encourage "real time" peer relationships.** Ensure that your child has opportunities to enjoy face-to-face peer interaction. Establish playdates, library readings, park outings for younger kids. Find sports that nurture team building, camping, group music, art, or dance classes as they get older. Kids desperately need to read each other and learn to connect to keep their empathy intact. Twelve-year-old Abby said: "We're not great at knowing how to connect with each other like shaking hands, looking eye-to-eye, and taking time to talk with others. We should be practicing it." Even during social distancing we can create small-group interactions. Zoom and Skype can be a substitute where kids can learn hobbies, hold book club discussions, play games, and do virtual projects together when real life connections are prohibited for health reasons.

Model Empathetic Listening

Listening fully is one of the best ways to help us feel with and understand another's views. While it doesn't guarantee empathy, listening gets you a whole lot closer. To succeed, kids have to put down those cell phones, abandon "I'm better than you" opinions, and focus on the speaker. Empathic listeners generally use what I call "Four Ls." Teach each "L" separately, and then provide lots of practice until kids can use all four Ls together.

1. **Look eye-to-eye.** Use eye contact to help the speaker know you're interested. Teach: "Always look at the color of the talker's eyes." Or tell your kid to look at the spot between the speaker's eyes or on the wall behind the speaker's head. The trick is to help your child practice gazing at the speaker's eyes without staring him down (which signals heightened alert or aggression) or looking away which connotes disinterest. The skill takes practice and do honor cultural values.

2. **Lean in.** Bend slightly toward the speaker, nod to show your interest, and smile. Welcoming body language lets the speaker know you care. Uncrossing your arms and legs makes you appear more relaxed and less nervous, as well as more receptive. You'll also be taken more seriously.

3. **Learn one common thing.** Think about what the speaker is saying without interrupting. Paraphrase his main idea: "You're saying . . ." "You think . . ." or "I heard . . ." Try to learn one new thing about the person or something you have in com-

mon. Share your discoveries: "We both like . . ." "We had the same . . ." "I didn't know you also . . ."

4. **Label the feeling.** Identify how the person feels helps verify if you are correct: "You sound stressed." "You seem angry." "You look happy." Show you care, if warranted: "Thanks for sharing." "Can I help?" "I'm glad you told me."

Beware: 35 percent of adolescents grade their parents with a D or F for listening.[28] Be the example you want your child to copy.

Put Yourself in Someone Else's Shoes

I love the scene in *Dead Poets Society* when the teacher (Robin Williams) tries to convey a point to his privileged high school students by jumping on a desk. "Why do I stand on this?" The boys attempt a few feeble answers. "No," he says, "it's because we must always look at things in a different way." Perspective taking is the thinking or cognitive part of empathy that helps us step outside our worlds and understand other people's feelings, thoughts, and desires.

Benefits of teaching this second ability are profound. Kids with perspective-taking abilities are better learners, earn higher grades,[29] are better adjusted,[30] and have healthier peer relationships (core to mental health). They are also more open, less judgmental, less likely to be in peer conflicts, get along better with others, and more popular,[31] all because they can grasp other people's needs.[32]

Kids *begin* to understand other points of view around the end of preschool and become more proficient by age eight, but the ability must be practiced and stretched. The fact is we are more likely to empathize with those "like us": people who share our same gender, age, income, education, race, religion, and that's why we must expand our children's comfort zones. After all, the world is diverse and our children are growing up in times when racism and social injustice are prevalent. So, how do we help kids step into the shoes of those *not* like them? One of the best answers comes from museum curators.

The United States Holocaust Memorial Museum in Washington, D.C., has an exhibition for young visitors called *Remember the Children: Daniel's Story.* I've toured the interactive exhibit several times, and always walk behind school-age kids just to watch their reactions. You literally step into the shoes of a young Jewish boy living in Germany during the Nazi era, and the story is narrated through his diary. As you step into his world, you "meet Daniel" and see his room, family, friends, school, desk, and books. As you read his diary entries from 1933 to 1945 you realize that you share the same thoughts, feelings, and needs.

Then halfway through the exhibit, the music grows somber, lights dim, and you realize something is happening to "your new friend like you." The Nazis arrive, Jewish families are sent to the ghetto, and you worry for Daniel. The final room is dark and chilling: you arrive at the Auschwitz-Birkenau concentration camp and see mug shots of three young Jewish boys. I've watched countless shaken children who can't believe what happened to "their friend." A boy whispered, "Is it Daniel?" Two girls held hands and cried. Another sadly shook his head. Tears, sighs, and sobs. "Me" turned to "we." Humanity!

The last room offers paper and pencils to leave notes; the wall is covered with children's letters.

"When I heard your story, I cried. I can't imagine how hard it was for you."

"We will not forget . . . ever. Love can conquer evil."

"I promise this will never happen again. We got your back!"

Children begin their exhibit journey meeting a Jewish boy who lives in a different country at a different time. But as they walk his life, Daniel becomes real, and they move from "them" to "us."[33] When Daniel is treated unfairly, they are mad; when he suffers, they want to help; and when he is exiled they are livid.[34] Such is the power of perspective taking. The museum experience proves that the ability can be nurtured using meaningful, age-appropriate ways.

Expect Your Child to Care

Science proves it: parents who express disappointment about uncaring behaviors raise kids with stronger moral identities and perspective-taking abilities. The approach is effective from toddler to teen, can be used anywhere (if done calmly and with dignity), and involves three steps that I call Name, Frame, and Reclaim.

1. **NAME the uncaring act.** Skip the heavy-handed lecture. Instead, deliver a firm statement that plainly explains why you disapprove of the uncaring behavior: "Yelling 'Liam can't hit' was mean." "Telling Jaki to move was insensitive." "Texting when Grandpa was talking was impolite."

2. **FRAME the impact**. Pointing out the impact of a child's behavior on another is a simple, proven way to nurture empathy. Your preschooler grabs a playmate's toy: "You made her sad." Your six-year-old ostracizes a peer: "How would you feel if someone did that to you?" When your child grasps the impact, switch to the victim's feelings. Your tween sends a callous text: "How do you think Sara feels reading that note?"

3. **RECLAIM caring expectations.** State clear disappointment in your child's behavior and explain your expectations. "I'm disappointed in your behavior because you are a caring per-

son." "You know our rules about kindness and can do better."
"I'm upset that you picked on so-and-so. I expect you to make
up to your friend." Don't feel guilty: science finds that one of
the strongest factors that boosts kids' caring actions is parental use of "disappointment statements."[35] So reclaim to your
child that you expect him to care and repair any harm caused.

Imagine How the Other Feels

UCLA psychology professor emeritus Norma Feshbach conducted
studies with hundreds of kids and found that role taking can increase
empathy's "thinking side" *if the experience helped children recognize,
relate to, and adopt the perspective and feelings of another.*[36] Feshbach's
strategies were also simple: like kids retelling stories from different
characters' views, acting out situations from classmates' perspectives,
and guessing what a peer might want as a gift (and why). Here are more
ways to help kids see "the other side."

- **Step into their mind:** "Think how the other person would
  feel if roles were reversed."
- **Use books:** "Let's tell the story from the three bears' view.
  What would they say?"
- **Switch roles:** "Pretend to be Sally. What would she say and
  do?"
- **Use props:** Act out what happened from the "other side" with
  shoes, chairs, scarves, hats.
- **Incorporate puppets:** "Bunny is Olivia; Teddy is you. Let
  them talk out a solution."
- **Use a chair:** "Sit in the chair. Pretend you're me. How do I
  feel?"

- **Find shoes:** "Put on my shoes. How do you feel when your son talks rudely?"

You can also use role taking so your child understands your view. Jill, a Flint, Michigan, mother, said that her teen was late but couldn't understand why her mom was so upset. So Jill told her: "'Pretend you're me. It's dark, I don't know where my daughter is, and she isn't calling me. What am I thinking and feeling?' My daughter sat in my chair, cell phone in hand, pretending to be me. She apologized, admitted that she never considered my feelings, and hasn't been late since!"

Boost Gratitude

Research with several hundred people confirms that gratitude enhances empathy, optimism, and helps us consider others' feelings.[37] It also reduces materialism, self-centeredness, anxiety, depression, and loneliness, so it improves mental health, resilience, and burnout.[38] Increasing perspective taking *and* gratitude helps kids consider the *thought* that goes into the giver's *deed*.

- *Family Gratitude Prayer:* Each person reveals something they are grateful for that happened during that day and the reason at mealtime or before bed.
- *A Gratitude Circle:* Each member names one person they're grateful for and the reason. Log everyone's comments in a family gratitude journal to review grateful memories together. Just two weeks of keeping a gratitude journal can improve health, reduce stress, and increase happiness.[39]
- *"Give Me Five!":* Younger kids can put up one finger for each thing they appreciate and why until they reach five. It helps encourage them to find goodness in any situation.

Put Empathy into Action

We can share and understand another's pain and needs, but the true measure of empathy is when we to step in to help, console, support, or reassure another. That glorious ability is the third part of empathy: Behavioral Empathy (or empathic concern), and the most important. Indiana University professor Sara Konrath collated self-reported empathy scores of nearly fourteen thousand students and discovered dismal findings. *Almost 75 percent of college students today rate themselves as less empathic than the average student thirty years ago.*[40] Of the three aspects of empathy we discussed earlier in this chapter, empathic concern is diminishing the fastest.

Every altruistic child I've interviewed said that they were changed the moment they helped someone face-to-face. Whether it was giving a blanket to a homeless man, a toy to a hospitalized friend, or reading a book to a senior citizen, kids said the experience changed them. Social psychologist Jonathan Haidt calls it "elevation" or a "warm uplifting feeling that people experience when they see unexpected acts of human goodness, kindness, courage, or compassion. It makes a person want to help others and to become a better person himself."[41] Ten-year-old Mia described her moment: "When I gave the kids in the shelter my extra book the look of gratitude in their eyes made me realize I'm a caring person. It made me feel good." Such moments can move children from A = Affective Empathy or C = Cognitive Empathy to B = Behavioral Empathy (or empathic concern). Or as Rachel would say: "Empathy in action."

There are surprise academic benefits to this sort of empathy in action, too. A Penn State University study found that kindergartners who showed signs of prosocial behaviors were twice as likely to graduate from college and 46 percent more likely to have a full-time job by age twenty-five.[42] But the main reason to increase children's empathic concern is that doing so will unleash a host of positive benefits including happiness, healthier relationships, and resilience, as well as filling their lives with joy and meaning—exactly what running on empty kids need to thrive.

1. **Start face-to-face.** Empathic concern is best activated face-to-face with projects relevant to the child (not ones that we love or will look "good" on a college application). Eleven-year-old Joshua explained: "We pack boxes for the needy at school. I gave mine to someone on the street. His look of gratitude made me feel good. It felt so good to know I can make a difference." So find a meaningful service activity that puts your child in direct contact with the recipient so he feels the joy of "doing good." It might be delivering toys that he collects to the children's shelter, reading at a senior citizen's home, or baking cookies for the homebound neighbor. Volunteer as a family at a local food bank, pediatric hospital, or help your child initiate a blanket drive to distribute donations together. Network with parents with similar-age children and find giving projects in your community to do as a team. But let your child be the giver.

2. **Point out the impact.** Ervin Staub, author of *The Psychology of Good and Evil,* found that children who are given the opportunity to help others tend to become more helpful—especially if the impact of their helpful actions is pointed out.[43] *Contributing in a meaningful way is also proven to reduce stress and increase resilience.* So help your child reflect on her giving experiences: "What did the person do when you helped? How do you think he felt? How did you feel?" A Houston mom said she takes photos of her child with recipi-

ents and frames them. She said, "The images brighten his day and remind him of his goodness."

3. **Praise caring.** We're so fixed on raising "academically elite" students that empathy is low on our parenting agendas. Things parents tell me speak volumes: "How do you expect us to teach kids kindness when they have so much homework?" a Greensboro mom asked me. She has it backward. Nurturing empathic concern begins with our intentional efforts that let our kids know we value caring at least as much as achievement. Whenever our children show "empathy in action"- like helping, caring, reassuring, assisting, and comforting—we need to acknowledge it so they know that we value prosocial behaviors.

4. **Provide ongoing caring opportunities.** Kids learn empathy through repetition. Whether it's helping a sibling, raking leaves for a homebound neighbor, lending a hand around the house, or collecting blankets to give to the shelter, children's empathic concern increases with recurrent opportunities. Find ongoing ways to inspire kids to practice helpfulness and caring with the same gusto that we have for their academics and sports. "Delivering food to the homeless helps my friends and I become a little more compassionate and think about what others go through besides ourselves. Knowing we made a difference was a great stress reducer," said Kaitlin, twelve, in San Jose, California.

5. **Teach how to CARE.** Empathic concern can dip if kids don't know how to care. Don't assume that they know how. I teach kids the four parts of CARE, and then we role-play different situations so they know ways to console, assist, reassure, and empathize. They always thank me. "Now I know what to do,"

a third grader said. Show kids how to care and they won't let you down.

⇒C = **Console.** "I'm sorry." "I know it's not true." "You didn't deserve that."

⇒A = **Assist.** Run for first aid. Call others to help. Pick up what's broken. Ask: "Do you need help?" "Do you want me to get a teacher?"

⇒R = **Reassure.** "It happens to other kids." "I'm still your friend." "I'm here for you."

⇒E = **Empathize.** "She did that to me and I was so upset." "I know how you feel."

One caveat here: empathetic kids can try to help everyone and feel guilty if they don't. If this is your child, give permission for her to step back and not try to solve everyone's problems. Mother Teresa's advice is poignant: "I never look at the masses as my responsibility; I look at the individual . . . Just begin—one, one, one."

HOW EMPATHY CAN BE YOUR CHILD'S SUPERPOWER

Emmy Werner's forty-year groundbreaking study described in the Introduction, followed 698 infants born on the Hawaiian island of Kauai and found that though a large number faced severe adversity (abuse, alcoholic parents, poverty, loss), one-third thrived because they learned "protective factors"[44] such as critical thinking, empathy, contributing, hope, humor, self-control, perseverance, and problem solving. But their most significant adversity buffer was an "I will overcome" view that was almost always inspired by an empathetic adult with an unfaltering belief in the child. Empathy can be a lifesaver. It was for one young woman who faced great adversity and blossomed into the ultimate Thriver.

Elizabeth was a blond-haired, blue-eyed girl who excelled in school, loved playing the harp, enjoyed jumping on the trampoline with her friends, and talking with her mom. She lived in a devout Mormon home with her five siblings and two loving parents. On June 5, 2002, she awoke to a man holding a knife to her throat. He told her not to make a sound or he'd kill her and her family, and kidnapped her. For nine months, the young teen was raped, starved, and in constant fear that her abductor would harm her family. But Elizabeth Smart survived, and her story is a testament to the power of resilience and empathy.

On the first day after being raped and brutalized, Elizabeth said she felt a fierce resolve grow inside her. No matter what happened, she was going to live. "This determination was the only thing that gave me any hope," she wrote. "And that is one of the reasons I am still alive."[45] A conversation with her mom a few weeks before the kidnapping proved pivotal.

Elizabeth was upset because she wasn't invited to a party. Her mother empathized, and gave the perfect advice. "There were two opinions that really matter," she told her daughter. One was God's and the other was hers, and "*I will always love you, no matter what.*" The realization of her mom's steadfast love—no matter what—helped Elizabeth endure. "In fact," she later recalled, "it proved to be the most important moment throughout my entire nine-month ordeal."[46]

We never know what obstacles our children will face. Research finds that 40 percent of children will experience at least one potentially traumatic event before they become adults.[47] But science confirms that letting our kids know that we love them unconditionally and seeing through *their* eyes can help them endure even the most difficult times. Sometimes if we're not there, a stranger's empathy can create miracles.

Elizabeth was rescued on March 12, 2003, because a bystander with heightened emotional literacy noticed the teen with her captors. He picked up Elizabeth's distress signs, saw something was "off," and called 911. Police arrived and demanded to know her name and where she was from, but Elizabeth was afraid to speak. One officer read her fear: he saw a teen too scared to answer, and empathized. So he walked toward her and gently put his hand on her shoulder, looked her in the eyes, and asked with a soft and assuring voice, "Are you Elizabeth Smart? Because if you are, your family has missed you so much since you were gone! They love you. They want you to come home."[48] For the first time in nine months of captivity, the young girl felt safe to say, "Yes, I am Elizabeth Smart." And because she knew her mom's love was unconditional, Elizabeth could finally go home . . . all because of empathy.

Every child I interview tells me they desperately need to hear more messages of unconditional love from their parents. "What kind?" I ask.

Remind us: "Whatever happens, I'm on your side."

Tell us: "I'm proud of you."

Say, "I love you *no matter what.*"

When it comes to empathy, we are our children's first and most influential teachers. Children crave our love, need our approval, and want us to empathize with their stress and feelings of emptiness. Doing so helps them develop that fierce resolve they need to thrive and handle whatever comes their way. The science overwhelmingly confirms that the single commonality of kids who triumph over adversity is always an empathetic, stable adult who helps them realize: "I'm here for you. You can get through this." It's up to us to deliver.

AGE-BY-AGE IDEAS TO INSTILL EMPATHY

Josh Yandt was going through a tough time at school: he was bullied, his dad died, and he became depressed. His mom decided that a change might help, and so the Canadian teen and his mother moved so Josh could start over in a new school. He so wanted to fit in, but tough times continued. He ate alone in the cafeteria, his depression lingered, and he missed his dad desperately.

"I was sick and tired of being a no one. I wanted to be someone," Josh said. "And I wanted to reach out to people and show who I was." His past experiences taught him how mean some kids could be. "It was almost like they hadn't been shown any kindness in their lives," he said.[49] So he decided that the best way to get to know kids would be to show them kind gestures . . . and what better time than the minute they walked into the school building?

The very next morning, Josh stood at the school entrance, opened the door for each student, smiled, and said "hello." Most kids snubbed him and walked right past; others thought he was "weird" and called him "doorman." But Josh ignored their taunts and continued holding the door day after day, week after week. It was his way of connecting but also letting folks know that he was no longer going to be invisible. And the kids couldn't help but notice Josh, since he was always there.

Slowly, his classmates began to open up to him and even return his greetings. Teachers and students alike began to feel the positive change not just toward Josh but around the whole school community: the kids were kinder and friendlier to one another, all because their new "doorman" was teaching them the power of empathy. So when Josh graduated, students choose the perfect gift: they removed a door, signed it, and presented it to him.

Josh proved that one of the best ways to teach empathy is by modeling it. Repeatedly practicing small, caring gestures like smiling, looking eye-to-eye, or even holding a door can open hearts, move kids from "me" to "we," and help them to thrive. And Josh Yandt would remind us that it all starts with "hello."

Symbols designate recommended age suitability for each activity: Y = Young children, toddlers, and preschoolers; S = School age; T = Tweens and older; A = All ages

- **Read literary fiction.** "There's a divide among people these days," eleven-year-old Jaden told me. "*The Outsiders* helped me realize how two different social groups can put aside their differences, and gave me hope." Research supports his views: the right stories, books, and films can improve children's capacity to understand what others are thinking and feeling.[50, 51] Younger kids: *Through Grandpa's Eyes* by Patricia MacLachlan; *Enemy Pie* by Derek Munson; *The Invisible Boy* by Trudy Ludwig; *The Hundred Dresses* by Eleanor Estes. School age: *The Sneetches* by Dr. Seuss; *Wonder* by R. J. Palacio; *Inside Out & Back Again* by Thanhha Lai; *Something Happened in Our Town* by Marianne Celano, Marietta Collins, and Ann Hazzard. Tweens: *Because You'll Never Meet Me* by Leah Thomas; *The Outsiders* by S. E. Hinton; *Restart* by Gordon Korman; *Refugee* by Alan Gratz; *Once* by Morris Gleitzman. Teens: *Enrique's Journey,* by Sonia Nazario; *Genesis Begins Again* by Alicia D. Williams; *Born a Crime,* by Trevor Noah; *The Hate U Give* by Angie Thomas; *Stamped* by Jason Reynolds and Ibram X. Kendi.
- **Teach "Connect 4."** My youngest son is the family Connect 4 champ. So when he worried about going to camp and making

friends, I jokingly said, "Play Connect 4." I explained (to his puzzled look), that he could do four things to make a friend: 1. Look eye to eye; 2. Smile; 3. Say hi; 4. Ask: "What's your name?" or "Where do you live?" If they smile back or answer, ask: "Do you want to play?" My son returned and said, "It worked!" and the strategy became our family's secret way to make friends. Face-to-face connection is key path to empathy, so practice a new version of Connect 4 with your kids. **Y, S**

- **Instill a caring mind-set.** A study found that people who believe that empathy can be developed extend far more effort trying to understand and share another's feelings than those who think it's fixed and can't be improved.[52] Tell your child: "Empathy can be stretched just like a muscle. It's like learning to play chess or learning a language: the more you practice, the better you become at understanding another's thoughts and feelings." Then acknowledge her caring efforts and attempts. "I notice how you're trying to help others. Did you see how happy you made your friend feel with your kindness?" Some parents have their kids track their kind deeds on index cards to "watch your kindness grow." Help your child understand that with effort, empathy can be improved, just like reading, math, and science. **A**

- **Imagine another's feelings:** Subjects in a University of Washington study watched a person react as heat was applied to his hand. (They didn't realize that the victim was pretending to feel pain; "heat" didn't exist.) When told to "Imagine how the victim feels," they reported noticeably more empathy.[53] So encourage your child to imagine how the other feels by asking empathy-stretching questions. **S, T**

⇒ *You:* "Imagine Kaila's feeling. Why does she insult everyone?" *Child:* "She doesn't feel good about herself?" *You:* "What can you do?"

⇒ *You:* "Pretend you're Steven. Why does he follow you?" *Teen:* "Because he wants a friend?" *You:* "How can you help?"

⇒ *You:* "Step into Dad's shoes. Why was he impatient?" *Kid:* "He's stressed because Grandpa's sick?" *You:* "What can you do?"

- **Widen circles of concern.** It's easier to empathize with those "like us": our gender, race, culture, education, age, and income, and that's why we must widen our children's social circles. Emma, a sixteen-year-old, said, "Growing up in an affluent, white community is limiting. I wouldn't be surprised if I wasn't a little shell-shocked when I go off to college." Expose your child from an early age to different types of people, music, food, worship, languages, and news outlets. Widen your own circles of concern and social networks so that your child realizes that you walk your talk. **A**

- **Find common ground.** Help your kids switch their focus from "What makes me different," to "What we have in common." When your child says: "His skin color is different." Answer: "Yes, it's lighter than yours, but look, he likes baseball just like you." Your child: "She can't read as good as me." Answer: "But she loves to play chess like you." Child: "He speaks funny." Answer: "He speaks a different language, but let's find one thing you share in common." The goal is to help your child find common ground with the person or group and catch stereotypes before they widen the empathy gap. **A**

- **Praise teamwork.** Don't succumb to a "winning is everything" philosophy that pits kids against each other and reduces empathy. Instead, praise team efforts. "I love how your group supports each other." "I'm proud when you helped that injured player." "Great job of bonding together to solve the problem." Then expect your child to encourage others with high fives, "Good job!" and "Great one!" Also look for opportunities to help kids collaborate and stretch them from "Me" to "We." And watch your behavior! Youth programs in a least 163 cities are so concerned about poor parent sportsmanship that they now require parents to sign a pledge of proper conduct while attending their kids' games! **A**

- **Take an imaginary balloon ride.** Phyllis Fagell, author of the must-read, *Middle School Matters,* suggests using visual imagery to open your child's perspective. If your child can't see a friend's side, ask your child to imagine sitting in a hot air balloon lifting her up into the sky. "Try to see things from a new vantage point. Can you see the situation clearer or imagine other outcomes?" Fagell also says using "maybe" can help. Your child might surmise: "*Maybe* Kelle forgot to put me on her invite list." "*Maybe* my teacher didn't realize I was raising my hand." "*Maybe* Grandma didn't hear me." If your child needs more distance, ask: "What advice would you give a friend in the same situation?" **S, T**

- **Think of the giver or the helper.** A study in *Psychological Science* found that writing a thank-you note boosts gratitude—especially if kids consider the recipient's response to their thoughtfulness. Prompt your child to think more of the giver.

"Pretend Auntie Jo is opening her mailbox. How will she feel when reading your note?" "What can you say and do when you open your aunt Susie's gift so she knows you appreciate her effort?" Practicing gratitude can help our kids step out of their shoes and consider others.[54, 55] **A**

- **Overcome discomfort about disabilities.** Helping kids feel comfortable with those who are "different" enhances empathic concern. Start by answering questions about a disability or difference that may cause your child discomfort or fear. One mom explained why an autistic peer flapped his hands: "It's called stimming; he uses it to calm himself." From then on if he flapped his hands, his classmates would say, "Do you need a hug, Johnny?" Their empathy kicked in and relationships opened. Stress commonalities—the interests, concerns, and values they share—not the differences. And find ways to connect in person. "Kim's blind but loves Harry Potter, like you." "He's in a wheelchair but also a Lakers fan." "You may feel uneasy at first. But once you get to know each other you'll be comfortable and have a good time." **S, T**

- **Try gratitude breathing.** Once your child learns deep breathing (see self-control) you can teach variations to boost empathy and gratitude. For instance: "Take a deep breath, count 'one' as you exhale and think of something you're grateful for like 'I'm grateful for my teacher.' Take another deep breath, count 'two' and as you exhale, focus on another thing you're grateful for: 'I'm grateful for my parents.' Keep breathing, counting, exhaling, and telling yourself things you're grateful for until you get to five, and then start over at one, either repeating your thankful list or adding new ideas." Your child can also think of someone kind or helpful, and mentally thank them while breathing slowly. **S, T**

TOP FIVE TAKEAWAYS

1. Kids are likely to be more empathic if they understand why empathy is important.
2. To teach kids empathy, you must show kids empathy. Model what you want copied.
3. Children must be able to identify different emotional states before they can become sensitive to others' feelings. Ask often: "How do *you* feel?" until you can ask, "How does *she/ he/they* feel?"
4. Kids exposed to different perspectives are more likely to empathize with those whose needs and views differ from theirs. Expand your child's caring circles.
5. If you want your child to feel for others—*expect* and *demand* your child to feel for others.

ONE LAST LESSON

The shotgun was hidden under a garment bag as the student entered the Portland, Oregon, high school. Moments later, a frantic evacuation was underway after a report of an active shooter.

But then something unique happened, all because of a quick-thinking Parkrose High School football coach: he grabbed the gun from the suicidal student—and hugged him for at least twenty seconds. "Obviously, he broke down and I just wanted to let him know that I was there for him," Keanon Lowe said.[56] A potential tragedy was halted by one man's presence of mind and enormous empathy.

The darkest hours can bring out the better angels in our nature, as long as our empathy can be activated when needed. This Character Strength is teachable and the best antidote for emptiness and stress. Empathy moves kids to better their lives with hope, kindness, and joy. And it can make our children's world more humane—the kind of place where they will thrive!

PART TWO

Developing Mind

"Competition is fierce and we're always trying to keep up. Adults keep telling us we can do well in life if we get good grades, but they also tell us that we have to do all these activities, pick the right college, and then get into it. But nobody teaches us how to cope."

—*Keila, sixteen, Atlanta, Georgia*

CHAPTER 3

Self-Control

Thrivers can think straight and put the brakes on impulses.

T HERE'S NOTHING NEW ABOUT PARENTS wanting their children to excel, but these days it's all about raising the superkid (a.k.a. "a mentally superior child"). We do everything to try to give even our young kids an "academic edge" by stocking up on flash cards, number charts, alphabet workbooks, pricey tutors, and rigorous and expensive preschools. But are all our loving efforts helping kids thrive in school and life? After visiting a plush private New York City school for three- to four-year-olds, I'm convinced we're putting our energy in the wrong direction.

I arrived midmorning to find twenty four-year-olds practicing their numbers in their workbooks. A teacher stood ready to correct mistakes while her assistant handed stickers to "hard workers." Most children were on task but there was always an adult ready to swoop in to manage. The whole morning focused on teaching numbers and letters: no dress-up, finger painting, sandbox, or a chance to develop curiosity, self-confidence, empathy, or self-control. ("There isn't time to teach 'those,'" the head teacher told me. "We have to get kids ready for kindergarten.") Every second was adult directed and academic driven.

I noticed a freckle-faced boy frantically twisting his brown locks and rubbing his forehead. I didn't blame him: Benjamin had been working for close to fifteen minutes—an unmanageable time length for most four-year-olds—and he was struggling to maintain control. The teacher noticed, pointed to the time-out corner, and Benjamin lost it. He ripped his worksheet, ran to the corner, slammed himself in the seat, and cried. A blond-haired girl sadly shook her head. "Benjamin just wants to play." I couldn't agree more.

I started searching for more effective ways of educating young children and discovered an early education curriculum called Tools of the Mind. While Tools rigorously teaches reading, writing, and numbers, their focus is more on *how* young kids learn rather than *what* to teach them. They believe that self-regulation is the secret sauce to school *and* life success. After watching hours of demonstration tapes, interviewing several teachers, and speaking with Deborah Leong, one of the founders, I'm convinced that the Tools approach may be exactly what young kids need to thrive.

There are noticeable differences in Tools classrooms, the most striking are that disruptions, tears, and tantrums are rare. As a result, behavior admonishments to punish misbehaving ("Sit still or you go to time-out") are nonexistent. But also absent are typical preschool behavior aids that reinforce positive behavior, like star charts ("Johnny gets a sticker for staying on task"). That's because rather than offering kids outside incentives to modify their behavior, children are instead taught tools to help them learn to self-regulate, plan, attend, focus, and remember. Their motivation comes from within, and those lessons are woven into every part of their learning. I kept thinking about how a child like Benjamin could benefit.

The morning began with each child developing a Play Plan to co-ordinate and monitor their own performance. The teacher, Mrs. Adair, sat with Arden, a spunky red-haired four-year-old, and asked, "What is your Play Plan for center time?"

"I am going to build a bridge with blocks," Arden said.

"Let's write your plan," Mrs. Adair replied, and printed: "I am going to be an engineer and build a bridge with blocks" on a large card. Then she helped Arden read it by slowly moving her finger under each letter. "Go have fun," she said, "and remember to keep your plan with you." And the four-year-old scurried off to build, with his plan for the morning at hand.

When Arden moved from his builder role to the space center, Mrs. Adair asked, "Are you sticking with your plan or changing it?" Arden looked at his plan, remembered that he was supposed to be building a bridge, skipped back to the construction play center, and remained there for more than an hour. These four-year-olds were developing planning abilities and using their written plans to remind *themselves* to stay on task and learn to read.

Then it was Buddy Reading time, when children sit in pairs listening to an audiobook and then describe the beginning, middle, and end of the story to each other. Elijah (holding a large picture of a "lip") and Charlotte (holding an "ear") sat knee-to-knee listening to *Corduroy*. The "lip" helped Elijah know it was his turn to speak; Charlotte remained quiet as the "listener" until their roles switched. Play Plans and Buddy Reading were ways Tools teachers used simple objects to help children remember what to do, stay focused, and attend to their task. But the children were also more engaged, curious, and excited about learning.

The most noticeable difference about a Tools preschool was how teachers addressed problematic behavior in children—like four-year-old Henry, who was prone to outbursts because he couldn't wait in the snack line. His teacher was patiently training him to quietly talk to himself to stay in control.

"Henry, tell yourself: 'I will stand in line, count to ten until it's my turn, and sit down. Holding up a finger as you do each task will help you remember your three things." Then she helped him practice repeating his three things quietly to himself a few times while holding up one finger ("I stand in line"), two fingers ("count to ten"), and then three fingers ("sit down"). After a week of practice, Henry could remember his three things without adult prompts, rewards, or threats so Henry could learn to be in charge of his behavior—and tantrums diminished.

I spent lengthy time interviewing Deborah Leong, a professor emerita of psychology and the cofounder of the Tools of the Mind program. She and cofounder Elena Bodrova began working together in 1993, and they developed the Tools curriculum on the theory that if we teach self-control first, learning will follow. Numerous studies prove that Leong and Bodrova are correct: their approach boosts not only children's reading, math, language, and learning engagement but also self-regulation.[1]

But while most parents don't have to be convinced that self-control is an *important* thing, it continues to surprise them that it's the *crucial* thing—it's the foundation of the Tools of the Mind program, and when self-control is taught, Leong said, amazing things can follow. Leong told me that she receives countless letters from parents who admit that it took a while to realize that self-control had to be a top child-raising priority. A mother thanking her son's teacher for helping her "see the light" is among Leong's favorites.

"A year ago, we avoided going out because Derrick ran around and embarrassed us," the mother wrote. "When you said you were going to help Derrick develop self-regulation, my husband and I didn't think it possible. He was such a whirlwind of activity!" But after a short time in the Tools of the Mind classroom, Derrick's behavior and outlook started to change. "He started going to bed when we asked and there was far less fighting. He even made his younger brother write a 'plan' for what they would do if an argument started—just like he learned in class."

Several years later, the mom wrote the teacher again to inform her that Derrick was at the top of his class academically and had been elected class president. She recognized that the Tools of the Mind approach emphasizing self-regulation and personal discipline had changed her child's life. Arming children with tools so they can learn to think straight and self-regulate is how we can help them handle life in an uncertain, challenging world. It's one more way we raise Thrivers.

WHAT IS SELF-CONTROL?

"We're so stressed and burning out for a lot of reasons.
But we're really a different generation and suffering
from poor mental health and having trouble coping."
—*Elijah, fourteen, Annapolis, Maryland*

Hope your child is mentally healthy, excels in school, has healthy relationships, and a productive career? Then make sure that your son or daughter learns self-control. The ability to control your attention, emotions, thoughts, actions, and desires is one of the most highly correlated strengths to success and a surprising untapped secret to helping kids bounce back and thrive.[2] It is also a better predictor of academic success than IQ or those SAT scores.[3] In fact, self-control influences virtually *every* area of our children's lives: it's that crucial.

If you've been reading anything about education or self-improvement over the last decade or so, the importance of self-control won't be new to you. Most of us are by now familiar with Walter Mischel's famous marshmallow test (in which he tests how long preschoolers can wait to gobble down a marshmallow, after being told not to eat it and then being left unattended). Studies showed that the children who waited longer—who had more self-control—were overall more successful the rest of their lives. But what I'm impressed with is the sheer volume of additional studies and research over the last several years that have refined and gone much deeper in investigating this phenomenon. If anything, these researchers have proven that our initial assessment about the importance of self-control as a key attribute of Thrivers has been *under*-reported—it's that important.

An ingenious study by Angela Duckworth and Martin Seligman measured the intelligence scores and self-control of a group of eighth-grade students at the start of the school year. Children's self-control was measured by self-reports, parent and teacher reports, monetary choice, and study habit questionnaires that all measured their ability to delay gratification. Then they collected the students' grades, attendance, and achievement-test scores at the end of the year.

Duckworth and Seligman found that IQ alone did not correlate to higher grades and academic success. Rather, the "secret ingredient" for the eighth graders was self-control—in fact, this third Character Strength was more than *twice* as important as intelligence in predicting academic achievement.[4] The highly self-controlled eighth graders also had higher grade point averages, earned higher achievement-test scores, were more likely to get into a selective high school, were absent less, and spent more time on their homework—even when their IQ scores were the same as (or in some cases lower than) their less motivated classmates. If we want kids to get better grades, we need to stop trying not only boosting their IQ but also focusing on enhancing their self-control.

Kids with stronger self-control are also happier and healthier, now and later. New Zealand researchers followed a thousand same-aged children from birth to age thirty-two. They found that the preschoolers who demonstrated self-control not only did better in school later in life[5] but they also had healthier relationships, were financially more stable, and ended up far less likely to succumb to substance abuse.[6]

Kids who can control their focus, impulses, and thoughts are better off almost any way you look at it. And that's why I'm concerned.

About ten years ago I started noticing a sharp drop in children's self-control. This was coupled with skyrocketing rates of stress, anxiety, and depression (especially among high performers in affluent communities). Without a strong sense of self-control, kids can feel overwhelmed, helpless, stressed, and depressed—often causing them to self-medicate or turn to self-harm.[7]

Educators told me they are also seeing those disturbing changes *at every age*. Early childhood: "Kids are more fidgety and quicker tempered." Middle school: "Kids have more trouble coping and focusing." High school: "Teens are stressed and overwhelmed." Our most prestigious mental health organizations agree that American kids' mental health and self-control have never been so low.

- American Academy of Child & Adolescent Psychiatry warns that one in every four or five youth in the U.S. now meets criteria for a mental disorder.[8]
- American Psychological Association says that teens currently report worse mental health and higher levels of anxiety and depression than all other age groups—including adults.[9]
- San Diego State University researchers report that twelve- to seventeen-year-olds experienced a 52 percent increase in major psychological distress, depression, and suicide since the mid-2000s.[10]

Unless the self-control epidemic is rectified, our children's chances for health, happiness, and success will be jeopardized.[11] Self-control is teachable even to preschoolers, and it's why we must teach this strength so kids can truly be Thrivers—not just so that kids get good grades but so that children are ready for the unpredictable world that awaits them outside the rigid confines of school.

WHY SELF-CONTROL CAN BE SO HARD TO TEACH

As self-control plummets, stress builds. Soon, kids' abilities to focus, make good decisions, delay temptations, and regulate behavior decreases. It becomes a flywheel of bad decisions, each one fueling the next until their ability to function ceases and they just shut down. There's a name for this kind of overwhelm: burnout! So why are so many young people facing burnout, at younger and younger ages? A lot of it has to do with the environment in which each of us is living today.

Technology Encourages Us to Multitask—Constantly

Kids may tell us they have no problem talking on their phone, sending texts, and reading emails simultaneously, but science refutes their claims. When our brain shifts focus between two, three, or four things, there are "switching costs" incurred each time we have to stop doing one task and start doing another. These costs include lessened cognitive abilities, diminished concentration, weakened focusing abilities, and reduced performance. In short, multitasking inhibits their (and our!) self-control and performance.

Researchers at London's Institute of Psychiatry discovered that persistent digital interruptions can decrease a child's IQ by ten points.[12]

And Stanford University found that multitaskers regularly switching between applications do not pay attention or control their memory as well as those who prefer to finish one task at a time. The problem: those multitaskers couldn't help but think about the task they're *weren't* doing.[13] (This probably sounds familiar to many multitasking parents who struggle with the same impulse!) Those who repeatedly task-switch between tech applications perform significantly worse on simple memory tasks.[14]

Yet, 50 percent of teens admit that they "feel addicted" to their mobile devices.[15] (They say they'd rather lose a finger than their phone![16]) Even when they are focusing their hardest and exerting maximum self-control, most kids can't focus on their school assignments for more than two minutes without using social media.[17]

The fact is self-control requires focusing abilities. When kids multitask, their academic performance *and* self-control are jeopardized. Nicholas Carr, author of *The Shallows,* points out that online time also is "crowding out" the time that kids might otherwise spend in prolonged, focused concentration as well as time with *us*, their families and loved ones! Research also shows that as people improve at multitasking, they become *less* creative in their thinking, and that is a tragedy.[18] Curiosity is what helps children to grow in mind, heart, and will, find their passions, be open to what is around them, and embrace change: it gives them the tools they need to thrive in an uncertain world. It's why we must recognize the impact of digital devices on our digital natives, especially after experiencing a pandemic that required a dramatic increase in online time for learning as well as connecting with one another.

We're Pushing Our Kids Too Hard, Too Fast

One of the fastest-growing markets is after-school reading and math tutoring for preschoolers and kindergarteners with the promise that the early learning push will reap an academic edge.[19] But does kinder-cramming really help? Not if you look at where the most literate and happiest kids are raised. UNICEF ranks Denmark and Finland near the top in both categories.[20] An undeniable part of those positive outcomes is because their educational approaches enhance their children's self-control.

Denmark intentionally starts kindergarten one year later than the United States, and they are at the 99.9 percentile in literacy when compared with the rest of the world. An analysis of thousands of Danish children "found that delaying kindergarten for one year dramatically reduces inattention and hyperactivity at age seven with strong negative links to student achievement."[21] They also had higher assessment scores. But not so with our kids: younger American children are having a hard time paying attention and maintaining self-control.[22]

Stanford studied a large sample of kids and also found that those who went to kindergarten early (born in August with a September 1 school cutoff) were 34 percent more likely to receive an ADHD diagnosis and treatment when compared with their older classmates. But a one-year delay in the start of school dramatically reduced inattention and hyperactivity by 73 percent for an average child at age eleven.[23]

I've worked three times in Finland at the invitation of their Ministry of Education and Culture, and I am always impressed with their educational system. Their students also reap the highest reading scores worldwide. Finnish schools have mandatory outdoor free-play breaks, give the *least* amount of homework of sixty-four world nations, and kids don't start school or formal reading instruction until they are seven.[24, 25, 26] Finland also has some of the happiest kids in the world. Their positive outcomes should make us rethink thrusting academics on our young children so fast, so soon. A more child-centered, less pushy educational approach may be exactly what our stressed, lonely, burned-out kids need to acquire self-control *and* thrive.

Kids Aren't Getting Enough Sleep

Let's face it, kids who don't get enough sleep are often cranky and forgetful, but sleep deficiency takes a larger toll.[27] Kids who don't get enough "z-z-z's" have greater problems with attention and memory, make more poor decisions, and show increased impulsivity (all indicators of low self-control).[28] Sleep deprivation also increases their likelihood of suffering from heightened stress, anxiety, and depression—reducing school performance, grades, and test scores. A UCLA survey found that high school students who sacrificed sleep to study performed *poorer*—not better—on a test, quiz, or homework the next day.[29] Tel Aviv University found that missing just one hour of sleep can be enough to reduce a child's cognitive abilities by almost two years the next day. So that means that a sixth grader who loses precious sleep the night before a big test could end up performing at a fourth-grade level; a senior will perform at a sophomore level.[30]

And American students appear to be the most sleep-deprived of kids from fifty countries.[31] The American Academy of Pediatrics calls teen "sleep impoverishment" a public health epidemic.[32] The CDC warns that almost 60 percent of middle school students and 73 percent of of high school students are experiencing sleep deprivation.[33] The lesson: kids need sleep!

Kids Aren't Playing Anymore

Think back to your childhood. Chances are it involved kickball, hide-and-seek, tag games, or rolling down hills of grass. Fun, carefree times when kids directed themselves instead of adults organizing them. That's rare nowadays. Today's kids are "play deprived," and parents even admit that we may be ruining their childhoods.

Over a decade ago, 830 moms across the United States were asked to compare their children's play with their own. Eight-five percent agreed that their own kids (ages three to twelve) played outdoors *far* less than they had as children. Seventy percent of mothers said they played outdoors at least three hours or more at a time, but their own kids played far less than half that amount.[34] One reason for the steep decline is the academic push on our younger set that is replacing grass, sandboxes, and dirt with tutors, lessons, and homework. Electronic entertainment, digital devices, fear (of kidnappings, shootings, predators), and parental micromanaging are others. Modern childhood has changed so drastically that Utah passed a law stating that parents won't be considered negligent by authorities *if* they let their kids walk outside alone or play without supervision.

But for kids play is serious business. Those kid-directed carefree moments nurture crucial social-emotional skills: creativity, problem solving, collaboration, and language. They also help our kids decompress, learn to enjoy their own company, and make sense of others and their world. It's why the decline in free-form play is considered a major contributor to the stark increase in childhood anxiety and depression. Play is also one of the best ways kids learn self-control and skills like following directions, focusing, negotiating rules, managing emotions, making decisions, paying attention, and putting the brakes on impulses. And it lets kids discover their strengths, learn to direct their own actions, and just plain enjoy life so they feel less empty and more confident.

It's all why restoring free play may be one of the best ways to reduce the mental health epidemic and raise joyous, independent, self-directed children. And the solution can be so simple. Just open the door and tell your kid: "Go play!"

HOW TO TEACH KIDS SELF-CONTROL

Okay, so maybe you've tried just pushing your kid off the computer and into the backyard, and your efforts haven't gone so well. In the pages that follow, I'll offer more specific ideas and solutions. The research is clear: self-control is a crucial Character Strength in a Thriver. But the good news is that self-control is extremely teachable—parents can instill this trait in their children at any age. The key to learning self-control is to instill three core abilities: attentive focus, which strengthens focusing and waiting capacities; self-management to learn coping skills to regulate unhealthy emotions; and healthy decision-making so kids make safe, healthy choices.

Strengthen Your Child's Ability to Focus on What Matters

Attention is what connects us to others, defines our experiences, deepens our curiosity, and determines what we tune in to and see. Though largely underrated, this ability is the linchpin of self-control and crucial in helping kids succeed in school as well as thrive in life. This ability is key to task completion, memory, comprehension, critical thinking, emotional intelligence, learning, mental health, academic success, and empathy. Daniel Goleman, author of *Focus*, points out,

"While the link between attention and excellence remains hidden most of the time, it ripples through almost everything we seek to accomplish."[35] The Multiplier Effect is profound.

1. **Reduce attention robbers.** If any apply to your child, take steps to fix the problem.

⇒F—**Food.** Minimize caffeinated or energy drinks and food with high sugar content.

⇒O—**Overscheduled.** Cutting just one activity can free time for kids to recharge.

⇒C—**Computers and screens.** Electronic screens and bright lights can delay the release of melatonin and make it harder to fall asleep. Turn digital devices off at least thirty minutes before bed.

⇒U—**Unrealistic expectations.** Too-high expectations create stress and reduce focus. Too-low expectations make kids feel "anyone could." Aim expectations slightly above your kid's performance level to strengthen focus and boost success odds.

⇒S—**Sleep deprivation.** Inconsistent sleep routines (including on weekends) as well as noise, heat, cold, light conditions, and electronics can rob sleep. Stick to routines.

2. **Stretch the "wait time."** Time your kid's current waiting ability, or how long he can pause before an impulse gets the

best of him. Slowly increase that time and stretch self-control over the weeks by teaching *one* waiting strategy. Then practice until automatic. A few:

⇒**Freeze:** "Tell yourself: 'Freeze. Don't move until you're back in control.'"

⇒**Distractor:** "We'll play the game when you read three pages."

⇒**Use phrase:** "Say 'One Mississippi, Two Mississippi' three times, then take a bite."

⇒**Count:** "Count slowly from one to twenty and then it will be your turn."

⇒**Sing:** "Hum 'Frère Jacques' two times and I'll be done and can help you."

⇒**Timer:** "Set an oven timer for twenty minutes and work until the buzzer goes off."

3. **Play waiting games.** "Kids have always learned self-control through play whether it's Simon Says or Red Light, Green Light," Katherine Reynolds Lewis, the author of *The Good News About Bad Behavior,* told me. "That's how they develop those muscles that manage their impulses and regulate their behavior."[36] So put down those flash cards and resist the urge to sign your kid up for one more activity. Instead, teach him—and his friends—to play Red Light,

Green Light, Freeze Tag, Simon Says, or Mother May I?
They could also practice waiting strategies from the previous tip while playing.

4. **Teach mindfulness.** Scientific evidence shows that practicing mindfulness (intentionally paying attention to the
present without judgment) increases resilience, enhances
focus,[37] stretches attention,[38] improves memory,[39] reduces
stress, and improves learning abilities.[40]

Here's a start:

⇒**Notice your thoughts.** Pause on a walk or throughout
the day and gently ask your child to "notice your thoughts."
Or "what your body feels like," "what your ears hear," or
"what is happening right now."

⇒**Pay attention to a sound.** Use a bell, chimes, or a sound
phone app. "I will make the sound and you listen carefully
until you can no longer hear it" (about thirty seconds to a
minute).

⇒**Beanbag buddies.** For younger kids, place a small beanbag or stuffed animal on their tummy. Say: "Give the animal a ride by breathing up and breathing down slowly.
Focus your attention on the buddy going up and down as
you breathe in and out." Use a pebble, Koosh ball, or any
lightweight, small object for older kids.

⇒**Use an app.** Try: *Sitting Still Like a Frog: Mindfulness
Exercises for Kids by* Eline Snel; *Still Quiet Place* by Amy
Saltzman; and *Planting Seeds: Practicing Mindfulness with*

Children by Thich Nhat Hanh. BJ Fogg, author of *Tiny Habits,* points out that emotions are crucial in creating habits, and suggests celebrating immediately after doing the desired behavior. So when you see success, go out for an ice cream with your kid. Celebrate!

⇒**Use mental diversions.** Temptations can rob kids' focusing abilities and decrease attention spans. Walter Mischel, of the famous marshmallow experiment, found that when he taught kids easy mental tricks, their focus and self-control improved substantially.[41] The trick is not to think about how delicious that marshmallow is but learn a distraction diverter. A few:

⇒**Identify the attention temptation.** Ask your child: "What will be the hardest part?" "What's the toughest thing to control? "What would tempt you most?" Temptations could be "Playing *Fortnite* instead of doing homework," "Eating cake instead of dinner" or "Shooting baskets instead of doing my chores." (Then hide the temptation!)

⇒**Change focus.** Mischel found the more abstractly kids thought about the marshmallow, the longer they could delay. Teach one of these tips: "Focus on the least appealing part of the distractor." "Don't think about the taste but focus on its shape or color." "Put a frame around the distractor in your head, like a real picture." (Those kids could wait almost eighteen minutes!)

⇒**Create "if-then" plans to avoid distraction.** *If* your kid has troubling resisting Instagram notifications, *then* turn them off while studying. *If* your son is tempted to text, *then* put the device out of reach until chores are done. *If* your daughter is enticed to eat cake first, *then* put it out after the main meal is done. Identity your *if* and *then*.

Teach Your Child How to Manage Their Emotions

I was speaking to teens about stress at an independent, private school in North Carolina. Their comments echoed teens from coast to coast:

"Stress is hitting our friends hard—we really worry about some of them," said Alex, fourteen.

"Most of us worry that our grades won't be high enough to get into college," offered Jim, fifteen.

"We're all stressed, but we don't know how to reduce it and it builds," said Susanna, sixteen.

Then I asked: "What can parents and teachers do to help you cope?"

One teen summed up why our current self-control lessons aren't working. "Everybody tells us to not be stressed," he said, "but they don't show you what to do instead. You don't learn that stuff from textbooks or lectures. Kids have to find what works for them, and then practice until it becomes a habit or we'll always be stressed."

Wise advice that we must heed. Today's kids are stressed at a record high: 36 percent of girls and 23 percent of boys ages thirteen to seventeen say *they feel tense or nervous daily or almost every day.*[42] Untamed stress is dangerous to health, reduces their Character Strengths and performance, and creates helplessness ("I can't do anything about it, so why try?") and burnout. But a significant number of kids' suffering can be prevented by teaching them coping skills to regulate unhealthy emotions. Teaching kids to ACT is a moral imperative.

1. **A—Assess Stress.** The first step is identifying stress signs. With gentle prompts, even young kids can learn their "body warnings." I interviewed five second graders at Milton Hershey School in Pennsylvania, a glorious and hopeful place for kids. Students are from low income families and their tuition is paid from an endowment left by Milton Hershey, the chocolate magnate. I sat on the floor with five precious second graders and asked: "How do you know you're stressed?" The kids instantly named their signs: "My tummy feels weird." "My head hurts." "My heart starts pumping." "My feet move around." Their teachers spent time helping those kids learn their "warning signals," so they were far more likely to catch and control unhealthy stress before it mounted. Here's how:

⇒**Recognize signs:** *"How am I feeling?"* Explain: "We all have signs warning us when we're losing control. Watching for them helps you reduce stress, be safer, and make better choices. Let's learn your signals that warn of your need to calm down." Brainstorm a few: *louder talking, flushed cheeks, clenched fists, faster breathing.* Then quietly (and respectfully) point them out the second you see your kid displaying them: "Your hands are in a fist. Are you getting upset?" "You're grinding your teeth. Are you feeling stressed?" "Your feet are moving. Are you angry?"

⇒**Identify triggers:** *"What's causing it?"* Next, help your child recognize things that typically cause him to get stressed or lose control. Like meeting someone new, giving a speech, being bullied, taking a test, trying out for an event, a doctor's appointment, going somewhere new, chang-

ing schools, friend problems, scary news, juggling responsibilities. Depending on the child's age you might keep an
ongoing list or point them out as they occur. Once stress
signs and triggers are identified, your child can use strategies to stay calm and in control.

⇒**Rate it:** *"How bad is it?"* Next, kids need to learn how to
rate the intensity of their stress and talk about it. Doctors
and nurses ask patients to rate their pain on a scale from
zero to five. (Zero means "no pain"; five, the worst possible.) Develop a similar scale with your child to depict the
intensity of her stress. Then when she notices a strong, unhealthy feeling, use the approach.

> *You:* "Name your feeling!"
> *Child:* "I'm worried . . . scared . . . stressed . . . sad."
> *You:* "Rate it! Tell me the emotion's intensity."
> *Child:* "I'm so relaxed I could be asleep. Zero." Or "I'm
> a volcano exploding! Five." Kids can also name the feeling
> level ("I'm at four") or hold up that many fingers.
> *You:* "Let's find a strategy to help you cool down your
> stress."
> The book, *Sitting Still Like a Frog* by Eline Snel encour-
> ages children to "summon the weather report that best de-
> scribes feelings at the moment" (like sunny, rainy, stormy,
> calm, windy, tsunami) as an alternative to a number scale.

2. **C—Calm Down with Slow Breaths.** Taking a slow, deep
breath and then slowly exhaling twice as long as the inhale is
one of the fastest ways to relax. Long exhales get more oxygen

to the brain and help kids (and us) make better decisions and stay in control. It's a powerful tip to teach kids. Gray's mom proves that we can teach even young kids the skill of deep breathing. Like most three-year-olds, Gray hasn't mastered self-control, so his mom is his regulator. The second her son *starts* to get upset, Krista says, "Breathe, Gray. Take a big breath. It'll get better." I watched, and like magic, Gray slowly gained control. "See, breathing works, Gray."

The secret is that his mom knows her son's stress signs and teaches him the breathing trick slightly *prior* to his meltdown. They also practice during his calmer times. Krista puts her hand on Gray's tummy so he learns to breathe deeply to relax. He is learning self-control at age three!

These tips help kids become their own regulators. Find what works for your child, and then practice over and over until it becomes a habit, and celebrate!

⇒**Feather breathing.** Learning to breathe slowly is often difficult for kids so use a feather to show how. Place the feather on a table and explain: "Take a big inhale from deep down in your tummy and breathe from your lips so the feather moves slowly across the table." Keep practicing until the child can blow the feather *evenly* and *slowly* across the surface. You can also teach slow breathing to younger kids with soap bubbles: "See how slowly and far you can blow your worries away without popping the bubble."

⇒**Belly breathing.** The child lies on her back and closes her eyes and breathes normally while paying attention to how she feels. Then she places one hand on her upper chest and one hand on her tummy and slowly inhales through her nose and into her stomach. The hand on her stomach should move upward while the one on her chest should remain still. Say: "Inhale for a count of four, then hold it in for a count of four." The child exhales by pushing air out from her abdomen. (The hand on her tummy should move downward.)

⇒**1+2+3 breathing.** Explain: "As soon as you feel your body sending you a warning sign that says you're losing control tell yourself, 'Relax.' That's one. Take a deep breath from your tummy and feel your breath slowly going up to your nose. Try to focus on your breath. That's two. Then let your breath leave your lips back *down* to your tummy as you *slowly* count to three. That's three." Put them all together and you have 1+2+3 breathing. For maximum relaxation: the "going down" breath should be at least twice as long as the "going up" breath.

3. **T—Talk Positively to Yourself.** Learning self-talk can help kids from becoming overwhelmed, reduce stress, and maintain self-control. I learned that trick from Navy SEALs while training mental health counselors on American Army installations. SEALs told me that they use positive self-talk to override their fears. Neuroscientists prove that the calming technique changes how SEALs' brains react in stressful situations: positive self-talk keeps them in control.[43]

Explain to older kids: "Saying a positive phrase to yourself helps you stay in control in tough situations. Positive words can override the fear signal in your brain and reduce your stress." Offer a range of positive comments, brainstorm others. "I got this!" "I can get through this." "Breathe!!!" "Stay calm. Carry on." "I don't like it, but I can handle it."

For younger kids, offer: "I think I can, I think I can" from *The Little Engine That Could.* Your child chooses *one* phrase she likes and then makes it memorable. Young kids could hang it on their mirror; teens might upload their positive expression as a screen saver. Encourage practice until it's automatic. The easiest way is to repeatedly use the phrase until your outer voice becomes your inner child's voice.

Teach Your Kids How to Make Healthy Decisions

I was at an upscale private New York City high school near the end of the school year, and the teens were understandably excited. They'd *all* been accepted to college, but I sensed nervousness.

"What worries you about leaving home?" I asked. The kids rattled off a bunch of things: "Choosing a roommate. Deciding on classes. Finding a doctor. Balancing a checkbook. Decorating my dorm." Their worry list continued until a seventeen-year-old spoke up.

"My parents do everything for me. My biggest worry is that I'm going to flunk life." This from a straight-A student just accepted to Yale. The rest nodded; they all worried about failing life because they didn't know how to live outside the nest. Their concerns were justified.

College is supposed to be that special time when kids spread their wings and fly off on their own. But each year the percentage of young adults moving back home after college is increasing: a few years ago, about 50 percent of recent grads planned to return to the nest—and that was before the 2020 coronavirus outbreak sent a whole generation of college students and young adults back home.[44] Though college debt and no employment are reasons, another is the inability to handle life. Too many are having a tough time transitioning to adulthood due to parental coddling. The stories I hear about university parents are especially worrisome. We aren't cutting the umbilical cord.

- A dad told me he watched a mom cut her college-bound son's steak in the cafeteria during a parent orientation at the University of Chicago.
- United States Air Force Academy cadets asked me how to "respectfully stop our parents from helicoptering us. We have to learn to lead and even go to battle!"
- Apartment managers said that parents asked for keys to their college grads' living quarters to decorate before their kids started their Harvard MBA program.

Today's college students (versus those in the 1980s and 1990s) score markedly higher on "maturity fears." Teens today are more likely to agree with statements like: "I wish that I could return to the security of childhood," and "The happiest time in life is when you are a child."[45] They're worried about growing up!

"Adulting School" is a growing business that offers classes to young adults, teaching them how to perform tasks like setting goals, managing money, making beds, and even folding laundry. Enough! Let's make a pack to stop hovering and build strong kids from the inside out. A stark commonality amongst Thrivers is that they develop autonomy so they can steer their own lives. That starts by helping our kids learn to take some control and make their *own* decisions. And that requires that we abstain from always managing, directing and supervising their lives. Ask your kids what they want to learn *before* leaving your nest, and then commit to teaching those skills.

Our role is helping our kids learn to handle life someday without us. We must unleash so that they can learn how to make choices, good decisions, and solve *their own problems*. But there's a caveat: once your child settles on a choice, *let it be*. Don't rescue! Your child will never gain self-control or decision-making abilities if you keep deciding for him. (And do halt the "You should have" or "I told you!") Each experience stretches self-control a tad more until kids are able to make decisions completely on their own. And that's how we raise kids who are confident that they can handle whatever comes their way and thrive.

1. **Identify your parenting style.** How do you usually act whenever your child seeks your help to make choices?

   Enabler: "You've had a big day. Let me choose for you."

   Impatient: "We're late, so I'll decide."

   Coddler: "I'll tell Sam that you're sorry. Don't worry!"

   Competitor: "Ryan's project is going to be good. Let's add more photos so yours is better."

   Rescuer: "I'll redo your science project. Your letters don't look right."

   If you recognize that your parenting style might be robbing your kid's self-control, identify *what he is capable of doing alone at his age and ability level*. Then learn a new mantra: *"Never do for my kids what they can do for themselves."* The next time you feel the urge to "fix," "help," or "smooth over," give yourself permission to step back and say no. When your kid asks for help when he is capable of doing something himself, say, "I bet you can do it all by yourself."

2. **Allow choices.** If your child is used to you deciding, find ways to increase opportunities so he gets to choose. The key question is: "What things are you choosing for your kid that he could choose for himself?" For instance, clothes, activities, purchases, schedules, chores, food, bedroom decorations, entertainment. Some things are nonnegotiable, but which age-appropriate choices can you put on your child so he gains self-control?

3. **Offer "either-or" decisions.** Start with having your child choose between only two options: "Do you want to play Chutes and Ladders or Candy Land?" "Do you want to go for a bike ride or a walk?" Next try three options: "Do you want cake, ice cream, or pudding for dessert?" You can increase the options and work up to more sophisticated problems later: "Which college will you choose?" Keep expanding the choice list.

4. **Ask, "What might happen if . . . ?"** One part of decision-making is focusing on possible outcomes. Help your child think about decision consequences by asking: "What might happen *if* you try that?" Also help him weigh the pros and cons of each possibility: "What are all the good and bad things that might happen *if* you choose that?" Older kids can list all the *ifs*, and then count whether there are more positives or negatives.

5. **Teach "Stop, Think, Act Right."** What kids say to themselves ("self-instruction") during tempting moments is a significant

determinant of whether they use self-control and say no to impulsive urges.[46] STAR (Stop, Think, Act Right) helps kids make better decisions. It takes patience and practice, but with time kids can learn to Stop, Think, Act Right so they maintain control and make wise decisions *alone*.

HOW SELF-CONTROL CAN BE YOUR CHILD'S SUPERPOWER

Michael Phelps is the most decorated Olympian in history with a total of twenty-eight medals. Most would assume that Phelps's success is due to natural talent, an innate swimmer's physique, or a genetic predisposition, but the mental tools he learned to become a world phenomenon are key to his immense success. How he developed self-control has great lessons for adults who work with kids.

"Growing up, I was someone who was constantly bouncing off the walls," Phelps explained. "I was not just always on the go; I simply could not sit still."[47] His mom kept getting phone calls from his elementary school about his self-control problems: not paying attention in class, difficulty focusing, trouble concentrating, not doing his work, and always hurrying. At age nine, Michael was diagnosed with attention deficit hyperactivity disorder, a mental condition that affects an estimated four million children and adolescents in the United States. Like millions of other American kids, he was prescribed Ritalin, though school reports continued to show a lack of improvement in his ability to stay on task. Some teachers told him he would never be successful at anything because he couldn't concentrate. But Michael found a unique way to channel his excessive energy: the swimming pool.

"I could go fast in the pool, it turned out, in part because being in the pool slowed down my mind," Phelps recalled. "In the water, I felt, for the first time, in control."[48]

His mom helped Michael stay focused at his swim meets by reminding him to consider the consequences of his behavior (like the time when he was ten, came in second, and got so upset that he ripped off his goggles and threw them angrily onto the pool deck). They came up with a signal that she could give him from the stands. "I'd form a 'C' with my hand, which stood for 'compose yourself,'" Debbie Phelps explained. "Every time I saw him getting frustrated, I'd give him the sign."

Phelps also developed relaxation strategies to handle the inevitable pressure of competitive swimming. "Mom and I used to go through relaxation and programming techniques at home. . . . tighten my right hand into a fist and relax it, then do it with my left hand," he explained.[49] Songs by Lil Wayne and Young Jeezy helped him "stay in the zone," so he listened to them before a race. And he learned ways to control unhealthy emotions. "My anger would build up inside," he remembered. "I would use that anger as motivation, especially in the pool. Looking back, I firmly believe these episodes taught me how to manage my emotions to my advantage."[50] And his coach put him through *every* scenario possible to make sure Phelps could deal with any possible obstacle that came his way. No helicoptering here: his coach knew that champions must learn self-control.

It took years of training, desire, dreams, and discipline, but the boy whose teacher once said he would "never succeed" proved him wrong. Michael Phelps would be first to admit it wasn't easy: "But with hard work, with belief, with confidence and trust in yourself and those around you, there are no limits."

Every kid will face obstacles—some more challenging than others. But developing self-control along with a parent's enduring love helps *all* kids navigate life's hurdles. Who knows if they'll win medals, but they will feel less empty, be more likely to thrive, and reap the Character Advantage.

AGE-BY-AGE IDEAS TO INSTILL SELF-CONTROL

> "We live in little bubbles of protection and
> rely too much on our parents and they do too much
> for us. We have to learn to handle our own lives."
> —*Aiden, fourteen, Salt Lake City*

A Nashville high school freshman shared powerful wisdom. "When I graduated from middle school my mom gave me Dr. Seuss's book, *Oh, the Places You'll Go!*" Scarlett told me. "She read me his final lines: 'You have brains in your head. You have feet in your shoes. You can steer yourself any direction you choose,' and told me I'd do great in high school. But I'm not doing well because I never learned to do anything for myself. Mom's still steering me. If she wants me to make it, she has to stop doing everything for me and hand me the wheel so I can figure out how to control my life."

Such truth! If we really hope our kids acquire self-control and succeed and thrive, we must slowly give them the wheel so they can steer themselves.

Symbols designate recommended age suitability for each activity: Y = Young children, toddlers, and preschoolers; S = School age; T = Tweens and older; A = All ages

- **Model self-control.** Before you try building your child's self-control, seriously reflect on your own behavior. For instance: How do *you* act in front of *your* kids when *your* self-control is lacking? Do *you* drive over the speed limit, media multitask, or buy things impulsively in front of your kids? How do *you* control *your* stress? We are living textbooks to our kids. Model what you hope your child catches. **A**

- **Create a self-control motto.** An Iowa dad was so concerned about the poor self-control of his sons' classmates that he spent a day researching mottoes about the Character Strength with his kids. Favorites were written on index cards, taped around their house, and then they repeated them daily. "It finally sunk in that self-control was expected in our house," he told me. A few: "Think, then act." "Nothing valuable comes from weak self-control." "Control yourself or someone else will control you." "If you lose self-control everything will fall." Develop a family motto and then repeat it until your kids know it! **A**

- **Talk about self-control.** Kids need ongoing mini-chats to understand the value of self-control. Questions to use: "What is self-control?" "Why is it important?" "Why do some people have more self-control than others?" "Have you seen someone lose self-control?" "What did it look like?" "What makes people lose it?" "What can people do to regain control?" "What makes you lose control?" "What helps you stay in control?" **A**

- **Watch films.** Movies are great ways to talk about self-control, like in *Star Wars* when Yoda and Obi-Wan teach Luke Skywalker self-control to keep him from the dark side. Younger kids: *Frozen, Kung Fu Panda, Finding Nemo, Fantastic Mr. Fox.* School age: *Charlie and the Chocolate Factory, Spider-Man, The Karate Kid.* Tweens and teens: *Harry Potter, Hacksaw Ridge, Seabiscuit.* **A**

- **Give a signal.** Some kids have a hard time changing focus between activities. That's why teachers use "attention signals" like clapping prompts, ringing a bell, or verbal cues: "pencils down, eyes up." Develop a signal, practice together, and then expect attention! A few: "I need your attention in one minute." "Eyes on me, please." "Ready to listen?" **Y**
- **Stress "pause."** Without putting brakes on impulses kids can make dangerous, irreversible choices. Slowing down gives kids time to think. Teach a "pausing prompt" your child can use in the real or digital world to remind himself to "stop and think before choosing!" **S, T**

    ⇒"If you're mad, count to ten before you answer."

    ⇒"When in doubt: stop, think, cool off."

    ⇒"Never push send on text or email when angry."

    ⇒"Is it helpful or hurtful? If hurtful, don't do it!"

    ⇒"Don't say anything you wouldn't want said about you."

- **Read mindfulness books.** Younger kids: *Breathe Like a Bear* by Kira Willey; *Master of Mindfulness* by Laurie Grossman; *What Does It Mean to Be Present?* by Rana DiOrio; *I Am Peace: A Book of Mindfulness* by Susan Verde. Older kids: *The Mindful Teen* by Dzung Vo; *Ultimate Mindfulness Activity Book* by Christian Bergstrom. **A**
- **Stay in the "now."** Clara is a sensitive, creative fifth grader who often overthinks situations, which exaggerates her wor-

ries and depletes her self-control. Her parents help reduce her overthinking with cues: "Be in the moment, Clara. Don't worry about what *might* happen. Think about *now* and you'll feel better." Her mom told me that it's taken countless "Be in the moment" reminders, but Clara now uses it alone. If your child magnifies worries, help her stay in the "now." **S, T**

- **Use an app.** Download an app to help your child practice self-control. *Young kids:* Breathe, Think, Do with Sesame, Daniel Tiger's Grr ific Feelings. *School age:* Super Stretch Yoga, Mindful Powers. *Tweens and teens:* Stop, Breathe & Think, Take A Breath. Also download relaxing music to listen to on their iPhone or iPad. **A**

- **Make space in hostility.** Staying cool in a social scene can be tough. A way to tone down social conflicts is to teach kids to put space between those in conflict. Explain: "You can say 'let's solve it later' to give yourself time to pause, think, and cool off." Brainstorm phrases to create space like: "Let's talk after recess." "How 'bout we cool off?" "Now isn't a good time." Your child chooses a line (or creates another), and practices until he can use it. **S, T**

- **Start a yoga or mindfulness group.** Redondo Beach moms said they started a weekly mother-daughter yoga group to help reduce their tween daughters' stress. Research confirms that yoga and mindfulness boost self-control abilities and improve mental health. Find an age-appropriate yoga or mindfulness DVD or seek classes in your area so you learn the technique. Then start a youth yoga or mindfulness group or do it with your family. **T**

- **Consider a gap year.** Taking a year off between high school and starting college can help kids learn to manage their own lives. It also gives them time to explore interests, travel, do an internship, hold a job, or just find themselves before heading off to college. Research shows that "gappers" who take a year off consistently *perform better in school and reap higher GPAs* than peers who graduated from high school and went straight to college.[51] **T**

- **Aim for twenty-one days.** Teaching a new way to control an impulse is not easy, especially if a child has practiced inappropriate ways. Choose one self-control area that needs improvement, show your kid the new strategy, and then practice it a few minutes every day for at least three weeks—or however long it takes. (Science now says it can take anywhere from eighteen to 254 days!) The possibility that your child will adopt the skill is far likelier because he's repeated practice: the exact way any new behavior is learned. Roy F. Baumeister, author of *Willpower*, points out: "The important thing is to practice overriding habitual ways of doing things and exerting deliberate control over your actions. Over time, that practice improves self-control."[52] That's what our kids need to obtain the Character Advantage. **A**

TOP FIVE TAKEAWAYS

1. Self-control is a like a muscle that gets stronger from regular daily exercise.
2. Taking a slow, deep breath and exhaling twice as long as the inhale helps kids gain control.
3. Odds that a child will adopt a self-control skill are more likely if he practices it over and over.

4. A child's ability to control attention, emotions, thoughts, and actions is one of the most highly correlated strengths of success and resilience.

5. We are living textbooks to our kids. Model self-control so your child catches it.

ONE LAST LESSON

"Adults need to offer kids a range of stress management
tools so they choose ones that work for them. And we
need to practice how to do it so it becomes a habit."
—*Elijah, fifteen, Phoenix*

Tarrytown is a picturesque village located in the Hudson River valley about thirty minutes from Manhattan. I was speaking to the students at Pocantico Hills Central School about character. I taught them several ways to put the brakes on impulses and explained: "Self-control is a like a muscle that gets stronger from regular daily exercise, but real and lasting change always comes from the *inside* out." Each student then chose a strategy to work on to develop their self-control muscles.

Then the staff challenged students to go home and practice their chosen self-control muscle builder that night. Those who did would let everyone know by wearing their school shirts the following day inside out. It was a powerful lifelong lesson about real and lasting change for kids as well as parents. After all, kids must learn self-control from the inside out, and we must unleash their abilities so they can. Best yet, the following day—and the next and the next—the kids wore their shirts inside out. They were acquiring the Character Advantage.

CHAPTER 4

Integrity

Thrivers have a strong moral code and stick to it.

NORM CONARD, A HIGH SCHOOL teacher from Uniontown, Kansas, believes that one of the best ways to teach children about developing a moral code is through studying history. Each year he encourages students in his social studies classes to work on an academic competition called National History Day.[1] His wish is that the project will help students learn history and research skills, yes. But Conard's greatest hope is for students to understand that they can be difference makers, just like the people they are studying. It's why his class motto is: "He who changes one person, changes the world entire."[2]

Several years ago, two freshman students in the class, Megan Stewart and Elizabeth Cambers, agreed to work together on the competition. When they asked for help in generating a project idea, Conard gave them a box filled with inspiring articles that he'd clipped over the years and kept handy for students. One was a clipping that mentioned a woman named Irena Sendler and it said she saved more than 2,500 Jewish children from the Holocaust. The girls figured the number was an error—it was more than double the number of rescued lives attributed to Oskar Schindler, after all, and wouldn't they have heard this story before if this woman had really saved so many young people?

"Dig deeper," urged Mr. Conard. So the girls did. They contacted Holocaust centers, libraries, and historical societies. No one had heard of her. Could it all have been a mistake, or a tall tale? One question kept them going: Did one person really make such a difference?

The girls continued a web search and found one hit about Sendler from the Jewish Foundation for the Righteous. Liz phoned the New York City organization, and they confirmed that the story was true, but they didn't have a lot of details. Now they had to know more. "Keep digging," Mr. Conard said.

Sabrina Coons, a junior, joined the team and the girls spent the day at the Midwest Center for Holocaust Education in Kansas City. There they found a photo of a five-month-old who had been smuggled from the Warsaw ghetto past Nazi guards in a carpenter's box: her whole family was later killed in Treblinka. The girls caught their breath: it said that the baby's rescuer was Irena Sendler. The history lesson was coming to life, and the facts were beyond their imagination.

Irena Sendler was a social worker and leader of a Polish underground group. When Nazis began rounding up Jews, the Polish woman was outraged at such cruelty. She disguised herself as an infection control nurse and entered the ghetto to persuade Jewish parents to let her save their children. Between 1942 and 1943, the four-foot eleven-inch woman smuggled babies, children, and teens past Nazi guards in toolboxes, suitcases, and old sewer pipes. Then the woman carefully recorded all the children's names on tissue paper and buried them in glass jars under an apple tree. Someday, she hoped to reunite the children with their parents.

Sendler was eventually caught, tortured, and imprisoned by the Nazis, but refused to disclose the names of those who helped. She later escaped and, amazingly, kept working with the Polish underground. By the war's end almost all the parents had died in the camps, but Sendler had saved over 2,500 children. Then she fell back into obscurity, becoming nothing more than a footnote in history. "How is that possible?" the girls wondered.

And so they consulted dozens of books, reviewed archives, and corresponded with Holocaust survivors. Finally, Liz contacted the Jewish Foundation for the Righteous again to ask where Sendler was buried, and received a shocking reply: she was alive in Warsaw, and they even provided her address. The girls immediately wrote her a letter.

"We walked to the post office to mail it, but wondered why is a woman in eastern Europe going to care about kids in rural Kansas?" Megan Felt told me. "But she responded! I'll never forget the day Liz came running down the hallway shouting, 'We got a letter!' We were so excited! The first line read, 'To my dear beloved girls.' It's still very close to my heart."

The girls were captivated by Sendler's integrity, and they had to tell her story. They penned a ten-minute play about her extraordinary experiences called *Life in a Jar* and presented it to their community. One audience member was so moved that he raised funds to fly the girls, their parents, and their teacher Mr. Conard to Poland to meet their hero. That was how the girls found themselves in Irena Sendler's small Warsaw apartment hugging and crying with her. And they were finally able to ask the one question that haunted them: What moved her to be so heroic?

"What I did was not extraordinary," she told them. "I was just being decent."[3] The woman even admitted that she still had nightmares wondering what more she could have done.[4]

The girls' play is still performed at hundreds of schools and organizations, and one teacher's motto: "He who changes one person, changes the world entire" is now understood not only by the girls but by hundreds of children who have seen the performance. Irena Sendler was nominated for the Nobel Peace Prize in 2007 and passed away in 2008 at the age of ninety-eight, but her legacy of integrity lives on.

But how did Irena Sendler develop such an unshakeable moral core? The answer came from Sendler herself, who said, simply, "It was how I was raised."[5] Irena grew up in a small Jewish town outside Warsaw, the only child of Catholic parents who taught her to respect all people regardless of their religion, social status, or nationality.[6] Her father was a physician known for his kind heart, who treated the poor, including Jews, free of charge, and always told his daughter, "If you see someone drowning, you have to jump in and save them whether you can swim or not." From a young age, Irena was often by his side watching and listening to his example. Young children can learn integrity early, and Irena was learning well.

We want our children to be good people and do the right thing, but what lessons help them develop strong moral compasses so they know what they stand for, stay true to their beliefs, and speak out for what's right? And how do we inspire kids to realize they can make a difference in their world? The road to integrity, as Irena's story shows, starts at home—and can have ripple effects in the world around us for generations to come.

WHAT IS INTEGRITY?

Integrity isn't made up of DNA (or a GPA) but of learned beliefs, capacities, attitudes, and skills that create a moral compass that children use to help them *know* what's right, *care* about what's right, and *do* what's right. This Character Strength sets boundaries, provides strength to resist temptations, and offers kids guidance on how to act the right way even when we're not there to keep them on track! And it gives them, and us, peace of mind when they do the right thing.

Children with integrity are true to themselves and honest with others, as well as tenacious, responsible, courageous, and resilient—the exact type of people we need in our callous, me-first world.[7] But national surveys show this strength in steep decline.

- Over half of teens admit to cheating on a test; 57 percent agree that "successful people do what they have to do to win, even if it involves cheating." [8]
- A national survey of 43,000 teens found stealing and lying rampant; 80 percent of kids admit lying to parents about something important.[9]
- 82 percent of adults feel today's kids today are more self-centered than in past generations.[10]
- School bullying increased 35 percent in three years;[11] one quarter of teens believe it acceptable to threaten or hit someone when angry; 31 percent believe physical violence is a big problem at school.[12]
- 70 percent of teens say they witnessed an increase of bullying, hate, and racially motivated messages.[13]

But despite those disturbing findings, 92 percent of kids feel "quite pleased" with their ethical standards and conduct; 77 percent even say: "When it comes to doing what is right, I am better than most people I know."[14] But here's the key: kids don't become good people through osmosis. Integrity must be intentionally taught, and parents are *always* children's first and best moral teachers.

WHY INTEGRITY CAN BE SO HARD TO TEACH

"It just takes one person to post something bad and
there's irreversible damage. We need to learn courage to do
what we know is right and stand up against cruelty, but that's
only going to work if we see ourselves as good people."
—*Stephanie, thirteen, Myrtle Beach, South Carolina*

The steady onslaught of immoral messages and horrific modeling is taking a toll on kids' moral development, regardless of age or zip code. Scandals of the rich, famous, and powerful lead daily headlines. Professional coaches steal opponents' plays. Political campaigns are nastier. Social media has become a platform for public shaming. Little wonder that our moral lessons aren't getting through.

An elementary student: "Integrity is the school's word of the month, but it's just on a poster. Nobody shows you how to do integrity."

A high school student: "Our school has an honor code, but why should I be the only one to follow it?"

A parent: "Kids' schedules are so jam-packed, how do you expect us to find time to talk about integrity?"

A teacher: "We talk about character at conferences, but parents only want to hear about how to help improve kids' grades and test scores."

A principal: "I recognize students for good character, but parents tell me it was taking away from class time and it doesn't help their kids get into Ivy League schools."

In our grade-obsessed culture integrity lessons are low on many parenting agendas. Here are reasons why "Ethics 101" must be a core part of child-rearing.

Adults Are Displaying Ethically Challenged Behavior

Forget the kids: three out of four Americans say that adults are less moral than we used to be.[15] Headlines support that verdict. In 2019 federal prosecutors charged thirty-three parents for alleged unethical behaviors including bribing university administrators, faking their children's test scores, creating bogus athletic records, fabricating biographies, faking disabilities, and paying others to take their kids' SAT exams.[16]

When it comes to getting your kid that coveted college acceptance, *nothing* is off-limits, but unethical behavior is a steep price to pay for parental bragging rights. What about the honest kids who work their tails off and lose their coveted, well-earned slots due to their classmates' dishonest parents? Kids *are* watching and learning from ethically challenged adult behavior, and their comments are telling. A Manhattan teen told me: "If you don't cheat and everyone else does, your school rank tanks. I'm the loser, because I'm honest." A seventeen-year-old from Sherman Oaks said: "I wrote my college essay. Other parents hired people to write them for their kids. They got admitted to top school choices, I didn't. What's the point of doing the right thing?"

One of the best ways to teach moral behavior is through example, and that puts many kids at a serious disadvantage. Too many parents, leaders, clergy, coaches, scout masters, and celebrities are members of the Hall of Shame.

We Don't Have the Language to Talk About Integrity

Researchers tracked the usage of character words in more than 5.2 million books published over the past decades and found that we literally don't speak, write, or read about character as much these days. Words like "conscience," "morality," "character," "virtue," "honesty," "kind-ness," "courage," and "honor" are declining;[17] terms related to "caring" and "concern for others" decreased the most.

And when we do talk about character with our kids, it doesn't nec-essarily mean what we think it does. David Brooks, author of *The Road to Character,* points out that the word "character" "used to connote traits like selflessness, generosity, self-sacrifice and other qualities that sometimes make worldly success *less* likely. Today the word is used to describe qualities that make worldly success *more* likely."[18]

We Are Disciplining Our Kids the Wrong Way

Many parents today vacillate between two diametrically opposite styles of parenting: on one hand, very strict "autocratic" parenting ("*Because I said so*") or, at the other extreme, very lenient "permissive" parenting ("*Whatever is fine*"). But science shows that neither autocratic or per-missive parenting styles are likely to help kids develop integrity.

Instead, we should be aiming for what science calls an "authorita-tive" style of parenting, characterized by warmth, reasonable demands and high responsiveness: "You know our rules—I know you can do better." The authoritative style is more likely to boost moral growth because it sets consistent family rules and firm limits, but it also en-courages open discussion to explain—and, when justified, revise—rules. Those parameters help kids develop strong moral selves and realize they are their own moral agents—and both are key traits of re-silience.

But here's what a lot of parents are getting wrong today: authorita-tive parenting doesn't necessarily equal the sort of hyper-*intensive* parenting that so many of us think we have to adopt to be on top of our game. Intensive-style parents are *very* involved with their kids at *all*

times—whether enrolling them in extracurricular activities, partici-
pating in their play at home, or advocating for their individualized
needs with teachers and professionals. Those are all good things, of
course, but in moderation.

If we don't step back and allow our kids the freedom to make their
own moral decisions—and, yes, probably fail sometimes—their character growth and ethical growth never have the opportunity to develop
on their own. This is how you end up with kids who lack moral compasses and do whatever it takes for personal gain. We've all heard of
helicopter parenting, but these parents have upgraded to Black Hawk
mode.

To embrace integrity kids must see it in action, recognize that it
matters, and have opportunities to display it. Only then will they grasp
that integrity is the true source of success that can get you to the top
and *stay there.*

HOW TO TEACH KIDS INTEGRITY

While the culture is changing, don't wave the surrender flag too quickly:
this Character Strength *can* be taught. The next sections offer lessons
to instill moral awareness, moral identity, and ethical thinking. Those
abilities help kids develop integrity and give them the Character Advantage, so they think, feel, and act with integrity, become their personal best, and thrive.

Model Moral Awareness to Your Kids

I was talking to a few Florida teachers about this subject, and all of
them mentioned the same student who had recently graduated from

their school: Mia. She "always did the right thing." She had "a strong moral compass." "She stood up for anyone treated unfairly." All of them wondered: How did Mia develop such integrity—and how could they get other kids to model it?

"You should interview her," they said. So I took the young woman to lunch and asked the question on her teachers' minds: "How did you develop such character?"

She smiled and said, "It was the way I was raised." At my prodding, Mia shared how her parents schooled her in character. It's a lesson for us all.

"Mom and Dad always talked about character and expected it of me, but I'll never forget a family meeting when I was six. The kitchen floor was covered with chart paper and markers. Dad told my brothers and me that we were going to decide what we stood for as a family. We brainstormed words like kind, caring, trust, generous, respectful while Mom wrote them down. Then Dad said we had to choose one that best described how we wanted to be remembered. We chose honesty. Our last name is Dunn, and so our family motto became 'The Honest Dunns.'"

I asked how she remembered the motto and Mia laughed. "It was impossible not to! My parents said it fifty times a day. When Dad left for work he'd say: 'Remember, be an Honest Dunn! When Mom dropped us off at school, 'Remember, we're Honest Dunns. We gave Honest Dunn huddles at night. They said that motto so much that we became it.

"I got married recently," she added. "Right before the ceremony, Mom called us all together for one last Honest Dunn huddle. Then Dad walked me down the aisle while I fought the tears. I knew we'd never live together, but I'd always be an Honest Dunn and carry their values in my heart forever."

"My parents said it so much we became it" is the best way to instill moral awareness in our kids. Integrity doesn't materialize from a one-time lecture but from repeated discussing, emphasizing, explaining, modeling, expecting, and reinforcing. Here are simple lessons to help kids understand what integrity is and why you value it, so they "become" it. Just remember the acronym, "teach."

- **T—Target your touchstones.** Reflect on the virtues you deem most significant and want to nurture in your kids and create your family's moral compass. Discuss your choices with your parenting partner. Try to identify a few on which you both agree. Then post your choices in your agenda to remind you to emphasize the touchstones like other aspects of your kids' schedule.

- **E—Exemplify character.** Modeling is one of the best ways to boost children's integrity, so assess your "moral talk." 1. How would my child describe my character to someone else? 2. Is it how I would like to be described? 3. If my child only saw my behavior today what would he catch? Then reflect on how to tune up your chosen moral touchstones in your behavior. The children are watching!

- **A—Accentuate with a motto.** Moral mottoes help kids define who they are as people, so create a family mantra like the Dunn family did. Call a household meeting and ask: "What kind of family do we want to become?" "How do you hope people describe us?" "How do we want to be remembered?" Brainstorm virtues that mean the most to your family and choose one or two that you all agree on. Then turn it into a short, catchy phrase. Keep saying the motto until your kids "become it."

- **C—Catch it.** Help your child understand character by "catching" them living the virtue—and then praise them for it. Use two steps. 1. *Name* the virtue. 2. Then *describe* what the child did to deserve recognition. "It took courage to be *honest* and tell Dad you lost his pen." "I like how *respectful* you were waiting for Grandma to finish speaking." "You showed *responsibility* by doing your chores and then going out."

- **H—Highlight it.** Find daily moments to reinforce the touchstone until your child adopts it as her own. Conflicts: ("We're working on *self-control*, so take a deep breath before talking to your brother.") Driving: ("Wasn't that driver *considerate* when he pulled over to let me in?")

Help Your Kids Develop Their Own Moral Identity

Laying out our own expectations for our kids is a huge part of the integrity puzzle. But equally important is giving them space to develop their *own* moral identity alongside and separate from our own—one that will sustain and maintain them even when we're not around.

I'll never forget my son's fifth birthday. One of his friends sprinted in screaming at the top of his lungs: "Where's the mom? I have to find the mom!!" Assuming the worst, I told Nate that I was the mom and asked what he needed.

"I gotta know your family rules," Nate said. "My mom said yours may be different from ours, and I don't wanna get in trouble. So, what are your rules?"

Caught off guard, I asked him to explain *his* family's rules.

"My mom really says 'Be nice' is our big rule," he said. "I already said a nice thing to Kevin when I walked in. But even if your rules are different, my mom says I have to always use the 'golden one.' I need to treat people like I want to be treated—real nice."

I assured Nate he'd do just fine at the party, because we had almost the same family rules. He smiled with relief, ran off to play, and I made a mental note to have lunch with his mom. I had to tell her what a fabulous job she was doing in helping her child recognize that though some people have different rules, the Golden Rule always applies. At age five, Nate was learning moral identity, the child's image of himself as a good person.

Stanford professor of adolescent development William Damon says that this second ability of integrity develops slowly in hundreds of little ways, like when our kids watch others, reflect on experiences, hear others' feedback, as well as from family, peers, school, religious institutions, and mass media. An image of a moral self begins to form in childhood when kids begin to analyze themselves and others and start to define "who they are." Younger children's self-identifiers are usually action-related skills and involve their interests: "I love soccer." "I play basketball." "I'm a good reader." But with age, kids begin to apply moral descriptors: "I'm kind." "I'm patient." "I'm an honest person." Inner definitions matter because moral identity drives behavior and attitudes, and it is always built from the inside out.[19] In short, kids act how they see themselves to be. Here are lessons to shape your child's moral self.

Kids aren't born knowing right from wrong, which is why we must constantly explain virtues until they internalize our messages. One way is using everyday discipline that "rights the wrong" and drives home the moral lesson. Pretend your child angrily yanks his controller from his friend's hand and his pal bursts into tears. Here's how to use the four Rs of moral discipline.

⇒ **R1: Respond** *calmly* to help your child think about his action. "Why did you take the controller from Sam like that? And it was also his turn."

⇒ **R2: Review** why the behavior is wrong. Say, "It isn't kind when you don't share." "Why do we have the motto 'Be helpful, not hurtful'?" or "What was wrong about what you did?" The key: don't just tell a child that his action was wrong; help him understand *why*.

⇒**R3: <u>Reflect</u>** on the behavior's effects. Ask, "Did you see how sad Sam looked when you grabbed the controller? How would you feel if he grabbed it from you? I'm disappointed in your behavior because I know you're a kind person." When your child has a lingering feeling that his actions were wrong, it's a sign that he is developing moral identity.

⇒**R4: <u>Right</u>** the wrong. Finally, help your child figure out how to improve so he doesn't repeat the same act. "How can you help Sam feel better?" "What will you do next time?" or "Let me know your plan because I expect you to be kind and that just wasn't like you." This final restitution step conveys to a child that you know that he is capable of righting a wrong, and must, because the action didn't match his moral identity and your family's moral beliefs.

Show Your Child How to Speak Out

Children must learn to think, ask, and answer questions to stimulate their moral views. But a ten-year study by Notre Dame sociologist Christian Smith found that most high school graduates lack insufficient moral reasoning and are unable to even consider moral problems in their everyday life.[20] Lectures, test taking, and fact memorizing don't help kids become deep, ethical thinkers, but the ancient teachings of Socrates, the Greek philosopher, hold promising answers and that's why many educators embrace their lessons.

I watched a middle school English teacher using the Socratic lesson model in Riverside, California. Her rules were clear: "Be respectful, speak clearly, participate a minimum of five times, and come prepared to have a scholarly conversation." Seventh graders sat in two concentric circles to facilitate their discussions. Past topics were ethically driven and relevant. ("What are functioning societies?" "What are responsibilities of individuals in society?" "How do decisions impact futures?") Questions were drawn from the book *The Outsiders*. "Is prejudice learned?" "Why do people exclude others?" "How can people be more inclusive?" For the entire period I watched twelve-year-olds reflect, discuss, and defend moral issues about racism and inclusion.

The Socratic process requires adults to step back, so kids learn to think and ask the right questions to develop ethical reasoning, and that's what these kids were doing. In fact, their teacher let students run their own dialogue and they appreciated the opportunity. "Most adults don't let kids share their views, but how will we learn to speak out if we don't practice?" one girl told me. "This helps kids become better people." The process is empowering because kids realize that their views count and will be listened to, and they have the chance to speak up.

Use the Three A's to help your child understand integrity and develop moral reasoning. The objective is to help your child find her voice and develop opinions so she can become an ethical thinker and confidently voice her views.

> **A1: <u>A</u>llow disagreement.** The best place for kids to learn to speak up and clarify their moral principles is at home, so why not start family disagreements? Set clear rules: *Everyone gets a turn and has equal airtime. Listen to each person's full idea. No put-downs allowed.* Topics can range from family concerns (allowances, curfews, and chores) to world issues (poverty, bullying, and immigration). Some families create a box for members to store debate topics. If your kid has a

different opinion or pressing question, let him respectfully share his view. The key point: you don't have to agree, but you must try to understand the other person's view. If you disagree, state your opinion respectfully and offer a strong "why."

A2: Ask questions. Maurice Elias, director of the Rutgers Social-Emotional and Character Development Lab, suggests using prompts to help kids think about moral issues and defend their views.[21] A few:

⇒Whom do you admire? List three of that person's admirable qualities.

⇒Describe an incident or event from which you learned a lesson the hard way.

⇒What three qualities do you value in a friend? A teacher? A parent?

⇒Who has been most important in your life in helping you establish your values?

⇒What are three important values you would encourage in your children one day?

⇒What is the one rule that you believe is important to live your life by?

⇒If we lived in a perfect world, how would people behave differently than they do now?

⇒Use books and real-life examples with younger kids: "Was (*character's name*) really to blame?" "What did you like about him?" "Did you see any of his strengths in your-self?"

A3: <u>A</u>ssert your beliefs. But kids also need our permission to speak up and recognize that we expect them to do the right thing. And we must teach kids that having integrity isn't easy, standing up for moral beliefs is hard, and peer pressure is intense. Practice together until you feel they can do so without guidance.

HOW INTEGRITY CAN BE YOUR CHILD'S SUPERPOWER

"They cannot shoot my dreams, they cannot
kill my beliefs, and they cannot stop my campaign
to see every girl and every boy in school."[22]
—*Malala Yousafzai*

Malala described herself as "a girl like any other." She loved cupcakes and pizza, cracking her knuckles, the color pink, sharing secrets with her best friend, and reading Jane Austen and *The Hunger Games*. But her childhood was unique. Malala grew up in the Swat Valley in Pakistan, one of the most dangerous places in the world, especially for girls. When the Taliban took control and declared a ban on girls' education, Malala refused to be silenced because she believed that education is a human right. At fifteen, she was shot in the head by the terrorist group on her school bus. She miraculously recovered, continues to fight for girls' education, and became the youngest person to win a Nobel Peace

Prize. But how did this young woman acquire such a strong ethical core and resilience? It was the moral lessons she learned as a young girl from her parents.

Samuel and Pearl Oliner conducted one of the most extensive studies of rescuers of Jews during the Holocaust and found striking similarities in how altruists are raised. Parents tended to have close warm, supportive relationships with their children, strongly emphasized kindness, modeled caring behavior, expected their children to apply the value to all people, and used moral reasoning to discipline.[23] This was remarkably similar to how Malala was parented.

Neighbors described Malala's family as "sweet, happy, and laughing a lot," and her parents modeled and expected kindness. "We must never forget to share what we have," her mother would remind her daughter.[24] She grew up in an atmosphere that reinforced strong moral values, *Nang* (or "honor") was among the most important. The few times she lied, the young girl was held accountable and required to give reparations. She never lied again.

Her father told her stories about great heroes like Mahatma Gandhi and Abraham Lincoln. He ran one of the schools in the region that instructed young girls and was an activist for the rights of girls to be educated. He also encouraged his daughter to sit and listen to his and his friends' political discussions, which helped ingrain her values. Her father became Malala's role model.[25] "He inspired me," she said.

Her parents also respected her freedom of thought and gave her self-confidence. "People ask me what has made Malala so bold and courageous, vocal and poised," her father once said. "I tell them, 'Don't ask me what I did. Ask me what I did not do. I did not clip her wings, and that's all.'"[26]

People are often surprised at the strength of Malala's moral beliefs but fail to realize that she was developing and practicing integrity from a young age. By the time she addressed the United Nations at the age of sixteen, she was living her ethical beliefs and no one—including the Taliban—could stop her. Strong integrity is nurtured with the right parenting lessons and experiences: Malala had the gift of both.

AGE-BY-AGE IDEAS TO INSTILL INTEGRITY

> "We never get praised for being just good people.
> It's all about our tests and grades. I guess the
> human part of us doesn't really matter."
> —*Olivia, eleven, San Diego*

Cambridge Elementary School in San Antonio has a beautiful rock garden under a large oak tree. The counselor, Diana Cashion, told me that the school's goal was to help each student "excel academically as well as become a confident, compassionate citizen with impeccable character." But teachers worried that parents, like most these days, focused on academics, putting character low on their priorities. So they gave parents homework: "Please talk to your child about their key Character Strength, why you admire it, and write your answer on this form."

Students returned their assignment the next day with exuberance: "My mom loved my kind heart!" "My parents told me they're glad I'm so responsible." "My dad appreciates my honesty!"[27] Then each child painted their identified Character Strength on a rock and placed it in the garden. That day countless kids proudly pointed out their rock. "Mine says I'm empathetic," one boy said. "My dad told me so!" I wondered whether kids would recognize their Character Strengths without that homework assignment. Our children need lessons that develop their "human sides."

Symbols designate recommended age suitability for each activity: Y = Young children, toddlers, and preschoolers; S = School age; T = Tweens and older; A = All ages

- **Acknowledge integrity.** Praise ethical behavior when your child displays it so he recognizes that you value it. Call out integrity, and then describe the action so your child knows what he did that deserves recognition so that he will be more likely to repeat the behavior. Using the word "because" makes your praise more specific. "That showed integrity *because* you refused to pass on that gossip." "You showed integrity *because* you kept your promise to go with your friend even though you had to give up the slumber party!" "That was integrity *because* you were honest despite everyone cheating. Integrity is doing the right thing even if not popular." **S, T**
- **Do "two goldens."** A key message is to help children realize that people with integrity treat *everyone* equally and in the way they would like to be treated. A Palm Springs mom told me that she wanted her girls to learn the Golden Rule so she encouraged her kids to do what she called "two goldens" every day ("two things you'd like someone else to do to you because that's the way you'd like to be treated"). They brainstormed simple "golden ideas" (like opening the door, smiling, asking someone to play). Then each night they shared what they did. The mom told me, "The more they practiced, the more they began to see themselves as people of character. Then we took it up a notch by brainstorming 'goldens' that

take courage and aren't always popular: like speaking up for someone treated unfairly, asking an excluded classmate to sit with them at lunch, or comforting a bullied peer. It's a joy watching integrity grow in my children." Try the idea with your children. **Y, S**

- **Play "What if?"** Hold a "What if?" chat for any moral infraction to right the wrong. If your child "borrows" something from a friend without asking, pose: "*What if* that happened to you? How would you feel *if* someone took something from your backpack without your knowing?" "*What if* everyone cheated (lied, cyberbullied, or plagiarized)? What can you do to build your integrity muscle?" Continue posing "what if" questions until your child understands that integrity isn't always easy but is necessary for people to trust you. And they will be more likely to do the right thing and take responsibility for their behavior—even if no one is looking. **S, T**

- **Create a hero box.** Norm Conard filled a box with stories of inspiring people and changed his students' lives. Create a family box of articles and discuss the person so your child grasps the impact of integrity. "Who inspires you?" "What virtue do you admire?" "How did it help others?" Check out the Giraffe Heroes Project (giraffe.org), *50 American Heroes Every Kid Should Meet* by Dennis Denenberg or *Real Heroes* by Lawrence Reed. Introduce your child to Irena Sendler, Hugh Thompson, and Malala Yousafzai in this chapter as well as in the book *I Am Malala: How One Girl Stood Up for Education and Changed the World.* **S, T**

- **Bring heroes to life.** One in four teens admits they are influenced more by celebrities than people they know,[28] and a Gallup Youth Survey found that a substantial number of American teens said they had *no* heroes.[29] Introduce individuals who can help your child understand integrity, including Abraham Lincoln, Emmeline Pankhurst, Mahatma Gandhi, Rosa Parks, John Lewis, Harriet Tubman, as well as real folks in your children's lives like Auntie Jo or the firefighter next door. Stress that it takes courage to maintain integrity and do the right thing, no matter what the consequences. The Shipley School holds a Hero Day where younger students make life-size cardboard cutouts of their heroes. (I'll never forget a fourth grader introducing me to his hero, Martin Luther King, Jr., and sharing the strengths he admired.) Teacher Sally Songy has second graders dress up as their hero. (My son was Dwight D. Eisenhower.) **Y, S**

- **Use virtue mantras.** Mantras can help children understand character. Find one about integrity that fits your family's values. "Honesty is the best policy." "Tell the truth." "Keep your promises." "Do what you say," or "Walk your talk." Then keep repeating and explaining the one phrase in context until your kids can use it without you. Our family's motto was: "Actions speak louder than words." My grown sons still end our chats with "I know, Mom, 'actions'!" **A**

- **Read books about integrity.** Books help kids recognize how people with strong integrity contribute to a society. Younger children: *Stand Tall* by Cheri J. Meiners; *The Boy Who Cried Wolf* by B. G. Hennessy; *My Name Is Truth* by Ann Turner; *The Golden Rule* by Ilene Cooper; *Horton Hears a Who!* by Dr. Seuss; *The Three Questions* by Jon J. Muth. Older kids and teens: *Nothing but the Truth* by Avi; *The Hate U Give,* by Angie Thomas; *Harry Potter and the Goblet of Fire* by J. K. Rowling. Family: *The Children's Book of Virtues* by William J.

Bennett, and *What Stories Does My Son Need?* by Michael Gurian. **A**

- **Establish an honor code.** The Taipei American School is an academically rigorous school in Taiwan, and their student honor council was onstage making a plea to peers to sign an honor code. They knew that success required sustained agreement from all, so they were making a case for integrity, and I cheered because their peers signed. Research shows that honor codes upheld by serious commitment to integrity work.[30] Set an honor code in your home, sports team, club, school, or community. Teacher Deb Brown asks students to sign each assignment attesting that it was completed with honesty and cheating went down. **S, T**

- **Identify a "kid-concern" cause.** Too often service projects are chosen based on what looks good on college résumés. Don't fall for the academic mania trap! Service learning can help develop integrity, *but the experience must be developmentally appropriate, meaningful, and match the child's interest.*[31] Find a project that matches your child's passion like volunteering at a local soup kitchen, helping at Special Olympics, or playing Candy Land with kids at a shelter. In fact, actions of moral exemplars are frequently ignited when they find causes aligned with their ethical beliefs.[32] **S, T**

- **Create an integrity-building network.** Pass your family touchstones on to grandparents, relatives, and others who care deeply for your child. Find coaches, teachers, scout masters, and club leaders who emulate integrity. Start parent groups to discuss raising kids with integrity or read books together like *The Moral Child* by William Damon; *Raising Good Children* by Thomas Lickona; *Building Moral Intelli-*

gence or *Thrivers* by me (use the discussion guide in the appendix). Get on board with parents of your child's friends and do service projects together. The more kids hear the *same* character message and are surrounded by people who model integrity, the more likely they will become people of character. **A**

TOP FIVE TAKEAWAYS

1. Children's moral growth is an ongoing process that spans the course of their lifetime.
2. Parents play a significant role in helping kids develop moral codes to guide behavior.
3. Integrity must be nurtured, influenced, modeled, and taught. Use your time wisely!
4. Kids must hear repeated messages about character. Keep explaining why it matters.
5. Moral development isn't learned in a vacuum but is influenced by parents, neighbors, peers, schools, and communities. Find ways to create a culture of integrity.

ONE LAST LESSON

Early in the morning of March 16, 1968, a twenty-four-year-old army chief warrant officer was flying a helicopter and spotted scattered bodies of Vietnamese civilians lying below. He realized Americans troops were shooting unarmed men, women, and children on orders from their superior officer Lt. William Calley. The young pilot faced a split-second moral decision: comply with his commander's instructions or defy military authority and help the civilians knowing that it might mean a court-martial.

Hugh Thompson, Jr., chose to do what he knew was right. He immediately reported the massacre and radioed for backup. Over the next few hours, he flew in the line of fire, helped evacuate civilians, and shielded villagers with his body. When superior officers ordered him to back down, Thompson refused and continued to offer medical support for the wounded. His courageous efforts led to the cease-fire order at My Lai and stopped the atrocities.[33]

So where did Thompson get his extraordinary character? "I just think it was my parents, and they taught me right from wrong," he said. "They always taught me to live by the Golden Rule: 'Do unto others as you would have them do unto you.'"[34]

Irena Sendler, Malala Yousafzai, and Hugh Thompson are three very different individuals who did extraordinary deeds. Each credited learning integrity from how they were raised, so when their moment came they had no choice but to do the right thing. Parents don't raise ethical children by accident; they are intentional and consistent in their efforts. And they use everyday moments to teach lessons about integrity, so their kids learn to walk and talk their family's beliefs and thrive.

CHAPTER 5

Curiosity

Thrivers are out-of-the-box thinkers.

THREE-YEAR-OLD SAM HOUGHTON INVENTED A double-headed broom by hooking a big elastic band over two brooms to sweep leaves faster, and became the youngest child to hold a patent.[1]

Thirteen-year-old Alissa Chavez was upset about toddlers dying when accidentally left in hot cars. She created a Hot Seat cushion with a sensor connected to the parent's smartphone to alarm them if their baby was still in the car.[2]

Riya Karumanchi was fourteen when she met a woman using a white cane but struggling to get around. The tech-obsessed Canadian teen engineered a device called SmartCane that vibrates and alerts the user of treacherous situations. "My initial thought was like, What? How is nobody working on this?"[3]

Kids of any age can be innovators. The tricky question is how to nurture children's creative gifts in an era of conformity, test-obsession, and extreme safety consciousness especially following a pandemic. I found some of the best lessons in one of the most innovative labs in the world.

If you've read a book on an e-reader, built a robot with your kids on

Lego Mindstorms, asked Siri for information, or ridden in a vehicle with child-safe airbags, you've experienced a sampling of the extraordinary inventions of MIT's Media Lab in Cambridge, Massachusetts. I spent the day observing these creative geniuses, and I learned that their success is based on four principles: peers, passion, projects, and play.[4] We can use those same principles to unleash our children's curiosity and resilience from toddler to teen.

Peers. The MIT lab is housed in a unique six-story glass building with no walls: just open space so all researchers can view each other from various vantage points. What you see and hear is an endless flow of ideas that have birthed some of the most original inventions in the world, like driverless cars, growing food in the desert, connecting the human brain to the internet. But immediately evident is intellectual diversity: computer scientists, musicians, neurobiologists, designers, artists, biomedical engineers, and architects all working together across academic boundaries to find solutions to humanity.

Curiosity flourishes when people—regardless of age—collaborate and build on one another's work. Too often we pigeonhole kids' learning into set subjects and pit them against each other in high stakes testing environments. If we want our kids to be open to diversity, they must be exposed to different opinions and learn to collaborate.

Shannon, a fifteen-year-old from Baton Rouge told me, "Kids don't know each other well because we're always doing individual work. We should be doing more team-building exercises that give us more time to be creative, follow our passions, and have fun." When peers learn from each other, the need to outperform the other diminishes because each kid's learning enhances another's performance instead of inhibiting it.

Passion. Eminent psychologist Mihaly Csikszentmihalyi found that when creative people are passionate about projects, they experience a state of total absorption and joy that he calls "flow." "You know that what you need to do is *possible* to do, even though difficult," Csikszentmihalyi explains. "You forget yourself, you feel part of something larger . . . what you are doing becomes worth doing for its own sake."[5]

In every lab I watched intensely focused, excited, and eager adults performing difficult tasks. I watched projects break, fall, and clearly not go as planned, but those failings never stopped them: the designers just picked up the pieces, altered their course, and kept on. They were rejuvenated and eager—even when faced with setbacks—because they were driven by their passion. That performance-enhancing formula also works for children.

Watch your kids when they are so absorbed that they don't want to stop: they're in that flow state fueled by their curiosity. Eighty-two percent of more than forty thousand American high school students[6] said they would "relish opportunities to be creative at school" and admit they're most engaged when activities are meaningful to their lives.[7] They're not getting these opportunities to express their imaginations and explore their interests in our grades-first academic culture. Our job is to find our kids' passions and nurture them.

The Sandy Hook school massacre inspired the robotics club at Benjamin Banneker Academic High School to find a solution to a problem they identified: "We wanted to know how we could stop intruders from entering our school," said Deonté Antrom, a junior.[8] The teens created an affordable emergency metal door-lock prototype called DeadStop that easily locks onto a door and stops entry into a classroom in the case of an active shooter. Their creative solution was driven by a need to help others and prevent a similar tragedy from unfolding in the same way in other schools. "We did it for other people," junior Anjreyev Harvey said, "not to put on our [college] application."[9] The students were awarded a $10,000 grant by the Lemelson-MIT Student

Prize to develop the invention further and got pro bono representation from a law firm to file for a patent. Their invention now sells for $15.[10] Innovation driven by passion to help humanity can produce profound results—at any age.

Projects. Have you noticed that kids are more energized when involved in projects they care about? It's because curiosity builds when kids are tinker*ing*, shar*ing*, build*ing*, draw*ing*, construct*ing*, play*ing*, develop*ing*, or doing what I call "ing-ing." Active engagement increases curiosity; passivity reduces it. Projects ignite curiosity; worksheets stifle it. That's why ing-ing is a key part of the lab. Everywhere I visited I saw MIT students excitedly work*ing* on projects together—whether develop*ing* concepts, design*ing* prototypes, mak*ing* improvements, or creat*ing* ideas. And their finished products were outstanding: Amazon Kindle, Clocky, Guitar Hero, Symphony Painter, Audio Spotlight, and XO laptop, just to name a few.

One reason for their exemplary creative performance is an understood MIT rule: everyone encourages one another to take risks. In fact, there are no "wrong" answers or "crazy" ideas: out-of-box thinking is relished. Challenges and setbacks are considered chances to rethink and explore options. "Great ideas don't come from playing safe," Frank Moss, former MIT Media Lab director, explains. "Rather, they come from thinking about things in a way that no else has."[11] It's why "That can't be done" or "It won't work" isn't part of the MIT vocabulary.

Unfortunately, our kids play it safe because they worry that their original ideas or wrong answers might jeopardize their college chances. A Florida science teacher told me that he wrote: "In this class failure is not an option but a requirement" on his smartboard. Students read it and were dumbfounded. "It took three months of convincing," he said. "They're just now starting to take risks and their originality is *finally* increasing. I also had to revise my lessons by putting kids in teams to

do projects. They kept repeating to each other, 'Mistakes are okay.'"
Curiosity flourishes when students are encouraged to think outside the
box, take creative risks, work on projects, and know that failure *is* an
option.

Play. My favorite lab at MIT was Lifelong Kindergarten, where
university and grad students work in the spirit of play from their kindergarten days. Counters, tables, and floors were covered with ham-
mers, nails, cardboard, metal, 3D printers, bolts, plastic pieces, and
whiteboards to help researchers create with the childlike thrill of discovery. Floor-to-ceiling shelves were filled with Legos—and the adults
were playing with them. The typical engineering tools of computers
and protractors were replaced with tactile, tangible *toys*! It almost
looked more like recess than a high-tech research facility.

But at the same time, they were talk*ing*, collaborat*ing*, tinker*ing*,
creat*ing*, question*ing*, and innovat*ing* products to better humanity.
"If we really want kids to develop as creative thinkers," says Director of
the Lifelong Kindergarten, Mitchel Resnick, "we need to make the rest
of school—in fact, the rest of life—more like kindergarten."[12]

Imagine how our play-deprived, digital-driven, stressed-out,
running-on-empty children would relish classrooms designed with
those four MIT principles. Kids tell me how hard it is to sit passively at
desks, listen to lectures, and do lengthy paper-pencils tasks. An eight-
year-old described her classroom as a "worksheet factory." Many educators recognize the curiosity deficiency and are adding those four P's:
peers, passion, projects, and play, but they are also finding a surprise
obstacle: their students.

A middle school Houston teacher implemented Genius Hour. Students pick a question that piques their curiosity, and then research the
answer over weeks or the year. I watched his introduction. "I know
you're curious about things," he said. "Each week I'll give you an hour

to learn about something you're passionate and curious about! What do you wonder about?"

The kids looked at one another, and then back to the teacher. Silence.

"Come on!" he asked. "It's your chance to find answers and be creative!" More silence.

Then one brave kid raised his hand and said what was probably on the students' minds. "No one ever asks us to be curious," he said. "We may need some time to think."

The teacher and I locked eyes and realized a sad truth: this Character Strength is such a low priority in children's ultra-packed, test-taking lives that they need permission to be curious. MIT has a formula to cultivate it, leading organizations verify that curiosity is imperative for our future, science says it helps kids be more resilient and lead more meaningful lives. Now it's time for adults to give kids their consent to be inquisitive, think boldly, and wonder about their world.

WHAT IS CURIOSITY?

> "We're forced to grow up too quickly and we're tired.
> We need more time to play and be kids."
> —*Isabella, eleven, Sherman Oaks*

Your son reads a book and comes across a new fact. Your daughter visits a museum and is fascinated with a concept she's never heard of. Suddenly, they want to know more! Curiosity is the "recognition, pursuit, and intense desire to explore novel, challenging and uncertain events."[13] Watch a toddler explore a new environment and you'll see this Character Strength in action.

My two-year-old grandson's curiosity is unstoppable. Hand him a wooden bowl and a plastic spoon, and the Rolling Stones have serious competition. Give him chalk and an easel, and watch out Picasso. If he sees a butterfly, he puts his world on hold. Sure, I'm biased, but the truth is *all* toddlers are creative geniuses with endless amounts of eagerness to learn and discover; to experiment and try. Their hungry minds are still guided by an open sense of wonder and unpolluted by "no, can't, don't," or worries about grades, scores, and résumé fillers. The trick is keeping our children's curiosity unleashed, because the benefits are profound.

- The World Economic Forum predicts curiosity, complex problem solving, and critical thinking will be *the most crucial* skills for our children's future.[14]
- 90 percent of respondents in a recent Pew Research survey[15] named creativity, collaboration, and abstract thinking as *essential* for the changing employability market.
- Leading world organizations and universities (including IBM, Harvard, and Bloomberg) name this Character Strength as an essential twenty-first century-skill.[16]

Curiosity is what helps children to be open to possibilities and motivates them to learn—both inside the classroom and beyond it. Students with greater curiosity have greater academic success than less curious peers.[17] In fact, a meta-analysis[18] of two hundred studies involving over fifty thousand students found that *curiosity is as important as intelligence* in determining how well kids do in school.

But this Character Strength also inspires children to think in new ways, make discoveries, and sparks interests and stirs creativity. It helps kids want to acquire new information, consider exploring new horizons, and inspires them to chase their dreams. It fuels children to find solutions, challenges them to explore diverse ideas, motivates them to follow their passions, and to greet each day with "What else can I discover?" That's why kids who score higher in curiosity consistently report greater psychological well-being: they feel fulfilled and less depleted because they're using their strengths and following their ambitions so they thrive.[19, 20]

And here's the best news of all: curiosity also has a Multiplier Effect. If you pair curiosity with any Character Strength discussed in this book, it's a surer formula for success. Simply put: curiosity amplifies children's talents, strengths, performance, and potential.

> *Curiosity + Self-Confidence* increases the openness to take
>   healthy risks and explore.
> *Curiosity + Empathy* opens and strengthens relationships.
> *Curiosity + Perseverance* deepens learning.
> *Curiosity + Integrity* can start a social movement.

Curiosity makes children's lives interesting, and provides necessary skills to thrive in a challenging world. And when kids face obstacles, this trait helps them think of ways to resolve their problem and find new ways to "pick themselves up and start all over again." It's all the reasons why we must nurture this crucial Character Strength in our depleted kids who are running on empty.

WHY CURIOSITY CAN BE SO HARD TO TEACH

Picasso said it best: "Every child is an artist. The problem is how to remain an artist once he grows up." Though curiosity *can* be learned, it can easily be unlearned. Helping today's kids maintain their hungry minds is now a global priority—and the lack of curiosity we're fostering in the next generation of children is a looming crisis.

George Land, with NASA researchers, tracked the creative potential of 1,600 young children over time. Ninety-eight percent of four- and five-year-olds scored at the creative genius level. Five years later, only 30 percent of the same kids were at that level; and at age fifteen, only 12 percent were creative geniuses. By thirty-one years of age, the percentage of creative geniuses had dropped to a mere 2 percent![21] Other research confirms that our children's creativity is in free fall.

Kyung Hee Kim, a professor of education at the College of William & Mary, analyzed thousands of creativity scores of children and adults over decades and found creativity steadily rising until 1990, then starting to decline and continuing to drop. "The decrease is very significant," Kim said. But "it is the scores of younger children in America—from kindergarten through sixth grade—for whom the decline is most serious."[22]

Curiosity diminishes for many reasons, including certain parenting styles that put kids' curiosity on a short leash. Luckily, science can show us the right lessons to nurture this crucial Character Strength.

We Rely Too Much on External Rewards

"What do I get if I do it?" "How much will you give me?" "I won't do it for less than ten dollars."

If you've heard any of these phrases from your kids, chances are they're suffering from a widespread epidemic called "hooked on rewards." Symptoms are expecting those gold stars, stickers, or monetary prizes for a job well done. But research[23] proves that tangible enticers can make kids *less* creative and *worse* at problem solving,[24] and the effect is even *more* detrimental for school-age kids than for college-age students.

- Preschoolers who previously enjoyed drawing were far *less* motivated to draw if they expected gold seals and ribbon rewards. Judges even rated their pictures as *less* aesthetically pleasing if they drew after receiving enticers.[25]
- Fifth and sixth graders praised for their creative-type tasks did *lower* quality work when compared with students who received more neutral-type comments.[26]
- Sixth-grade students graded on the results of their work—instead of simply encouraged to focus on the task itself—decreased in performance, creativity, and interest in the task at hand.[27]

Alfie Kohn, author of *Punished by Rewards,* analyzed hundreds of studies and concluded that enticing children with incentives ultimately does more harm than good, especially when it comes to their curiosity.

"Do rewards motivate people? Absolutely," Kohn said. "They motivate people to get rewards."[28] Curiosity is internally driven, so announce a "No rewards for every little thing" policy, and then expect your kids to do their best—without those enticers.

Parents Are Micromanaging

We say we don't, but science shows that we treat kids differently based on their birth order, and it's why our youngest are more likely to become our most creative. An analysis of eleven thousand teens by the National Longitudinal Survey of Youth found that we are far less strict with our youngest—we relax a bit more, don't hover as much, and don't set nearly as many rules as we do with our oldest.[29] And so our youngest (Charles Darwin, Harriet Tubman, Copernicus, and Mozart are a few) turn out to be more laid-back, more willing to see another point of view, and more creative.[30, 31] Youngest kids also take more risks, are more original in their thinking, and are likelier to question authority: all qualities of the curious.

Studies also find that *less intense parenting* produces more creative kids. Children rated as creative by teachers were compared with those who were not considered highly creative.[32] Researchers found that parents of highly creative children had fewer rules and less rigid timetables and schedules than parents of not unusually creative kids.

While we should hold kids accountable, we also need to step back and micromanage less: too many restrictions hinder curiosity. Decide your non-negotiables (generally ones regarding safety and your moral code), and then slowly unleash from those excess rules to give kids freedom to explore, learn self-sufficiency, and feel less depleted and more fulfilled.

We Have Lost the Time to Tinker

My entertainment on a recent three-hour flight was watching a preschooler and his most prepared mother sitting next to me. Mom's "flight goodie bag" included workbooks, craft sets, flash cards, and electronic gizmos. From the time they buckled up until touchdown, there wasn't a second her child wasn't occupied—and every activity was parent directed. While we mean well, filling our kids' schedule minute by minute with adult-managed activities jeopardizes their curiosity and thriving potential. Solo, undirected times when kids let their thoughts wander often produce the most profound personal and creative insights.[33] "Alone moments" are also when kids can gain fresh ideas, spin creative thoughts, or just decompress.[34] Curiosity can't be rushed or have time limits, and needs lots of trial and error.

Our kids' fast-paced lives don't leave intervals for quiet reflection, let alone cloud watching. In fact, 7 percent of U.S. schools no longer provide daily recess time for young kids, trading in monkey bars for more test prep.[35] But it's not only classwork—the heaps of extracurricular activities we sign our children up for (all in the hopes of making them well rounded) are instead causing them to fall flat and feel depleted. All this well-meaning scheduling further reduces the opportunities for kids to just tinker. And if there *are* any free moments, kids admit to spending them on electronic devices, which are not the greatest curiosity boosters.

Look at your child's schedule: Is there unstructured downtime where your child's mind can just wander? Cutting just one activity a week can free up time for kids to unleash curiosity.

HOW TO TEACH KIDS CURIOSITY

Curiosity must be developed to prepare our children for an uncertain twenty-first century and help them thrive. The good news is that this Character Strength is not innate but stretchable. Using these science-backed lessons will teach three abilities that raise stronger, world-ready kids who feel fulfilled: a curious mind-set, creative problem solving, and divergent thinking.

Develop a Curious Mind-set

Parents can make a big difference on their children's character and future success *if* they help them develop mind-sets that are open to curiosity and the capacity to imagine, create, and invent ideas. Orville

Wright (who made aviation history with his brother Wilbur) said: "The greatest thing in our favor was growing up in a family where there was always much encouragement to intellectual curiosity."[36] Steve Jobs's father set up a workshop in the garage with a space for his son to tinker. Steven Spielberg said his life changed when he was sixteen and his father gave him a camera.[37] Matt Damon's mom said he "played pretend games for hours every day for many years, making up stories, taking on roles and reworking his experiences in creative ways." [38]

I asked kids to describe the type of experiences most likely to satisfy their hungry minds and spur their curiosity. From sandbox to prom age, they inevitably named open-ended, active, kid-driven experiences a tad on the unusual side.

"Science projects, because we figure stuff out. Yesterday we put raisins in bubbling water where they dance but sink in drinking water. Then we guessed why!" —Johnny, seven, Rancho Mirage

"Our media lab! We get to design our own website about a topic we're passionate about. I'm creating one on animal endangerment." —Gianna, eleven, Kansas City

"History! Our teacher makes us pretend to be in a place in our text. We close our eyes and picture ourselves at the Battle of Bull Run and imagine what we looked like, wore, behaved, and felt. She makes history come alive!" —Sally, sixteen, Dallas

Such opportunities help kids believe in their creative abilities and keep their curiosity vibrant. These seven factors are proven curiosity builders that we can use in our homes and schools.

C **Child-driven.** The activity piques the child's interest or passion.

U **Unmanaged.** The child, not the adult, is planning, structuring, or directing the learning.

R **Risky.** The task is a little uncertain and a bit out of the child's comfort zone.

I **Intrinsic.** The activity is driven by the child from the inside out, and not motivated by a reward.

O **Open ended.** The end is unknown and there's more than one answer or possibility.

U **Unusual.** The task is novel, with the chance to explore or experience the unknown.

S **Solitude.** There is time to contemplate, daydream, and gather thoughts or rejuvenate.

But it's one thing to want to instill curiosity in your child, and quite another to understand how to weave these lessons into everyday life. And those lessons are even more crucial in our unpredictable, safety-conscious pandemic world. Here are some specific ideas for getting curious with your kid and teaching him or her how to approach life with a curious mind-set.

- **Provide creative-building moments.** Review the seven curiosity boosters and assess how many are part of your child's daily experiences. Which are lacking? What can you do to increase curiosity boosters into your child's regime? How will you begin?
- **Use open-ended toys, gadgets, and games.** Creative kids thrive on experiences where they can let their imaginations go wild and don't have to worry about "right" answers. Offer

unstructured, open-ended products to let your kids' minds go free, like marking pens, finger paints, sugar cubes, yarn, popsicle sticks, paper tubes, and masking tape to create constructions. (My boys loved finger painting on our kitchen counter with instant pudding.) Keep a batch of homemade Play-Doh in the fridge. Provide flashlights and sheets to fling over chairs to make forts, castles, and caves. Offer paper clips and pipe cleaners and challenge your kids to see how many unusual ways they can use them. Or introduce mud, sand, and water and let your younger kids' creativity soar.

- **Ask, "I wonder?"** Verbalizing our own curiosities gives kids permission to be inquisitive. So start by saying your queries out loud to your child: "I wonder why the lake is frozen?" "I wonder what would happen if bees became extinct?" "I wonder why the sky is blue?" Then encourage your kids to share their own wonders, and challenge them to find the answers to keep their inquisitiveness alive by using the next tip.

- **Stretch inquisitiveness.** Instead of "That won't work," try: "Let's see what happens!" Instead of giving answers, ask: "What do *you* think?" "How do *you* know?" or "How can *you* find out?" As you read a book, watch a film, or just walk by someone, model inquisitiveness with "I wonder" questions. "I wonder *what* he's doing?" "I wonder *where* she's going?" "I wonder *why* they're doing that?" "I wonder *what* happens next?"

- **Create a tinkering space.** Curiosity thrives at any age with playful, active, hands-on, ing-ing experiences, so create a tinkering area like at MIT or in Steve Jobs's garage where your kids and their friends can let their imaginations soar. Two twelve-year-olds at a Los Angeles middle school told me their favorite part of the day was the after-school Tinker Club. The girls showed me tables covered with broken cell phones, key-boards, computers, stereos, and radios to take apart, reas-semble, and tinker away. "We get to take stuff apart and figure stuff out," one explained. "It's how we learn innovation." Gather wires, hooks, magnets, hammer, nails, levers (and whatever else); old cameras, computers, cell phones, DVD players, and gadgets for kids to take apart and put together. Also, check your community for innovation labs, children's discovery museums, or makerspaces.

- **Allow solitude.** Creative kids need time to daydream, play, and imagine. Keep an eye on your child's weekend or after-school schedule, and carve in downtime without digital devices. You may need to help your kid learn to enjoy his own company. Stock a basket with items like the ones below, and introduce them gradually to see where your child's interests lie.

⇒*Leonardo da Vinci Box:* Glue, paper towel rolls, popsicle sticks, paper clips, tinfoil

⇒*Frank Lloyd Wright Box*: Hammer, nails, wood, lever, measuring tape, sandpaper

⇒*Frida Kahlo Box:* Paper, crayons, pencils, paint, paint-brush, canvas, colored markers

⇒*Meryl Streep Box*: Hats, scarves, old shirts, torn sheets, bath towels for capes

⇒*Louisa May Alcott Box:* Paper, pencils, and a notebook or journal

⇒*Taylor Swift Box*: Sound-making objects, including paper tubes, wax paper, rubber bands, bowls, wooden spoons, musical instruments

Brainstorm Creative Problem Solving

Problem solving sparks curiosity, generates ideas, develops divergent thinking, solves challenges, and increases resilience. And even preschoolers are capable of learning to problem solve.[39] Widely respected psychologists George Spivack and Myrna Shure found that when young children learn the skill, they are less likely to be impulsive when things don't go their way, more caring, less insensitive, better able to make friends and achieve greater academic success. There are fun ways to teach this essential twenty-first-century skill, and I've learned the best lessons from kids.

Odyssey of the Mind is an international creative problem-solving program for kindergarten through college. I've coached three elementary school teams, and I am convinced that the process is one of the best ways to get kids' creative juices flowing. Kids work yearlong in teams up to seven members on one problem ("from inventing a factory machine to writing a new chapter to *Moby Dick*").[40] Then—*without adult help*—kids create their script, sets, costumes, props, and perform their solution to adult judges. And the criterion for winning: creativity!

My role was helping kids learn to collaborate, think outside the box, capitalize on each other's strengths (ideal teams have members with diverse strengths like music, art, science, design, drama, and writing), and identify their problem to solve. One year a member told the team that he was worried about trees: "They're close to extinction!" he announced. Well, the fifth graders were livid and decided that their performance would address the "tree problem." I taught them how to brainstorm, and then I stepped back as they created their play. I was amazed as I watched their risk-taking, problem-solving, and creative abilities grow through the process—I was seeing MIT Media Lab's four principles (peers, passion, projects, play) in action.

Their final performance was a testament to the kids' creativity. Johnny Appleseed (one team member named Sarah) introduced the tree problem, two boys (both named Adam) traveled through time (through a sheet with a hole) to describe a future without trees, three "forest rangers" (Mohsen, Uval, and Maritza) offered creative ways to reduce endangerment, and then Byron Williams, one of the team members, closed by singing a song that he wrote to the tune of "We Are the World."

> "Now it is time to sing our 'tree song.'
> And there are lots and lots of words to say, so let's start singing.
> It's a choice we're making; we're saving our own lives.
> So, leave our trees alone for our world."

Byron stunned the audience with his stirring lyrics and majestic voice. Seven diverse fifth graders had unleashed their curiosity around their joint passion, and prevailed. The team placed third in the state that year, and the competition taught them important life lessons, but it took me two decades to fully realize their value. I just delivered a keynote to teachers in my hometown, and a young man stood waiting at the bottom of the stage steps holding a photo. I instantly recognized the image: my fifth-grade Odyssey team! The man smiled, pointed to the boy dressed as a tree, and then back to himself. It was Bryon! He taught music for several years, was now a third-grade teacher, and came to my speech because he wanted to tell me the value of the experience.

"Odyssey of the Mind helped us discover our creativity," he told me. "It gave us the chance to learn to work together to solve a problem we cared deeply about. It's exactly what kids need today."

Sometimes parenting lessons take time to understand. As their coach, I now realize that a big reason for their creative growth was because they repeatedly practiced brainstorming: what all kids need now and later to thrive.

Brainstorming ignites kids' creativity, better prepares them to handle challenges, bounce back from adversity, and is teachable. First, explain brainstorming: "Every problem has a solution. The trick to getting unstuck is to brainstorm or 'spark your brain' for solutions." Then share five brainstorming rules. Each letter in the acronym SPARK stands for one rule. Posting the SPARK rules helps kids remember them until they can use them without visual reminders or our guidance.

> S—**Say the problem.** Clarify to yourself or others what needs resolving.
>
> P—**Positives only.** Set a no-judgment zone. Put-downs and criticisms stifle curiosity.
>
> A—**Add on to create more options.** Piggybacking is fine. *Every* idea counts.
>
> R—**Rapid-fire ideas.** Say the first thing that comes to mind. A fast pace sparks creativity.
>
> K—**Keep storming until there are no more ideas or the time limit you set to brainstorm expires.** Choose what you and the group can agree to.

Then practice SPARK using age-related problems with your child or as a family. A few: "What shall we name our puppy?" "Why is lying wrong?" "How can schools be more relevant for kids?" Your child can use the rules to solve his own problems or use them with others so he learns collaborative brainstorming. Then from this moment on, anytime your child is confronted with a dilemma, *don't solve it.* Instead, unleash his creative powers: "Spark your mind and think of what *you* can do to solve it! I know you can."

Take Creative Risks

I was observing an AP history lesson in an elite, affluent Boston school. The teacher was engaging, knew his subject, and cared about his students. The lesson was on the Holocaust, and he wanted kids to think deeply, so he posed thought-provoking questions beyond the text.

"Why is it important to confront the brutality of this history?"

"What is the meaning of human dignity?"

"What are creative ways to ensure that the Holocaust is never forgotten?"

His smart, well-educated kids knew the material, but I saw hesitancy. Few raised their hands, and those who did shared only tentative, brief remarks. No intellectual curiosity or original ideas were voiced. Meeting their teacher's approval and earning high marks trumped taking the risk to think differently. One student explained later, "I didn't want to say something that might jeopardize my grade." Their behavior showcased a troubling new trend.

Many teachers worry that students are "idea cautious" and hesitant to stray from the status quo.[41] Grade obsession and résumé adulation are partly to blame. Kids put so much energy into test taking, merit gathering, accolade accumulating, and gold-star collecting that sharing original thoughts that might lower a grade and jeopardize college entry is simply deemed not worth it.

University faculties also notice the disturbing change. Former Yale professor William Deresiewicz labels today's college batch "excellent sheep." He contends that our educational system "manufactures students who are smart and talented and driven, yes, but also anxious, timid and lost, with little intellectual curiosity and a stunted sense of purpose." [42] Not the profile of kids who thrive, feel fulfilled, or will be ready to live in an uncertain, highly competitive world.

Jean Twenge, a psychologist at San Diego State University and authority on intergenerational differences, sees yet another troubling trend. College students are also obsessed with emotional safety and don't want to be exposed to "offensive" ideas or even to people who disagree with them.[43] By 2017, a poll found that almost 60 percent of college students said it was "important to be part of a campus community where I am not exposed to intolerant and offensive ideas."[44] If a controversial speaker is invited on campus, students feel they should be allowed "safe spaces," so they aren't subjected to derogatory or offensive views. (Some colleges set up "safe rooms" filled with cookies, bubbles, Play-Doh, calming music, and videos of frolicking puppies.) Students also demand protection from words and subjects that may cause discomfort in class, and they expect university professors to warn them of emotionally charged ideas—like racial violence in *Things Fall Apart* and physical abuse in *The Great Gatsby*. Keep in mind that those findings were *prior* to the coronavirus outbreak that required extreme measures—sanitizers, masks, social distancing, hand washing—to protect everyone's health. The impact of the pandemic on children is still a great unknown, but research on resilience says that a crisis only amplifies preexisting conditions. Children's concerns for emotional and physical safety will most certainly be higher.

Overprotection is a toxic recipe for curiosity and thriving. It increases kids' fragility, dependence, stress, and risk aversion, reduces resilience, kills creativity, and expands emptiness. Part of preparing kids for the twenty-first century is helping them be comfortable with divergent views: after all, that's how curiosity grows, empathy strengthens, civic engagement is learned and autonomy forms. It's why we must stop trying to sanitize kids from every imaginable discomfort, and we should start when kids are young—not college bound or in dorm rooms. But how can we tell our kids it's okay to risk—and even fail— sometimes?

- **Give permission to stray off course.** Curious kids are passionate about their original ideas and willing to defend them, but must feel support from adults so they can deviate from the norm. Do you convey such support to your child? Does your child know that you admire originality? Have you explained that failure is part of life? Are you backing away from always protecting or rescuing your child from mistakes or challenges? If we want to raise world-ready, curious kids who thrive and don't feel empty, we need to give them space to take creative risks, embrace originality, and develop out-of-the-box mind-sets.

- **Stretch comfort zones.** Risk-averse kids need small steps to venture outside their comfort zones until they feel secure sharing original ideas. Start by encouraging your child to take low risks: "Raise your hand just once tomorrow." "Write down your thought first so you have courage to share it with the class." "Tell your teacher your thought after class." Then gradually stretch his confidence until he can take creative risks alone.

- **Institute family meetings.** Regular family meetings help kids learn to speak up, solve problems, and learn divergent thinking. Topics are endless: curfews, chores, sibling conflicts, homework, as well as real-world stuff. Kids can also practice the skills in this chapter. Encourage your kids to voice opinions, but *hold* your judgment so your kids can learn to speak independently. Do set rules so kids feel safe to share divergent views.

⇒Each member's opinion is equal and *everyone* has the right to be heard. You may disagree with a view but must do so calmly and respectfully.

⇒Schedule regular meetings: ideally, once a week lasting twenty to thirty minutes.

⇒Determine how decisions are made (majority or unanimous consensus).

⇒Rotate roles so each member is assigned a different position each week: chairperson, parliamentarian, secretary, time keeper, and cheerleaders to encourage.

- **Encourage divergent disputes.** I listened to Robert Zimmer, president of the University of Chicago, speak recently about the need to better prepare students for the complex situations they will face in the world. He was adamant that today's kids must learn to challenge their own and others' assumptions, and effectively argue their positions. He later told a congressional hearing: "If the education that we provide does not give students the opportunity to acquire these abilities, they will be underprepared to make informed decisions in the complex and uncertain world they will confront upon entering the workplace."[45] I wholeheartedly agree, and debate is a great avenue to prepare children to be comfortable with divergent views. It can also help kids practice arguing their opinions, spot fake news, and identify argument gaps in their opposers.

⇒**Alter discussions with younger kids.** Topics could be: "What should our next family read-aloud be?" What should we have for dinner?" "Which are better pets: cats or dogs?" A Florida dad holds fun debates with his twin six-year-olds, with one rule: "Any answer is fine, *but you must give a reason.*" His son's answer to the best pet question: "Dogs are best *because* they can bark to protect you." (Telling kids to say "because" in their answer reminds them to give a reason.)

⇒**Teach effective dissension for older kids.** Watch films such as *The Great Debaters, Rocket Science, Speech & Debate,* Intelligence Squared Debates (on TV, podcasts, and YouTube), and presidential debates to see creative (and poor) debaters in action and help tweens and teens learn divergent thinking skills. Schools often have debate clubs for older kids. Do share Desmond Tutu's advice: "Don't raise your voice, improve your argument."

• **Encourage constructive arguments.** Most kids try to avoid disagreeing, but constructive arguing can help them consider alternate opinions, learn independence, and boost curiosity. It also helps kids be *less* risk averse, *more* willing to voice original thoughts, and more comfortable hearing divergent opinions. "If no one ever argues, you're not likely to give up on old ways of doing things, let alone try new ones," declares Adam Grant, author of *Originals*.[46] Grant also says that though most creative people grow up in homes full of (healthy) arguments, few parents teach their kids how to argue constructively. So teach older kids to argue constructively with three steps using the acronym ARE.[47]

⇒A—**A**ssert. Be brief, and share the main point of your opinion with facts. "I think . . ." or "I read . . . heard . . . believe . . ." Ten-year-old Sam's assertion: *"I think I deserve a bigger allowance . . ."*

⇒R—**R**eason. Next, support your assertion with a valid or proven reason: the "because" part of the argument. Sam's reason: *". . . because I'm a year older . . ."*

⇒E—**E**vidence. Finally, offer proof for your reason, the "example" part of an argument. Sam's evidence: *". . . and get the same amount and do twice as much."*

Developing divergent thinking takes practice. So help your kids learn ARE with family discussions and debates. Possible topics: "Television does more harm than good." "Plastic bags should be banned in grocery stores." "Cell phones should be allowed at school." "It's better to be a leader than a follower." "School should be year-round." Also, take any controversial issue, real kid dilemma or news story, and let the debates begin! Kids can take turns arguing the pros and cons of each issue.

HOW CURIOSITY CAN BE
YOUR CHILD'S SUPERPOWER

Parenting is never easy, but our ultimate role is helping our kids become their personal best and making them ready for whatever life throws at them. Nourishing their curiosity increases those odds, but to do so we must step back, stop hovering, and tailor our parenting to our kids' passions. That's the formula two parents used to nourish their child's gifts, and it paved his path to success.

Pauline and Hermann worried about their first child from the beginning: his head was deformed at birth, and they feared developmental issues.[48] Their son was also slow in learning to speak. When he finally did talk at age three, he whispered words softly to himself before saying them aloud. They consulted doctors and assumed the worst, but they also discovered that their child was curious, and nourishing his strength was how they helped him thrive.

The boy marched to his own drummer and loved to wander, and Pauline encouraged his explorations and encouraged his freedom at a young age. His mom taught him to play violin and piano and frequently played classical music as a brainstorming technique to help his creativity flow.[49] His father knew his son was curious about moving parts and bought him a pocket compass. When he wanted to know why the needle never moved, Hermann explained that the Earth is like a giant magnet . . . and the boy's curiosity with science endured.

School was challenging and the boy had a hard time sitting still. He hated memorizing and learning by rote, daydreamed often, and frequently questioned his teachers. Creative kids are less likely to become the teacher's pet; students who follow directions and do what they're told are favored.[50] So it was little surprise that the boy's creativity wasn't valued in school. (One educator even told him outright that he would never amount to much.) His hunger to learn came not from the classroom but from his family, who fostered his curiosities.

He enjoyed making constructions, so his mom and dad supplied decks of cards to build giant houses. He loved watching his uncle design gadgets, so they let him tinker at his father's electrical workshop. He was fascinated by science, physics, and geometry, so a family friend supplied books. He was fascinated with problem solving, so his parents bought him textbooks. And his curiosity thrived.

The child was Albert Einstein, one of the world's most creative geniuses. "I have no special talents. I am only passionately curious," he once said. While our goal is *not* to try and raise an Einstein, Marie Curie, Mozart, or Frida Kahlo, we can identify our kids' curiosities, strengths, and passions so they are eager to learn and let their imaginations soar. Pauline and Hermann Einstein offered the lessons to do so.

AGE-BY-AGE IDEAS TO INSTILL CURIOSITY

"The load of four AP classes plus marching band and theater
eats up a lot of free time to do things I'm passionate about. So,
my stress goes up and I feel empty."
—*Robin, fifteen, Torrance, California*

Symbols designate recommended age suitability for each activity: Y = Young children, toddlers, and preschoolers; S = School age; T = Tweens and older; A = All ages

- **Offer creative characters for younger kids.** Children's books with characters who face problems and creatively solve them are great for discussing curiosity. For younger kids: *Curious George* by H. A. Rey; *Zoey and Sassafras* by Asia Citro; *Papa's Mechanical Fish* by Candace Fleming; *Rosie Revere, Engineer* by Andrea Beaty; *Windows* by Julia Denos; *The Curious Garden* by Peter Brown; *Beautiful Oops!* by Barney Saltzberg; *The Most Magnificent Thing* by Ashley Spires; *On a Beam of Light: A Story of Albert Einstein* by Jennifer Berne; *Curiosity: The Story of a Mars Rover* by Markus Motum; *Cabinet Curiosities,* by Markus Motum. Also: *What Do You Do with an Idea?*, *What Do You Do with a Problem?*, and *What Do You Do with a Chance?* by Kobi Yamada. **Y, S**

- **Limit technology.** A number of top technology gurus— including Steve Jobs, Apple cofounder, Chris Anderson, chief executive of 3D Robotics, and Bill Gates, former CEO of Microsoft—strictly limited their children's screen time: they worried that electronic devices will reduce curiosity.[51, 52] Decide what amount is appropriate for your family, and then set specific times when electronic devices are *off*-limits. Consider using screen-time-tracking and parental-control apps to monitor which devices are used for how long and by whom. Then replace plugged-in time for nurturing curiosity during the free, unplugged times using ideas in this chapter. **A**

- **Pose creative challenges.** Divergent thinking is a form of creativity that solves problems with originality instead of settling for conventional answers. Proposing creative challenges helps children develop the ability. Over time, they inspire kids to take creative risks, think out of the box, consider multiple ways to solve problems, and contemplate "What if I did this . . . or tried that?" Offer needed materials, and then pose one weekly creative dare to your family by posing the question "How many different ways can you . . ." **S, T**

⇒use a paper clip? (offer a box of paper clips)

⇒move from here to there? (end of driveway, your bedroom, across the grass, etc.)

⇒build something from a box of pipe cleaners?

⇒draw shapes from a circle? (or triangle, square, rectangle, etc.)

⇒use a spoon and a bowl?

⇒make something from string (or yarn) and scissors?

⇒create things with cotton balls and glue?

⇒use a paper towel tube and masking tape?

⇒use a paper bag, scissors, and marking pens?

⇒use a paper cup and popsicle sticks?

- **Show movies depicting curious minds.** In the film *The Martian*, astronaut Mark Watney (Matt Damon) is stranded on the surface of Mars and must figure out how to survive. He is the epitome of a curious mind: constantly tinkering and problem solving, and he ultimately survives due to creativity.

Movies can help kids realize that curious folks don't instantly come up with answers but hang in there! Younger kids: *Alice in Wonderland, Finding Nemo, The Lorax, The Incredibles, Home Alone, October Sky.* Older kids: *A Wrinkle in Time, The Imitation Game, Dunkirk, Hidden Figures, Apollo 13.* **A**

- **Encourage questions!** Curious kids generally ask seventy-three questions a day.[53] Unfortunately, most children's inquisitiveness peaks at age four because we discourage them, and so their questions cease. Keep encouraging curiosity by fielding their questions with four tips:

  1. *Encourage:* "I love your questions!" "Great thought!" "Please don't stop asking!"
  2. *Clarify:* "Do you mean . . . ?" "Are you asking . . . ?" "Can you repeat so I understand?"
  3. *Find the answer:* "Not sure, but I'll find out." "Great question! I bet Grandpa knows."
  4. *Solve together:* "Who can we ask?" "Let's google it." "Let's go to the library." **A**

- **Use a hand problem solver.** Help your child realize that mistakes aren't failures but opportunities to learn. When my kids were young, they loved using a hand problem solver. I told them: "When you have a problem use your hand to help you think of solutions. Hold your thumb up and "Say the problem." Next, hold up pointer, middle, ring man and "Name one solution for each finger." When you get to pinky "Choose the best idea and do it." After a while, they were "storming their brains" and solving problems solo-style. **Y**

- **Play the solution game.** Help older kids practice brainstorming by playing the solution game. The object is to generate multiple solutions to a problem. Setting a time limit adds challenge: "Let's see how many ideas we can come up with in three (or whatever) minutes." Use an oven timer or cell phone stopwatch to keep track. Appoint one child to tally responses and then compare with previous games. Problems should be suitable to children's ages and can be real or make-believe. "How do you respond to kids who name call?" "What are no-cost ways to thank someone?" "What advice can you give the president to save the whales?" Remind your child: "Don't worry how silly your idea sounds. Say it, because it may spin off another idea." **S, T**

- **Seek open-ended learning opportunities.** Curiosity flourishes with open-ended, hands-on, child-guided experiences. School possibilities might be project-based learning, outdoor education, design thinking, service learning, science projects, Odyssey of the Mind, National History Day, theater, art, debate, music, and robotics. Or try extracurricular activities in scouts, religious groups, discovery museums, camps, or team sports. Also, join forces with like-minded parents and then create projects that match the interests and passions of your children. Just make sure the project is *child directed.* **A**

TOP FIVE TAKEAWAYS

1. Curiosity flourishes with open-ended, hands-on, child-guided opportunities.

2. Children must feel supported by adults to deviate from the norm and be creative.

3. Kids are more likely to think outside the box and take creative risks when not rewarded.

4. Curiosity and peak performance are driven by passion: help children find their passions.

5. When people collaborate and build on one another's work, curiosity increases.

ONE LAST LESSON

In researching curiosity, I read dozens of studies and interviewed top scholars, but the best answer on how to cultivate it came from a precocious eight-year-old.[54] I met Adam El Rafey at an international education conference in Dubai where I was invited to speak, but he stole the show. The young, gifted boy was worried that schools squelch curiosity and shared his concerns in his ten-minute talk to educators and political leaders.

"We are not allowed to be as creative as we can be," he told delegates. "Schools should not limit a child's creativity by asking them to follow only one particular way like coloring inside the lines." He mentioned famous abstract artists who "don't color inside the lines, and I'd say they've done pretty well for themselves," Adam pointed out. "So why should we?"

He had a message for parents: "No idea is 'ridiculous' and should be dismissed. Explain things to us in full detail," he urged. "We might just surprise you in how much we understand."

And he wished education was more personalized. "Schools really need to focus on teaching us how to think for ourselves, dreaming big and thinking differently. So instead of focusing on teaching us what is known, teach us how to make the unknown possible."

Our children's curiosity is nose-diving and an eight-year-old was standing on a stage reminding adults to prioritize it. We must reimagine children's education and readjust our parenting to unleash our children's curiosity to keep up with the times. Adam said it best: "Kids must learn to think for themselves, dream big, and think differently." It's up to adults to heed his advice. Doing so is one of the best ways to raise Thrivers with the Character Advantage.

PART THREE

Cultivating Will

"Parents need to give kids opportunities
to experience life and learn from our failures
without always being told what to do.
We have to learn life on our own."

—*Tate, thirteen, Boise, Idaho*

CHAPTER 6

Perseverance

Thrivers finish what they start and don't need gold stars.

E ACH SUMMER SINCE 2012, MORE than a hundred male and female students from Lake Highland High School in Florida depart for Outdoor Odyssey Leadership Academy in the Allegheny Mountains. Students I interviewed said that seven-day wilderness experience was life changing.

"When I got home it felt weird because I was a man and not a boy anymore," one teen told me, still excited about the experience when I talked with him months later. "I could overcome my fears because I found out that I had grit."

T.S. (Tom) Jones, founder and executive director of Outdoor Odyssey, is a former major general in the United States Marine Corps who believes that effective leadership requires mental, moral, and physical elements. His philosophy is "Growth Through Adversity," and he believes that progress happens when you step outside your comfort zone. It's why Jones repeatedly reminds teens: "You're going to do things this week that really challenge you, but if we didn't put you out of your comfort zone, we failed."

That process starts the moment the teens arrive, when they are separated from friends, split into smaller teams of twenty-one same-gender students, and assigned mentors. Then the activities begin: climbing rock walls, scaling rope nets, walking on wires thirty feet in the air, rafting through white-water rapids in the rain, and taking long hikes. These are scary activities, the teens face real danger, and they're operating without a safety net—except the safety provided by their own fortitude, and by each other. And those experiences turn out to be exactly what burned-out, nature-deprived, helicoptered kids crave.

"One reason our generation is so stressed is because we're coddled by parents. If you're always rescued, you're robbed of learning how to succeed on your own," Andrew C., a camp graduate, told me. "Each Odyssey experience helps you become surer of yourself, because you push yourself out of your comfort zone and your confidence grows. You learn that you're stronger than you think." It's the ultimate environment for developing perseverance and resilience.

Developing perseverance also requires that kids learn to handle challenges and follow through without adult rescue. "If a teen has a problem, Odyssey counselors tell us: 'This isn't our problem but yours,'" June, a former Odyssey grad, explained. "Phones aren't allowed, so we can't call our moms. We learn to communicate with each other. And when you succeed at solving the problem, you realize you're capable of doing things that you never believed you could do. That's when you really grow as a person."

Jenna attended the camp as an eight-year-old following the death of her mom, and said the experience gave her a new lease on life. "I was a depressed young girl, but Odyssey helped me find my inner strength, and I learned it in the Bear Cave. Counselors led us into a small, tight, dark tunnel with a flashlight, where we had to crawl through on our stomachs. I thought it was impossible," Jenna recalled, "but the counselors encouraged me, and I realized, 'I have grit and strength to get through so much more than I ever thought.' I was finally okay with being Jenna."

Perhaps the easiest Odyssey character-building lesson is for adults to stop coddling and always doing for our kids. It's the message I repeatedly hear from students. "You learn grit by being exposed to adversity so you have the chance to realize that you are more capable than you thought," said Amy.

"Odyssey forces you to experience growth through adversity because they put you into situations that you may not feel comfortable," Emma told me.

Seventeen-year-old William summed it up: "Facing adversity in little steps is what kids need. We have to know that we're capable human beings."

"Things of real value make you the person you want to be—things like your character that you have to really work at and develop," General Jones reminded the campers. And that is the very message that is key to every lesson we teach our children about this crucial strength.

WHAT IS PERSEVERANCE?

"Learning you can figure things out on your own is how you learn perseverance and confidence. A big problem in our generation is that everyone wants to do things for us."
—*David, fourteen, Des Moines, Iowa*

Every parent wants success for their child, but science shows we may be using the wrong lessons. Angela Duckworth, now a psychology professor and MacArthur Fellow, began searching for the magic success formula as a middle school math teacher. She noticed that some kids (whom she considered to have lower "natural" mathematic ability) actually outperformed those who displayed a greater innate facility with numbers. Why?

Duckworth tracked 164 middle schoolers over the school year and found a secret: students' self-discipline scores were better predictors of their GPA than their IQ.[1] The kids who stuck it out—even when they didn't understand a concept at first—were the ones who were succeeding in her classroom. But would the children's perseverance forecast success in other circumstances?

To find out, Duckworth developed a "grit scale" for people to rate themselves, with statements like "I finish whatever I begin," or "I have overcome setbacks to conquer an important challenge." She tested freshman West Point cadets: low grit scores were a better predictor of who would drop out than their academic grades, high school rank, athletic ability, or leadership scores. She tested Green Berets: grit was what distinguished men who made it through the grueling boot camp. She tested Scripps National Spelling Bee contestants: grittier kids went further in the competition. And she followed undergraduates at an Ivy League university: grittier students (despite lower SAT scores) achieved higher grade point averages than their less gritty classmates. Her studies continued, but one constant remained: it was always the grittier—not the smarter or more talented—who succeeded.

The terms "grit" and "perseverance" are often used interchangeably in these pages, and that's by design. But I see a distinction between the two. Grit is a popular term that's become part of mainstream vocabulary and defined as having two components: passion *and* perseverance.[2] I agree, but I believe other Character Strengths also energize perseverance. That's why kids who shine are more likely to use their personal strengths, self-control, and optimism to cope with setbacks, and curiosity to stretch their willpower and get to the finish line. Caring (empathy) or feeling deep concern (integrity) about the issue stretches determination even more. Character Strengths are *always* amplified when combined to reap the Multiplier Effect and the reason I use the term "perseverance." It can never stand alone.

Perseverance helps kids keep on when everything else makes it easier to give up. To a child, that might be the Little Engine That Could, who answered every challenge up that mountain with "I think I can, I know I can." To a parent, coach, or teacher, perseverance is a kid who hangs in there and just doesn't give up, and so he is far more likely to shine.

What's more: perseverance is not fixed or entirely determined by genes, but just like with the other qualities we've discussed so far in this book, it can be stretched and improved with the right lessons. And the benefits of strengthening this trait can be enormous. This character trait boosts children's resilience, mental health, performance, confidence, self-control, self-sufficiency, and hope. Simply put: *the ability to stick to a task and a long-term goal Is the greatest predictor of success and stronger than IQ, academic achievement, SAT scores, extra-curricular activities, and test scores.* Perseverance keeps kids on track, gets them closer to their dreams, and helps them thrive—and that's why we must add teaching perseverance to our parenting lessons.

WHY PERSEVERANCE CAN BE SO HARD TO TEACH

Perseverance is the trait that pushes the envelope to help kids thrive and often makes the critical difference in whether they succeed or fail. But we may need to seriously recalibrate our current parenting and education. The wrong lessons that aren't science-backed rob kids not only of developing their true passions but also zap their "grit reservoir."

We Don't Give Kids Enough Deliberate Practice Time

In our winner-take-all society, parents desperately try to give kids "a success edge" and believe the answer must be *more* teams, *more* coaches, *more* activities. But research on peak performers negates those claims. With not enough time to deliberately practice his passion, ability or talent *decreases* a child's intrinsic motivation, perseverance, and his potential to shine. Overextended schedules and excluding true passion are causing too many kids to give up their dreams and fall short of their thriving potential.

From a fifteen-year-old: "I want to be a videographer. My teachers say I'm really good at it, but with all my activities I don't have time to develop it."

From a thirteen-year-old: "I love swimming, but I'll never get good because my parents have me do three sports so my résumé looks good."

From a seventeen-year-old: "My passion is drawing, but with all the AP classes I have to take to have a chance at a decent college, I haven't taken one art class."

Anders Ericsson was a cognitive psychologist at Florida State University who studied world experts. He found that great performers (like a Tchaikovsky, Wilma Rudolph, Jerry Rice, Itzhak Perlman, or Serena Williams) focus on *specific* aspects of their strength, and then *deliberately* practice for years to develop it. Their extraordinary accomplishments aren't due to superhuman abilities, inborn strengths, memory, high IQ, money, or rewards but intentional, focused practice—and that takes perseverance.[3]

Angela Duckworth, in her must-read *Grit: The Power of Passion and Perseverance,* also points out that improving in any area requires perseverance, yes—but it's not just about the quantity but also the *quality* of time spent. To get the benefits of this Character Strength, the practice must involve not *more* time but *better* time. Being involved in multiple activities with no time to practice reduces success odds.

We're Setting the Wrong Expectations

Mihaly Csikszentmihalyi, eminent psychology professor at the University of Chicago, worried that too many talented kids were giving up their abilities. He led a five-year study of two hundred talented teens to understand why some continue cultivating their talent while other equally gifted kids quit and never develop their potential. Csikszentmihalyi found two conditions especially dangerous to disengagement: anxiety and boredom. Anxiety occurs primarily when adults expect *too much* from kids, but boredom happens when adults expect *too little*.[4] "When curricular experiences are out of sync with students' abilities, not only does motivation decrease but also achievement," says Csikszentmihalyi.

Optimum expectations are when the child "takes on challenges that are just at or above his skills." Right expectations also increase perseverance and help the child achieve "flow" (being so involved in the task that a sense of time is lost). If you want your kids to stick with a task and maintain grit, you must set the right level of expectations that align with their interests, talents, or abilities. Our job is to find the class, teacher, activity, sport, or task that is challenging for the child but not overwhelming—in Goldilocks terms: not too high or too low but just right. Unfortunately, too many kids are pushed beyond their capabilities too fast, too soon and give up their talent or ability that could help them thrive.

We Rescue Our Kids from Failure

Without experiencing failure, kids can't develop perseverance or learn how deal with inevitable challenges that help develop resilience. Over-parenting and "rescuing" in America is pervasive, especially in affluent areas where parents pay schools steep prices to ensure their kids *don't* fail. Dominic Randolph, headmaster of Riverdale Country School in the Bronx, New York, points out, "In most highly academic environments in the United States, no one fails *anything*."[5]

Parents readily admit that they pay hefty private school tuitions so their kids won't stumble. A Greenwich mom with two kids enrolled in a prestigious academy told me: "For the amount we pay for their education, I expect high grades and Ivy League acceptance." A Sarasota dad with sons in a small, elite high school said: "I know I'm raising my boys in a cocoon, but I want to cushion them from failure as long as possible." But rescuing doesn't do kids any favors.

Decades of research show the kids whose parents *do* let them fail are *more* resilient, *more* motivated, *more* excited about learning, and ultimately *more* successful than kids whose parents swoop, hover, and rescue. Mark Seery of the University at Buffalo, State University of New York, examined a national sample of people and found that those exposed to some adverse events reported better mental health and well-being outcomes than those with no bumps or adversity. In fact, those who experienced little or no hardship were *less* happy and *less* confident when they grew up than those who had experienced setbacks.[6]

Each time we rescue or fix we send children a deadly message: "We don't believe you're capable of doing that alone." So our kids learn to step aside, depend on us to pick up their pieces, and the gap between thrivers and strivers widens. While thrivers develop agency; strivers feel more helpless. Instead, step back and subscribe to a new behavior:

"Never do for your child what your child can do for himself." Your kid will thank you someday.

HOW TO TEACH KIDS PERSEVERANCE

If our kids are to succeed, they must learn to hang in there, not quit, and keep on. Perseverance is the Character Strength that helps them endure long after we are gone—and it's what they'll need in our fast-paced, highly competitive, constantly changing, uncertain world. Three teachable abilities nurture perseverance: a growth mind-set, goal setting, and learning from failure. The lessons that follow will also help your kids be stronger, more successful, and better able to thrive because they know they can rely on themselves.

Cultivate a Growth Mind-Set

Stanford psychologist Carol Dweck believes that people have two types of mind-sets: "fixed" or "growth." Her research into mind-set theory began four decades ago when she taught math to elementary and middle schoolers, and much like Angela Duckworth, would notice several years later a clear split in students' learning behaviors. Despite similar abilities, some students seemed helpless and gave up at the first sign of difficulty (even if they were rewarded for success on easier problems), while others solved far more math problems, put out effort, and kept trying when problems got tough. It was Dweck's first indicator that a focus on *effort* can reduce helplessness and foster success. And her research continued.

In another study, Dweck asked fifth graders to think out loud while solving difficult problems. Some reacted defensively, browbeat

themselves ("I never did have a good rememory [sic]"), and their performance deteriorated. Others zeroed in on solving their mistakes.
(One told himself: "I should slow down and try to figure this out.") The
"fixers" didn't dwell on their failures but rather thought of mistakes as
problems to be solved . . . and so they persisted.[7] Dweck recalled an
especially memorable kid. When confronted with a hard problem, he
rubbed his hands together, smacked his lips, and said, "I love a challenge!" And as predicted, the fixer group far outperformed the other,
more defeatist group that dwelled on their own mistakes.

Dweck developed a hypothesis: what separates the two classes of
learners is how they view their intelligence. Those with growth mind-
sets believe that their character, intelligence, talents, and abilities can
be improved with education, effort, good strategies, and help from
others. They see in themselves a potential to do better. Those with fixed
mind-sets, however, are convinced that those qualities are carved in
stone: achievements are due to their inherent intelligence rather than
any additional work they put in.

And those two distinct beliefs have remarkable impact on whether
kids succeed or fail. Dweck's research shows that growth mind-set kids
tend to learn more, thrive on challenge, acquire deeper knowledge, and
do better—especially in hard subjects—compared with equally able
students who believe their intelligence is a fixed entity. These growth
mind-set kids are also less likely to give up and more likely to push
on—even if they fail or if the going gets tough—because they know it's
just a matter of ramping up the effort until they triumph.[8]

While genes may decide your child's starting spot at the gate, good
old perseverance and a growth mind-set can influence his or her fin-
ishing place. The best news: just like all the other qualities we've studied, growth mind-sets can be nurtured in children, with the simple
lessons that follow.

1. **Redefine success as a "gain."** Our test-obsessed culture has our kids labeling themselves as "scores," so redefine "success" to your child as a four-letter word spelled G-A-I-N: an improvement (or "one step higher" for younger kids) over past performance due to personal effort.

Then help your child identify his personal GAINs. "Last time, you got nine words correct, today you got ten! That's a GAIN!" "Yesterday you hit one run; today you got two. That's a GAIN!" "Last month your math grade was seventy-three percent; this time it's seventy-nine percent. That's a GAIN! All your efforts are working because you're improving!" Then ask: "What did *you* do to get those gains?" Always help your child compare his performance with *his* previous attempts and not to others' scores.

2. **Add "yet."** Kids can develop negative, harmful "I can't" or "I'll never get it right" mind-sets. When you hear "can't, never, won't" comments, respond with a growth mind-set phrase that helps your child know that with effort, he will improve.

Child: "I can't do it." Parent: "No, you can't do it 'yet'!"
Child: "I'll never get it." Parent: "You don't know it now. Keep practicing!"
Child: "This is too hard." Parent: "Keep working. You're getting closer."

3. **Hold growth conversations.** We're quick to ask: "What was your grade (or score or rank)?" Ask instead about effort so your child knows you care about his work ethic and learns the value of a growth mind-set. A few examples:

"What did you do that made you really think?"

"What new things did you try?"

"What was challenging?"

"What mistake did you make that taught you something?"

"What did you try that was hard?"

Then make sure you share your own learnings!

4. **Praise effort, not the end product.** Another Dweck study of over four hundred fifth graders found that when praised for their intelligence ("You're so smart!" or "What a brain you are!"), they became concerned about failing and were *less* likely to attempt new challenges.[9] But when praised for effort ("You're working so hard!" or "You're really hanging in there"), they worked harder and were *more* likely to succeed. Why? Fixed mind-set kids didn't feel they had control over their intelligence; those with growth mind-sets understood that they could control how hard they work, and so they improved. The lesson: *to stretch a growth mind-set, praise your child's effort, not the end product.*

"When you discover how to do a new problem, your science brain grows!"

"Wow, you're really working hard at that!"

"That was clever how you tried different ways to solve that problem. Nice work!"

"I loved how hard you worked on that project. What helped you improve?"

And if your child excels without challenge, Dweck suggests saying: "That was too easy for you. Let's see if there's something more challenging that you can learn from."

5. **Use growth mind-set reminders.** Stanford analyzed 265,000
students learning math online to see if feedback improved
their performance,[10] by randomly putting them in five groups
and sending different messages. Students receiving growth
mind-set feedback learned at higher rates than those receiving generic ("Good job") or no feedback. So find routine ways
to offer growth mind-set messages. A Dallas dad posts a re-
frigerator sign: "Improvement comes with practice!" A Reno
mom puts a napkin note in her child's lunch: "Brains get
stronger when you work them harder." An Austin dad texts
his college teen: "The more you work, the better you get."

Set Realistic, Manageable Goals

Stanford University psychologist Lewis Terman was known as the "father of gifted education." He believed IQ to be the sine qua non for
success, and he held that our country's future welfare hinged upon
educating superior children.[11] And Terman was on a mission to prove
it. He identified 1,500 gifted children and tracked them for the rest of
their lives. The study became the longest running longitudinal study
on the gifted in the world. But the psychologist discovered he was
wrong: high IQ, test scores, GPA, or elite college attendance did *not*
determine a child's future success. What set the most successful children apart was their ability to set realistic, manageable goals—and use
perseverance to meet those goals.

Goal setting is teachable, and it turned out that most of Terman's
peak performers not only learned this skill but they learned it *early*—
before leaving high school.[12] Our mistake is that we wait too late to try
to instill this crucial ability in our kids. The sooner we begin teaching

those lessons, the sooner kids will be on the right path to thrive and succeed.

Effective goal setting is teachable, but must meet five factors. The child should:

1. Have the necessary skills, ability, resources, mentors, and knowledge to succeed
2. Not need excess help
3. Have enough time to succeed
4. Display the interest and passion to persevere
5. Be in control. Ask: "Do you have power over that? A goal must be something *you* can control."

If no is the answer to *any* question, help your child choose another goal or refine the selected goal so it is more realistic and meets the five factors. Now you're ready to teach goal setting.

- **Define "goal."** An easy way to explain goals is to link the term to hockey, soccer, or football. Say: "A goal is like a target or something you shoot for. Goals aren't just for sports but also something you shoot for to be more successful in life. Planning what you need to work on is called goal setting, and the skill will help you in school, at home, with your friends, or later in your job." Asking a child to name something he wants to "have, be, or do" helps him think of possibilities, and then choose one goal he's willing to work on.

An Austin middle school teacher told me: "Kids are more willing to try skills if they recognize they are important in real life." So he shares articles with his students about successful people who use goal-setting principles. Michael Phelps set goals since he started competitive swimming. Phelps said, "When I was younger, I used to scribble my goals out by hand. Now I might type them on my laptop."[13] You might encourage your child to track his goal progress in a journal or Word document like Phelps. Share articles about goal setters or read the story of Phelps in the Self-Control chapter.

- **Teach "I will + what + when."** Goals usually start with *I will* and have two parts: a *what* (what you want to accomplish) and a *when* (when you plan to achieve it). One easy way to teach that lesson is by "purposefully modeling" your goals to your child. Suppose your laundry room is piled high with dirty laundry. Say to your child: "I will get these clothes washed and dried by three o'clock." (*What* = washing and drying the clothes + *when* = by three o'clock.) Or describe your plan for the day: "I will call Karen to thank her for the cookies the minute I get inside." (*What* = call Karen to thank her + *when* = as soon as I get inside.) Once you model "I will + what + when" you can teach it to your child using the next goal formula strip activity.

- **Use goal formula strips.** Cut a paper strip at least three inches by twelve inches (wider for a younger child). Fold the strip lengthwise into three even sections. Section 1: Print *"I will."* Section 2: Print *"What."* Section 3: Print *"When."* Then help your child set a goal using the goal formula. First ask, *"What* do you want to achieve?" (He prints or draws his goal in section 2.) Then ask, *"When* will you try to achieve your goal?" (He prints or draws his aim. *"I will learn five math facts in fifteen minutes." "I will read ten pages in thirty minutes."* Or *"I will clean my room in ten minutes."* Kara M., an Iowa mom, holds a family goal-setting session each Sunday night. Each member names their goal, writes it on a Post-it using the goal formula, and tapes it to the door. She says everyone usually succeeds "because all week long we encourage one another."

- **Add *how* for older kids.** Listing what needs to be done to succeed in a sensible order makes goals manageable. Provide several paper slips or sticky notes to help older kids learn to plan their goals. Parent: "What is your goal?" Kid: "I want to get more batting hits." Parent: "How will you succeed?" Kid: "Ask Coach for help. Watch videos of good batters. Practice thirty minutes every day." The child writes one task per note, puts the "how-to plan" in sequence, and sticks them together. Each time a task is finished, the child tears off a note until none remain. Teens can list their *how* tasks, and check off their progress.

- **Keep triumph logs.** Goal victories, large or small, deserve celebrating, but praise effort: "You hung in there!" "You got a little better every day because you didn't quit!" Twelve-year-old Carolina said that she and her brothers have small notebooks that her parents call "triumph logs" where the siblings describe their goal victories and the effort they took.

Teach That Mistakes Are Just Problems to Be Solved

Children cannot learn to persevere unless they learn how to deal with failure. But I admit my own kid might have missed that lesson if I hadn't been at the door waiting for him to come home from first grade. The story I told in *Parents Do Make a Difference* resonated with readers and bears repeating.

My son was hiding a crumpled paper behind his back so I gave him a big hug, gently took and smoothed it, and was surprised to see why he was distressed. He'd missed five words on his spelling test, which were easily identified with large red check marks. I knew I needed to reassure him that mistakes are part of life. So I began: "Wasn't it nice that your teacher took the time to put these red check marks on your paper?" I ignored his skeptical look and continued, "You do know why your teacher took the time to make those check marks?" He shook his head, obviously confused with where I was going (who could blame him).

"She wants you to study those checked words so you won't make the same mistake. She must really care about you." He gave me a quick hug, and ran to play. But a few weeks later he was holding a package while dashing to the bus. I asked what it was, and he excitedly explained, "It's a present for my teacher: a red pencil!" My mouth flew open. "Now she'll always have one to mark my mistakes so I won't make the same ones again!"

Peak performers accept mistakes as part of their path to success, and it's why they stick longer to tasks and don't give up as quickly. They've learned the lesson that a mistake doesn't mean a "life sentence" of failure but is instead a temporary setback. But how you can impart this concept to young people?

1. **Model mistakes with "I learned."** When you do err, own up and tell your child your mistake and what you learned from it. If your dinner menu was a disaster, admit it to your family (before they tell you), and then say what you learned from your mistake. "I messed up on making this cake. *I learned* to read the whole recipe before adding ingredients." "I was late but *I learned* to hang my car keys on the hook every time." "I got lost but I *learned* how to plug in the directions."

2. **Erase: "Mistakes are bad."** Children cannot persevere unless they know that mistakes are part of life. Talk about your child's mistake without criticizing, showing anger, or shaming. Then give constructive feedback on how to improve. "Everyone makes mistakes. The trick is figuring how to learn from them so you don't repeat the same error. Let's look at your spelling test again and find how to correct it." Give your kids permission to fail!

The best way kids learn that mistakes aren't fatal is feeling our acceptance to their errors. When your child makes a mistake, show support. Lars, age twelve, shared the best response: "Tell your kid you love him whatever their grade or score. That's what my mom does, and then she helps me figure out what to do to improve." How are you helping your kids recognize that mistakes aren't fatal?

3. **Don't call it a mistake.** Thrivers often give their mistake a nickname like "glitch," "bug," a "temporary" so it won't discourage them to quit. Help your child come up with a word to say to himself whenever he encounters a mistake. Any word will do, then encourage him to say it often so he'll use it when he blunders. A Toronto teacher taught students to call mistakes "opportunities." An hour later I saw a boy make a mistake and try to erase it. The student next to him whispered, "Remember, it's an opportunity!" The smile on the boy's face was priceless, and proof that the lesson worked. Help your kids see mistakes as opportunities!

4. **Create turnaround plans.** Some kids can't see their way out of failure and so they repeat the same mistake and give up easily. Amy Morin, in her book *13 Things Mentally Strong*

People Don't Do, shared a study published in the *Journal of Experimental Psychology: Learning, Memory, and Cognition* that found as long as students were given a chance to learn correct information, they could learn from previous mistakes. "When kids thought about potential answers, even if those answers were incorrect, their retention rates for the correct answers improved once their mistakes were corrected."[14] It's why we must help kids learn to correct the mistake instead of labeling, shaming, or excusing the child.

A Denver mom helps her child create a "turnaround plan." Parent: "What was your mistake?" Child: "I flunked my math test." Parent: "What's your turnaround plan?" Child: "I could study a little every night and not wait until the last day." Parent: "Let's write your plan down so you remember!"

5. **Teach "bounce back" statements.** Navy SEALs taught me a great tip they use to overcome adversity: they say a short, positive statement inside their head at the moment of challenge. Help your child identify a statement and then encourage him to repeat it until he can use it alone. Statements kids say that work: "It doesn't have to be perfect." "I can learn from my mistakes." "Everybody makes mistakes." "I can't get any better unless I try it."

HOW PERSEVERANCE CAN
BE YOUR CHILD'S SUPERPOWER

In the beginning, Michael Jordan was just another kid from North Carolina. "Of all the kids in my family, I probably was considered the one least likely to succeed," Jordan admitted.[15] But somewhere along the way, he became one of the greatest basketball players of all time, earned two Olympic gold medals, was inducted into the Naismith Memorial Basketball Hall of Fame, and became an exemplar of perseverance.

There's no question that Michael Jordan's family's work ethic factored into fostering Michael's grit and future success. "I truly believe in commitment and integrity and honesty," his mother said.[16] And Deloris Jordan instilled guidelines in her home.[17] Doing chores, making your bed, hanging up your clothes, and completing homework were expected and reinforced. Michael learned integrity, responsibility, and a strong work ethic.

His parents also wanted their kids to be self-sufficient when they left home. "If something was broken in our house, my father would teach himself how to fix it," Michael recalled. "My mother was the same way. How could their kids not have the same approach, be it in school, a job, or playing a game?"[18] Michael learned self-reliance and grit.

The parents also taught goal setting. If a sibling said they were going to make the honor roll, the child had to explain how he intended to succeed. A plan was required to achieve each goal. There was also no shame in falling short of the goal, as long as the child had done their very best. "If you haven't failed," Deloris told her kids, "you may not be trying hard enough, you may not be setting your goals high enough. Failures actually strengthen us."[19] Michael learned that mistakes were learning opportunities.

When Michael was devastated for failing at his first attempt to be part of a varsity basketball team, his mom told him to go back and discipline himself. She also made a family rule that no one could say "I can't." "'Go try it'—that was a slogan for us," Deloris Jordan said. "If you try, then you can't fail. You have failed if you don't try."[20] And Michael learned that failure was an opportunity to improve his performance.

Michael's parents were demanding *and* supportive. Studies prove that a demanding + supportive parental style in equal parts = the sauce to success. Add grit *and* strong character to the mix and children's success potential amplifies. Michael excelled.

"It's up to us, as parents, to teach our children a higher standard," said Deloris Jordan, "no matter how hard."[21] Michael Jordan certainly exceeded all standards in his sport—and set quite a few himself—but when we're instilling perseverance in our kids, the goal is not to necessarily raise super elites. Whether your kid is NBA-bound or just shooting hoops in the driveway, instilling growth mind-sets, teaching goal setting, and learning from failure helps all kids thrive—especially in our trophy-giving, fame-driven world. It's also how we raise champions of heart, mind, and will.

AGE-BY-AGE IDEAS TO INSTILL PERSEVERANCE

Harold Stevenson, who was a University of Michigan psychologist, sought to answer what many Americans ask: "Why do Asian students do better academically than American students?" [22] He conducted five intensive cross-national studies analyzing student achievement in the United States, China, Taiwan, and Japan and found that on the whole, Asian kids work longer and harder than their American counterparts. In short: Asian kids tend to stick to difficult tasks longer than American kids.

Stevenson found a critical reason lies in what parents emphasize in their children's learning. American parents are more concerned about the end product: the kids' grades or scores. Asian parents stress their effort in the task: "Work hard, and you'll be successful," and so their kids recognize success is based on their effort. This actually empowers them to work harder. The perseverance-building lesson: focus on the effort, not the end product.

Symbols designate recommended age suitability for each activity: Y = Young children, toddlers, and preschoolers; S = School age; T = Tweens and older; A = All ages

- **Read and discuss perseverance.** Younger kids: *Fortunately* by Remy Charlip; *The Day the Crayons Quit* by Drew Daywalt; *The Little Engine That Could* by Watty Piper; *Beautiful Oops!* by Barney Saltzberg. Older kids: *Timmy Failure* by Stephan Pastis; *Fast Talk on a Slow Track* by Rita Williams-Garcia; *Hatchet* by Gary Paulsen. Teens: *The Hunger Games* by Suzanne Collins; *A Long Way Gone: Memoirs of a Boy Solider* by Ishmael Beah; *The Boys in the Boat* by Daniel James Brown. **A**
- **Model effort.** Modeling any Character Strength is the most effective teaching method. When you do a hard task, make sure your child overhears *you* say: "I'm going to persevere until I succeed." "I'm hanging in until I figure out how to program." "I'm going to every lesson until I can play golf." Pledge to show your child that you don't give up when things are hard. **A**
- **Teach "one thing."** Mr. White, my elementary school music teacher, was a verified mistake fanatic. If I made one error, I had to start the piece all over from the beginning. I loved piano, and then hated it because I'd dread making one mistake. If it hadn't been for my next music teacher, Mrs. Thompson, I would have turned in my metronome. She helped me find my "stumbler" (your "one little problem, Michele"), and we'd de-

liberately practice the mistake over and over in a *fun*, relaxed way until I had it right. Then I'd play from the beginning and breeze through Beethoven loving every minute.

Mistakes can derail kids from getting to the end and succeeding. So don't let your kid catastrophize his problem ("I'll never get this right!"). Instead, help him zero in and identify his stumbler. Make a plan to correct it and practice, practice, practice that one little piece until voilà: success! Parent: "I videoed you kicking. Your foot is over to the left so the ball won't go into the net. Let's practice one thing: straightening your foot to see what happens." **S, T**

- **Offer examples of "bounce back" individuals.** Too many kids think fame and fortune are due to luck or money and forget that peak performers excel because of hard work and refusing to give up! Kids need to hear about famous people who suffered setbacks, but used perseverance to succeed. Review the stories of Elizabeth Smart, Albert Einstein, Michael Jordan, Malala Yousafzai, Michael Phelps, Ruby Bridges, and Jim Abbott in this book: all used perseverance to excel. *Fantastic Failures* by Luke Reynolds and *Mistakes That Worked* by Charlotte Foltz Jones have more examples. Or share other examples of folks who bounce back with your kids. A few:

  ⇒ Thomas Edison's teachers told him he was "too stupid to learn anything."

  ⇒ J. K. Rowling's book *Harry Potter* was turned down by twelve publishers.

⇒Theodor Geisel's (Dr. Seuss) first book was rejected by more than twenty publishers.

⇒Oprah Winfrey was told by a TV producer that she was "unfit for television news."

⇒Steve Jobs was fired from Apple but returned with the iPod, iPhone, and iPad.

⇒Walt Disney was fired from *The Kansas City Star* for "lacking imagination." **S, T**

- **Teach "chunk it."** Some kids give up because they feel overwhelmed with "*all* the problems" or "*all* their assignments." Chunking tasks into smaller parts helps kids who have difficulties focusing or getting started, or are overly concerned that "everything's right!" Tell your younger kid to chunk it by covering all his math problems with paper except the top row. Lower the covered paper down the next row and the next as each row is completed. Older kids can write each assignment on one sticky note, in order of difficulty, and do one task at a time. Do encourage your kid to do the "hardest thing first" so she won't stress about it all night. Confidence and perseverance build as kids complete larger chunks alone. **S, T**

- **Use the right expectations.** Perseverance thrives with the right expectations, so ask yourself these questions when deciding on an activity or class for your kid. "Is this something my child is interested in or shows a talent for, or is it something I want more for myself? (Who is pushing whom?) Is he developmentally ready for the task, or am I pushing him beyond his internal timetable? Is the coach or teacher warm, skilled, and tuned in to my kid? Is the commitment worth the time, finances, and energy for both my child and family?" **A**

- **Teach "don't give up" phrases.** Help your child learn phrases gritty folks say like "I can do it!" "I'll try again." "Don't give up!" "I won't quit." "Hang in there." "You'll get it. Keep at it!" A San Antonio teacher prints "Don't give up" statements on a poster and encourages students to choose one to say several times a day. She reminds them: "The more you repeat it the more likely it will help you succeed." A Montana dad said that his family started a "Never give up" motto. They spent an afternoon brainstorming anthems about perseverance and ultimately decided on "In this family, we finish what we start." They wrote their verse on index cards, taped them on their bedroom walls, and say it often. **A**

- **Create a "stick to it" award.** Find a stick at least the length of a ruler to acknowledge "stick-to-it-ness." Print "Stick to it" across it with a black marking pen. (A Seattle family uses an old broomstick; a Chicago family uses a dowel.) Then everyone is on alert for members who show stick-to-it-ness. Each night (or weekly) gather your family to announce members who didn't give up, explain what they did to deserve the award, and print their initials on the stick with a marking pen. Kids love counting how often their initials appear on the stick and recalling moments when they didn't give up! **Y, S**

- **Use the "hard thing rule."** Angela Duckworth recommends the hard thing rule for parents who would "like to encourage grit without obliterating their children's capacity to choose their own path." In fact, she uses it with her own family. It has three parts.[23] First: everyone—including Mom and Dad—has to do a hard thing that requires daily, deliberate practice to improve, like yoga, piano, running, football, science, ballet, or anything that takes effort. Second: you *can* quit, but not until the season is over, lessons are paid, or some other "natural" stopping point occurs. You can't quit the day the coach benches you, you get a D on your test, or you have to miss a party because of rehearsal the next day. Third: each person gets to choose their hard thing because they alone know their interests, which will give them reasons improve. **S, T**

TOP FIVE TAKEAWAYS

1. Perseverance flourishes with open-ended, hands-on, child-guided opportunities.
2. To stretch your child's growth mind-set and perseverance, praise effort, not the end product.
3. Thrivers use mistakes as success tools so they stick to tasks longer and don't give up quickly.
4. A demanding *and* supportive parental style in equal parts is the formula for perseverance.
5. Chunking tasks into smaller parts helps kids who have difficulties focusing, getting started, or feeling overly concerned that "everything's right!" And they're more likely to succeed.

ONE LAST LESSON

I was observing a classroom of children with learning disabilities and was intrigued with the long strips of colorful yarn tied to the students' chairs. The yarn activity began after their teacher read *Knots on a Counting Rope* by Bill Martin, Jr. to her class—a story of a blind boy who is facing enormous physical obstacles (his "dark mountains") but who doesn't give up. Her students constantly faced difficulties, and she wanted to encourage them to reach their dreams.

The teacher told students: "Everyone in their life faces a dark mountain, but if you don't give up, and try your best, you usually succeed."

Then the teacher gave each child a piece of yarn and instructed them to tie a courage knot each time they made it across a dark mountain. She also told them valuable advice: "Success usually requires a lot of practice, trying strategies outside your comfort zone, and asking others for help." Days later, the students' yarn lengths were covered with knots, and they asked if I wanted to hear about the dark mountains they'd overcome. Did I!

"This knot is because I was sick for a long time and afraid to come back to school, but I did!" one boy said triumphantly. "Robby called and told me he missed me," he whispered.

"I just moved here and didn't know anybody," a red-haired girl said, "so the kids said I should tie a knot because I asked them if I could play with them—they let me!"

"I have a stuttering problem and had to give a speech in front of the class," a girl explained. "I gave it, and the kids all clapped."

What struck me was not only the pride of the knot tiers but also the reaction of their classmates: their faces were beaming with pride as well! They understood how hard it was for their peers to earn those knots because they felt their vulnerabilities themselves. The teacher's lesson stuck with her kids: facing adversity takes courage, but with perseverance, not worrying about mistakes, and asking others for help if needed, you'll make it one step at a time. Our kids need that lesson to help them learn to thrive!

CHAPTER 7

Optimism

Thrivers find the silver lining.

T**ODAY'S CHILDREN ARE LIVING IN** fear-based times—terrorism, lockdown drills, climate change, TSA screenings, and pandemics are the new normal. We try to shield them, but these kids are digital natives with instant access to viewing disturbing news, and it can take a toll. One out of three children aged six to eleven fears that Earth won't exist when they grow up. Girls worry more.[1]

I sat down with a group of middle school students at an elite Dallas school to hear their views about the world and scary news. A seventh-grade boy began: "It's not one thing, but a lot of bad stuff that keeps happening, and it makes us think that the world is mean and scary."

An eighth grader chimed in: "There's bunches of worries: climate change, viruses, bullying, domestic violence, racism, and shootings."

"Our entire school career is a memory of lockdown drills," said a twelve-year-old.

"We're more negative because bad news is so accessible," another boy explained. "Parents try to hide scary stuff, but it comes straight to our cell phones."

A small, thoughtful girl nodded. "Sometimes I worry about waking up. It's hard to stop thinking about bad stuff."

The kids continued sharing dismal stories, and then one quiet boy spoke up. "My friends and I were just saying that parents are too scared to let their kids play outside. It's sad. We kind of lost our childhoods." They all agreed. Pessimism about their world was the common theme.

I left them realizing that kids desperately need optimism. Educators agree, and I've made a practice over the past several years of searching out those teachers who are doing a great job of instilling optimism in their students. That's how I found myself in Mrs. Sandler's second-grade classroom on Long Island, New York, one snowy February day a few months later.

She found herself worried, just as I was, about her students' unfounded concerns about everyday issues and their propensity to often go to the most extreme, most negative outcomes. "Their pessimistic thinking really derails their performance," she said. She'd recently done some research into the issue, and she'd stumbled across psychologist Tamar Chansky's book *Freeing Your Child from Anxiety* for lesson ideas for how to teach optimism to these stressed-out second graders.[2] When she invited me to watch her lesson, I eagerly took her up on the invitation.

The concept Sandler was focusing on with the children that day was the idea that worries can grow, but "we can also shrink them." Then she asked, "Who has a big worry they want to share?" A girl with long pigtails immediately raised her hand. "I'm afraid of sleepovers."

The teacher put a cardboard box on the table, about the size of a large computer screen. "Okay, let's all help Chloe. Pretend this box is your biggest worry about the sleepover, and we'll help you shrink it. All you have to do is tell us why you're worried."

Chloe said, "I'm scared of the dark and worried I won't know where their light is." Sandler asked students to give their peer ways to shrink her worry, and they did.

"Ask your friend to show you."

"Bring a flashlight."

"Sleep with your sleeping bag by the light switch."

"Great ideas!" Mrs. Sandler said. "Which one works, Chloe?" The girl agreed to bring a flashlight, drew her "worry shrinker," and put the card inside the box. "Your worry isn't as big now," the teacher said. "Let's keep shrinking your worries." Mrs. Sandler put a second, slightly smaller box on the table—about the size of a laptop.

And Chloe shared another worry: "I might not like the mom's food." Again, the kids had solutions.

"Bring a granola bar with you!"

"I packed a peanut butter sandwich to my last sleepover."

"Just eat before you go!"

Chloe decided to put a granola bar in her bag, drew the worry shrinker, and put it in the second box.

Mrs. Sandler pulled up an even smaller, third box, and for a third time students helped their friend reduce her sleepover apprehensions. When the fourth and final box nested inside the others, Chloe was noticeably relieved. "I'm going to the sleepover," she pledged, and we all applauded. But I was also clapping for a teacher who helped all her students reduce their pessimism—just by putting their worries into smaller and smaller "mental" boxes until manageable. Science supports her lesson: one of the best proven ways to reduce worries and build hope is by giving children a sense of control[3]—something our pandemic generation will need to thrive.

WHAT IS OPTIMISM?

"Society and people are more hostile today.
It's just a different world from what our parents
grew up in so it's harder to be optimistic."
—*Ava, fourteen, Nashville*

Optimistic kids view challenges and obstacles as *temporary* and *able to be overcome,* and so they are more likely to succeed. But there is a dramatically opposing view: pessimism. Children who are pessimistic see challenges as *permanent,* like cement blocks that are impossible to move, and so they are more likely to quit.

Psychologists used to believe that attitudinal change isn't possible, which is why the research of psychiatrist Aaron Beck at the University of Pennsylvania over the past several decades was so significant. Beck completely revolutionized our perspective on optimism and the ability each of us has to shift our mind sets. Beck believed that how we think (cognition), feel (emotion), and act (behavior) interact. In short, *our thoughts determine our feelings and our behavior,* not the other way around. So, if we change negative, inaccurate thoughts, we can alter our feelings and behavior, and thereby improve our odds of handling whatever comes our way.

"We can choose to focus on the positive or the negative," Beck once said. He taught people how to shift their emphasis to the positive, and reap the mental-health results that followed. His method is called Cognitive Behavior Therapy (CBT), which has been widely popularized in the last few decades and proven effective in countering depression and anxiety, even in children. The best news: CBT is teachable. But just telling a child, "Be positive!" does not work. Our lessons must follow the science, and doing so can reap amazing results. The first step is often changing our children's negative mind-sets.

"I *never* get chosen." "Nobody *ever* invites me." "I *always* fail." No matter the experience, pessimistic kids have a "What's the point?" mind-set.[4] They give up easily, believe anything they do won't make a difference, assume they won't succeed, and rarely see the good parts of life. Then if by chance they do something well, they discount the accomplishment: "It wasn't that great." "It was luck." "No big deal." And in the process, they shortchange themselves from happiness and their potential to succeed.

Many kids admit to having pessimistic mind-sets. Fourteen-year-old Jenna told me, "I catastrophize things a lot, like I'm going to do really bad on a test, not get into a good college, or flunk a project. It really derails me."

Ned, a twelve-year-old from Boston, shared a similar view. "If you get a bad grade, it's overwhelming."

Kara said, "You get this mind-set that you're doomed. It would help if you could rewind your thoughts so you don't think things are so dismal, but nobody teaches that stuff." The kids know that if left unchecked, pessimism can spiral into cynicism, helplessness, and depression, plant seeds of underachievement, and influence every arena in their lives and reduce their chances to thrive.

Their dismal views are a stark difference from optimistic kids, who are far more likely to think about bad events in terms like "sometimes," "yet," and "almost." It's no coincidence that optimists are also less depressed, more successful at school, more resilient and better able to bounce back from adversity, and even physically healthier than pessimistic kids. But benefits continue: this strength also unleashes children's academic potential, character, and positive mental health. And the need for optimism has never been more crucial: data shows that

20 percent of young people today will experience depression at some point—that is double the rate of depression experienced by their parents. But science is on our side: we *can* teach lessons to help kids be less pessimistic and more optimistic.

University of Pennsylvania psychologist Martin E. P. Seligman conducted nineteen controlled studies worldwide, in which more than two thousand eight- to fifteen-year-olds were taught to think more realistically and flexibly about their daily problems. Over the next two years, students' optimism levels increased, and their risk for depression was cut in half, but they also discovered that optimistic, resilient kids *learn better.*[5] This chapter offers proven lessons to help our kids feel more fulfilled, less burned out, and to see the sunnier side of life.

WHY OPTIMISM CAN BE SO HARD TO TEACH

"We're more skeptical, negative, cynical,
and pessimistic because there's so much accessible bad
news like mass shootings, even to younger kids."
—*Charlie, fifteen, Chicago*

Pessimism is becoming the way our children view the world, and that means that their ability to thrive is at stake. Here are three factors that squelch this crucial Character Strength in kids.

We Live in a Fear-Based Culture

Every week that goes by finds us needing to explain yet another horrific event to our kids: terrorism, predators, hurricanes, violence, pandemics, and mass fires. Many parents tell me, "There's no place kids are safe anymore." In 2019 the hot back-to-school parent purchase was a backpack with removable bulletproof inserts (available in multi-colors) to shield school-age children from rounds of handgun fire.[6] Then in 2020, we loaded our children with plastic gloves, face masks, and hand sanitizers to protect them from COVID-19. We kiss them goodbye and send them to school while we fear for their safety. We are living in a culture of fear, but what effect does it have on our children?

I found the answer while touring schools in Nagorno-Karabakh, a small region and site of a war between Armenia and Azerbaijan in the late 1980s to 1994. A few years ago when I visited schools and families in the region, the fear was palpable: bullet holes were evident, land mines active, and military tanks visible. But as I write this, once again, the region is a war zone. A dad I met there sought my advice. "I was a frightened boy during the war, but my six-year-old shows my same fears today. Can he catch my fear?" My answer was, unfortunately, yes.

Our fears and anxieties *do* spill over to our kids and can over time erode their positive outlook on life. They learn from our general life outlook and make our style their own.[7] Twelve-year-old Madison told me, "My mom is always telling us not to be anxious, but it's hard not to when she's a basket case every time she hears anything bad."

We have to keep our own pessimism in check. Our cynicism can make us more fearful, anxious, and angry: a toxic trio that derails effective parenting. These negative views spill over to kids, who in turn become more fearful, anxious, and angry. Researchers now say that anxiety disorders affect one in four kids between thirteen and eighteen years old;[8] anxiety continues to be the primary mental health problem facing children and teens today. One study by psychologist Jean Twenge found even typical schoolchildren today—without any diagnosis— have baseline stress levels higher than psychiatric patients in the 1950s.[9] We must keep ourselves calm to help our kids.

Active Shooter Drills Cause Everyday Stress and Trauma

Every student group tells me that active shooter drills are traumatizing. "Our entire school career is a memory of lockdown drills," said twelve-year-old Elijah.

A girl with large brown eyes nodded. "Tomorrow we're learning to hide in a closet from active shooters. Sometimes I worry about waking up."

"We've had lockdown drills since kindergarten," another girl added sadly. "Tomorrow we're learning how to barricade a door and what kinds of things to throw if we're attacked. It gets to you after a while." Yes, it does.

While we must keep our kids safe and help prepare our kids so they know what to do for worst-case scenarios—like in a hurricane, pandemic, tornado, earthquake, fire, or shooting—we don't need to scare the pants off of them and boost their anxiety. But that seems to be what we're doing with active shooter drills. Teachers tell me younger students always carry cell phones "in case we get shot." Teens say the drills are so real that classmates are in tears and can't sleep. "We watched a video of a shooting at school; classmates were lying in the hallway with blood around them," one recalled. "Nobody said it was fake. I can't get the image out of my head."

The nation's two largest teachers' unions, the American Federation of Teachers and National Education Association, assert that current active shooter drills are too terrifying and cause harm to students' mental health, and they want schools to revise or eliminate them. Their requests include never simulating an actual shooting; giving parents, educators, and students advance notice of any drill; working with mental health officials to create age-appropriate and trauma-informed drills; and tracking the effects of drills.[10] And teachers aren't alone in their concerns.

Two criminology professors who created a database of 171 mass shootings also feel the costs of drills for children outweigh the benefits. "You want the adults in the building to be trained to know what to do," said author Jillian Peterson. "But training the children who are the potential perpetrators doesn't make sense with our data."[11] Let's teach kids precautions, prepare them for emergencies, and do whatever we can to prevent a shooting, but we don't need to make drills so realistic. We are creating traumatized children who fear for their lives.

Kids Are Exposed to Frightening Media Images Nonstop

A survey conducted by MTV and the Associated Press of more than 1,300 teens nationwide found that only 25 percent feel safe from terrorism. The vast majority admit that their world is far more worrisome than the world their mom or dad grew up in. One reason is that troubling images saturate their media landscape.

Constantly hearing and seeing frightening images does more than just increase anxiety; it also alters kids' views of their world and reduces optimism. Previous generations of parents could turn off the television set so their children didn't see scary news. These days, frightening images feed straight into kids' cell phones. This is the first generation to view live war feeds, terrorist attacks, daily pandemic death counts, and school shootings on personal screens. Violence portrayed in films has tripled since 1986.[12] Negative headlines are 63 percent higher than positive ones.[13] Children see about 8,000 murders by the end of elementary school, and about 200,000 violent acts by age eighteen, and those images are graphic and highly disturbing.[14] Many kids tell me one of the most disturbing images was the May 25, 2020 video of a white Minneapolis police officer kneeling on the neck of George Floyd, a Black American, while he was handcuffed, lying facedown, begging for his life while repeatedly saying, "I can't breathe," for almost eight minutes and calling out for his mother.

The late George Gerbner, dean emeritus of the Annenberg School of Communications at the University of Pennsylvania, coined the term "mean world syndrome" to describe when mass media violence–related content makes viewers believe that the world is more dangerous than it actually is. It's not the quantity of violence, Gerbner warned, but how it all adds up to reinforce and normalize a view of the world as "mean and scary"—exactly how too many kids perceive their world.

HOW TO TEACH KIDS OPTIMISM

All these challenges our kids face when trying to find an optimistic outlook on life are very real. But just as with all the other Thriver traits we've studied in this book, optimism can indeed be taught, despite the cynical world in which we all live. There are three proven abilities parents can instill to nurture optimism and give kids the Character Advantage: optimistic thinking, assertive communication, and hope. All are teachable and crucial for kids living in a rapidly changing world.

Model and Teach Optimistic Thinking

Terrorism. Hurricanes. Bombings. Mass shootings. Fires. Global warming. Earthquakes. Pandemics. We're jittery, but what about our kids? An Iowa mom's story shows that even our youngest are adopting a gloom-and-doom view about life.

"I had to tell my six-year-old that his best friend died of cancer. I wasn't prepared for his response. He looked at me in shock, turned completely white and said, 'Lucas is gone? I didn't know kids my age died of cancer. I thought they were only shot at school.' How do I help my child gain hope about our world?"

One of the best answers is in an overlooked source: history books.

From September 1940 to May 1941 nightly bombing raids by Nazi Germany took place in London and other British cities. Over three hundred tons of bombs were dropped on London for eleven weeks; one-third of the city was destroyed and thousands were killed, but Britain prevailed.

Imagine what it was like to parent a child during the Blitz. Each night shrilling air raid sirens warned of incoming attacks, and each night parents turned off lights, covered windows, put on gas masks, and did whatever they could to save their family. The Brit motto was "Keep calm and carry on," and that they did. But how did parents help their kids remain optimistic despite the terror? I uncovered their secret lessons quite unexpectedly.

Several years ago, a reporter interviewed me about helping kids deal with trauma. I told her that kids mirror what they see and repeat what they hear, so they learn pessimism or optimism from us. She blurted out: "That's how my grandparents did it!" She explained that she had lived in London during the Blitz as a young child with her brother and grandparents, and in the course of our conversation she told me a bit about those frightening times.

"We should have been terrified, but my brother and I always believed we'd make it. Now I know it was because my grandparents modeled optimism! As the bombs went off, our normal nightly family routines continued. We told stories, sang songs, and played Ring Around the Rosie. My grandparents constantly sang, 'Life is good; together we'll get through anything.' And we did, because they gave us hope."

Her grandparents applied a key parenting lesson: kids who thrive in tough times have caring adults in their lives who model a positive life outlook. Teaching children optimism begins with us. Children adopt our words as their inner voices, so over the next days, tune in to your typical messages and assess the life outlook you offer your kids. On average would you say you're generally more pessimistic or optimistic? Do you usually describe things as positive or negative; half full or empty; good or bad; through rose- or blue-tinted glasses? Would your friends and family say the same about you?

If you see that you're tilting to the half empty side, remember that change starts by looking in the mirror. If you see pessimism, write why becoming more optimistic would help. Reread it often to boost your change commitment. You might also find a lesson you'd like to learn in this chapter and teach it to your child. With practice you'll discover that both you *and* your kids become more hopeful about life.

Change is hard, especially when trying to alter a well-oiled, negative mind-set.

Be the example of what you want your child to learn. When an optimistic mind-set becomes your own you're ready to help your kids learn this Character Strength. Here are three steps to reduce kids' everyday pessimistic thinking *before* they become habitual, and replace them with an optimistic mind-set.

Step 1: Catch Pessimistic Thoughts. Every kid says negative thoughts, but be concerned when pessimism becomes your child's typical operating mode: "Nobody *ever* likes me." "Bad stuff *always* happens to me." "It's *never* worth the effort." "I'll flunk like *all the other* times." Ungrounded pessimistic thinking erodes optimism, sets kids up for failure, shortchanges their thriving abilities, and increases emptiness.

It may take your child a while to tune in to her *never, always, all the time*-type thoughts. So create a private code like, pulling on your ear or touching your elbow, that only you and your kid understand. The code means she's said a negative comment. Then encourage that she listen to her pessimistic comments. Creating a name for your child's pessimistic voice helps her control it. Names can be whatever resonates with your kid: "My Stinkin' Thinker," "Miss Bully," "Mr. No," "Fun Stopper," "Bossy Pants," "Negative Nelly." Teens' labels are sometimes quite explicit.

Younger child: "I'm going to help you listen to your Stinkin' Thinker, and talk back to it so *you* have power, not your voice." They can draw a picture of the voice and role-play talking back to it with puppets and toys.

Older kid: "Remember when you got that grade and said you were dumb? You don't feel that way now, right? Give that bossy voice in your head a name so you can talk back to it and stay in control."

Sometimes kids need evidence of how often they are pessimistic before they're willing to change. Help your kid count negative comments for a set time: "For the next five minutes (or brief period) track how many times you say negative things out loud or inside your head." Wearing a watch or bracelet can help kids remember to tune in to their thoughts. Younger kids can count on their fingers. Older kids can move coins from their left to right pocket per negative statement, make tally marks on paper, or track on their cell phone.

Watch for moments your kid *does* utter even an ounce of optimism. Then salute her positive attitude and tell her why you value it. "Your math is hard, but saying 'I'm getting better' was optimistic. Hang in there!"

Step 2: Challenge Inaccurate, Pessimistic Views. Next, help your child assess whether the statement is accurate (sometimes they are), and challenge those that are not. Teach your kid to talk back to their critical voice by using yourself as an example. Feel free to fictionalize as long as your child gets the point. "When I was your age about to take a test I'd hear a voice inside say, 'You're not going to do well.' I learned to talk back and tell it: 'I'm going to try my best so I'll do okay.' Pretty soon the voice faded because I refused to listen. When you hear that voice, talk back to it. Say: 'That's wrong,' 'I'm not listening,' or 'Stop it.'"

Pessimistic kids typically think the worst could happen. Ask: "What's the absolute *worst* that could happen?" Then help your child weigh if the outcome really is that bad, and see the good side.

Child: "I flunk the test and get an F for a final grade."

Parent: "You flunked *one* test. What can you do so your final grade isn't an F?

Child: "I could study more."

Parent: "Okay! Let's work out a plan for how you will you study better."

Another way to get kids out of negative thinking traps is offering balanced perspectives. Just make sure your statement is accurate. If your child hears your gentle counter enough, he may adopt it to refute his own negative thoughts.

Suppose your kid won't go to her friend's party. "No one *ever* likes me." *Balance it with:* "Kara must like you or you wouldn't have been invited."

If your son didn't make the team. "Kids think I'm *always* the worst player." *Counter it with:* "They know you're great at skiing so tell them that you haven't practiced baseball as much."

Your daughter fails her science exam. "I *never* do anything right." *Refute it with:* "You're good in math so let's work on improving your science grade."

Step 3: Change Unrealistic Pessimistic Thoughts. Kids can get trapped in pessimistic thinking patterns and see only the downside. As pessimism becomes more entrenched, they can overlook or downplay positive thoughts. The last step is helping kids replace their negative thinking to more accurate, optimistic views. Whenever a family member makes a sweeping negative statement (like "I *always*..." "I *never*..." "*Every time* . . ." *learned in Step 1*) another should gently remind the speaker, "Reality Check!" until the child can prompt himself. The strategy helps kids not only catch pessimism in themselves and others but also to reframe them with more positive, realistic views. And that is the critical, final step in helping children develop optimistic mindsets.

Child: "I *never* get good grades in school."

Parent: "Reality Check! What about your history scores?"

Child: "I *always* get left out."

Parent: "Reality Check! What about Kevin's birthday party. You were invited."

Then help your child replace negativity with positive word choices. Write "almost, yet, closer, next time, try" on a chart. Then prompt your child: "That was your pessimist voice. What word can you use instead?"

Almost: "I *always* flunk." Change to: "I *almost* have it right."

Yet: "I'll *never* learn." Change to: "I'm not there *yet*."

Closer: "It's *hopeless*." Change to: "I'm getting *closer*."

Next time: "I'm *so* stupid." Change to: "*Next time* I'll study more."

Try: "I *won't* make it." Change to: "I'll *try* it."

Changing habits is hard, so watch for moments your child *does* utter even an ounce of optimism. Then acknowledge her optimism and why you value it. "Your rehearsals are hard. But saying 'I think I'm getting better' was optimistic. Hang in there!"

Show Them How to Stand Up for Themselves

Growing up is never easy, but in today's world bullying and peer pressure have never been rougher. Almost 40 percent of teens in a Boys & Girls Clubs of America survey of 46,000 teens said that peer pressure was the greatest cause of stress.[15] One in five American students aged twelve to eighteen reported being bullied at school during the previous six months.[16] Not to be able to stand up for yourself can make a child feel helpless, start a dangerous spiral of pessimism, and increase stress, anxiety, depression, and feelings of emptiness.

Martin Seligman, author of *The Optimistic Child,* points out that pessimism "hardens with each setback and soon becomes self-fulfilling."[17] Kids worry a lot about peer harassment, but when I teach assertive communication strategies, their pessimism seems to fade because they learned tools to replace it. We can start teaching these lessons in assertive behavior to children as young as toddlers. Then don't stop until your kids know how to confidently stand up for themselves and feel hopeful—not helpless—about their world because they are more in control. Self-advocacy is a proven trait of Thrivers.

Help your child learn to self-advocate by teaching each step in CALM separately, until he can master all four elements. Emphasize that while you can't control what another person says or does, you can control how you respond. It will take time, but with practice you'll improve.

Part 1: C—Chill. Unless kids stay calm, they'll never be taken seriously. If you child has trouble staying calm, review strategies in the self-control chapter. She may also need to take a deep breath or walk away until she can get herself in control. Tell your child two quick ways to appear calmer and more confident: 1. Uncross your legs and arms; 2. Make your voice sound not too soft (meek) or harsh (angry).

Part 2: A—Assert. If you always defend your child she won't develop inner confidence and will rely on you! Thivers learn to self-advocate. From this moment on, step back and help your child learn to speak for herself.

- **Develop comebacks.** Brainstorm a few assertive lines that your child can say in difficult situations like: "Not cool." "Cut it out." "Stop." "That's not right." "I don't want to!" Firm, short statements work best. Stress that they are to *never* insult back.
- **Say or show "no."** Timid kids have tougher times speaking out. So tell her to say no. She can also place her hand straight out in the universal no position and not say anything. Stress that if someone wants her to go against her moral code or what your family believes (see integrity) saying "No" or "No, I don't want to" is just fine.
- **Teach "I messages."** Beginning an assertive message with "I" not "you" helps kids stick to the issue and not insult the person. It works best with a friend (not a harasser or bully). Start with "I" then say what you feel, need, or want to happen. "I feel upset that you took my turn because it wasn't fair." "I want you to stop teasing me because it hurts my feelings." "I need you to stop copying my work."

Then look for daily moments for your child to "be in charge" and practice assertiveness. If your child is timid and always hangs around a bossy playmate, provide him the opportunity to find a less overbearing pal so he will be more likely to speak up and gain confidence.

Part 3: L—Look strong. Most assertive communication has nothing to do with spoken words but messages we send with our body language. Kids are taken less seriously if they look vulnerable: slumped shoulders, head down, shaking knees, hands in pockets. So teach these assertive body language senders.

- **Head:** Stand tall and hold your head high.
- **Eyes:** Hold your head high and look eye to eye. A simple way to appear assertive is using eye contact because your head is held high and you look confident. So always look the person in the eye. If your child is uncomfortable with eye contact, he can look at the middle of the person's forehead or spot between their eyes.
- **Shoulders:** Pull shoulders down, back straight.
- **Arms and hands:** Arms at your sides; hands out of pockets and uncrossed.
- **Feet:** Stand with feet planted firmly on the ground about twelve inches apart.

Help your child practice looking strong head to feet in the mirror. Photograph him "looking strong from head to feet" to review often. Role-play "hesitant" and "confident" so he sees the difference. Point out actors using "assertive" (strong) and "wimpy" (timid) postures.

Part 4. M—Mean it! When intimidated or nervous, kids use a timid or yelling tone: both are ineffective so you need to help your child practice assertive voice tone. Stress to them that their voice can make them sound confident or timid. Demonstrate by saying "cut it out" in a strong, firm (not yelling or angry) voice, then in a softer, quiet, meek-sounding one. Ask: "Which voice would another kid listen to more? A stronger voice is most effective, so let's practice."

Then make sure your child has the opportunity to practice his voice and not be squelched by a domineering brother or sister (or even other parent). Do reinforce any assertive effort: "That was tough telling your friend you had to leave early to make your curfew. I'm proud you were able to stand up to them and not just go along."

Believe That the Future Is Full of Hope

I've worked in dozens of schools, but an experience in Hershey, Pennsylvania, haunts me. The town, home to Hershey's Kisses, is idyllic and suitable for a photo-op. Streetlamps are even shaped like Kisses; it's even registered as "The Sweetest Place On Earth."

The district hired me to speak to their staff about character education. I always first interview students in smaller groups representing a cross section of races, cliques, cultures, and incomes so I can get a pulse on their concerns. Once teens know I'm there to listen, not judge, they open up.

"What's keeping you up at night?" I asked them.

The answers came tumbling out, one after the other: "I won't get the scholarship." "Peer pressure." "Getting into college." "Stress."

Then I asked: "What worries you about the world?" They sat up, leaned in, and listed their concerns so rapidly that I had trouble keeping up.

"Global warming." "Pandemics." "Terrorism." "Violence." "Nuclear war." "Hate." "Shootings."

Their worry list went on and on. But one teen's question stopped everyone.

"Do you believe we'll live to see the future?" he asked. "I'm not very hopeful: I don't think our generation will." They all nodded: each had the same doom-and-gloom view about life, and it was no different from the hundreds of groups I'd interviewed before. Kids are pessimistic about their world and it's diminishing their capacity to thrive. While we can't assure safety, we *can* keep children's hope alive, and you probably watched one of the best ways on television as a child.

If I could wind back time to a favorite family memory, it would be watching *Mister Rogers' Neighborhood* with my three young sons. Nobody addressed television audiences in such a gentle, calm, honest way as Fred Rogers. For thirty-three years, this much-loved television host brought optimism, love, and joy into my home and countless others. He offered hope. Mr. Rogers always walked in with a big smile and hummed that upbeat tune: "It's a beautiful day in this neighborhood. A beautiful day for a neighbor . . ."

Then he took off his jacket, hung it in the closet, zipped on his cardigan sweater, replaced his dress shoes with blue sneakers, fed the fish, and taught my kids another profound but simple lesson about life. At the end of each episode, Rogers sang: "It's such a good feeling, to know you're alive. It's such a happy feeling you're growing inside." By the time the show ended my kids and I were psyched to handle whatever came our way.

Mr. Rogers's optimistic outlook is needed in these jittery times. With each new bombing, virus, hurricane, terrorist attack, fire, hate crime, tornado, or mass shooting we wonder, "What shall we tell our children?" Fred Rogers had the perfect answer:

"When I was a boy and I would see scary things in the news, my mother would say to me, 'Look for the helpers. You will always find people who are helping.' To this day, especially in times of disaster, I remember my mother's words, and I am always comforted by realizing that there are still so many helpers, so many caring people in this world."[18]

I used that strategy with my own kids after 9/11. "Look for the helpers," I told them, and my boys wiped their tears, nodded, and promised to find them. During the pandemic we pointed out how first responders, doctors, and nurses were helping to keep them safe. Using the "Fred Factor" is how we can keep our kids' hearts open, believe that their world is good, and kindle their hope.

Keeping an optimistic "glass is half full" outlook about the future is crucial for mental and physical health. Hopeful children are happier, more satisfied with life, and more willing to try. And these "high-hope kids" have greater academic success, stronger friendships, and demonstrate more creativity and better problem-solving abilities,[19] and lower levels of depression and anxiety.[20] I've learned some of the best ways to fight pessimism and maintain a hopeful attitude from teens.

1. **Monitor news consumption.** Teen after teen expressed concern about late-breaking "scary" news without parents monitoring it. They also worried that their younger siblings have even more access to the internet than they did at that age. Constant gloomy news can impact kids' life outlooks. Their ideas: "I upload uplifting YouTube documentaries during hard times," said Sara, twelve. "I focus on the good stuff: the rescuers, neighbors reaching out, people donating blood," said Ricky, thirteen. (Sounds like Mr. Rogers!) "Parents should put their kids' smartphones away until the news improves," said Cara, sixteen.

2. **Read inspiring books.** "Learning that other people overcame tough times gives me hope," Darren, age fifteen, told me. Scientists concur and find that hopeful kids draw on memories of past success when confronted with obstacles.[21] The kids I talked with have the following suggestions:

Emmanuel's Dream by Laurie Ann Thompson. A disabled boy born in Africa helps kids learn that anything is possible if you believe in yourself. **Y, S**

The Story of Ruby Bridges by Robert Coles. A six-year-old Black girl, escorted by federal marshals, walked through a mob of segregationists to school with hope! **S**

A Long Walk to Water: Based on a True Story by Linda Sue Park. A memorable portrait of two children in Sudan who endure every hardship imaginable. **S, T**

I Am Malala: How One Girl Stood Up for Education and Changed the World (Young Readers Edition) by Malala Yousafzai. A young girl's voice can inspire change. **S, T**

Just Mercy (Adapted for Young Adults) by Bryan Stevenson. A young lawyer is dedicated to fighting against racial inequality, excessive punishment, and mass incarceration. **T**

Educated: A Memoir by Tara Westover. A young girl, kept out of school, leaves her survivalist family and earns a Ph.D. from Cambridge University. **T**

3. **Listen to uplifting music.** Natalie, age fourteen, from New York City told me: "I keep a playlist of upbeat inspiring songs. I listen mostly to Elton John's 'Goodbye Yellow Brick Road,' and when I do well on a test I crank up 'I'm Still Standing.' *For younger kids:* "Don't Give Up" by Bruno Mars; "Let It Go" by Idina Menzel; "Don't Worry Be Happy" by Bobby McFerrin. *For older kids:* "Let It Be" by The Beatles; "Eye of the Tiger" by Survivor; "Defying Gravity" from *Wicked*; "Stronger" by Kelly Clarkson; "Unwritten" by Natasha Bedingfield; "Brave" by Sara Bareilles; "Firework" by Katy Perry; "Somewhere" by Jackie Evancho.

4. **Tell kids: "It'll get better!"** Teen after teen said: "Parents need to tell their kids over and over, 'We'll get through this.' And 'I'll love you *no matter what*. Tomorrow is another day.'" Adam, age fifteen, reiterated that statement, saying, "Kids are under such pressure and don't want to let their parents down. Let them know that you love your kid *more than the grade*." Help your child take a step back to look at the big picture so they can put things in perspective.

5. **Develop a healthy motto.** Many kids told me that it helps to use an upbeat mantra to say to themselves to counter pessimism. "I got this!" "It's rough, but I can do it." "I can handle it." Some teens showed me their smartphone screen saver with their motto downloaded. Help your child develop a positive mantra.

6. **Volunteer.** Kids agreed that lending a hand can help you spread a message of hope and kindle optimism. "It makes you feel good knowing you can make a difference," Roberta, age fourteen, told me. "But make sure the giving project is something your kid *wants* to do and isn't just to look good on a college résumé," Jenna, age sixteen, added. "Tell parents to get

their kids' friends involved," Adam, age seventeen, agreed. "We want to spend more time with friends, and volunteering is a great way to be together."

HOW OPTIMISM CAN BE
YOUR CHILD'S SUPERPOWER

On November 14, 1960, four federal marshals escorted six-year-old Ruby Bridges to the all-white William Frantz Elementary School in New Orleans. The first grader made history as the first African American student to integrate an elementary school in the South, but it wasn't easy. A large adult crowd waited outside the school every day to shout obscenities and intimidate the young girl as she walked to the front door. One woman always screamed, "I'm going to poison you. I'll find a way."[22]

Once she was inside, Ruby still wasn't safe. The other parents insisted she not be in the same classroom with their white children, so she spent the year alone with one teacher, Barbara Henry, who supported her. Miss Henry recalled that Ruby never complained or missed a day of school, held her head high, and remained upbeat. Despite loneliness, tension, and hostility, the child maintained a hopeful outlook and was a portrait of resilience.

How did she make it through that long, torturous year?

"I really believed as a child that praying could get me through anything," she recalled.[23] "My mother brought us up to believe that God is always there to protect us. She taught us there is a power we can pray to anytime, anyplace. Somehow it always worked."[24]

Like most Thrivers, the six-year-old developed a coping skill to help her stay in control and remain hopeful. And so twice a day before facing those angry crowds, the first grader would say a prayer: "Please

God try to forgive those people. Because even if they say those bad things, they don't know what they're doing."[25]

Research finds that resilient, optimistic individuals often rely on spirituality or prayer as a source of support in times of difficulty.[26] Another commonality of Thrivers is that they have caring adults in their corner who offer hope. Miss Henry became much more than just a teacher to Ruby. "She was more like my best friend," Ruby explained. "I knew she cared about me. She had a polite, kind manner that I admired. In fact, I began to imitate her. Little by little I grew to love Miss Henry."[27]

There was also Mrs. Smith, the wife of her pediatrician, who spent time with Ruby to keep her spirits up. On weekends the woman would take the child to her home, where the whole family was kind and supportive. Years later Ruby recounted, "Now it's clear to me that those visits showed me a better side of life and made me feel that I had to do better for myself."[28]

At a young age, Ruby Bridges demonstrated qualities of heart, mind, and will as well as self-confidence, integrity, empathy, self-control, curiosity, perseverance, and optimism—the very strengths we address in this book. Those Character Strengths—plus caring adults who champion kids—are the winning equation to help kids thrive. Ruby Bridges is proof.

AGE-BY-AGE IDEAS TO INSTILL OPTIMISM

"Current events are usually about shootings and violence. If we heard more about stories about kids doing good things to help the world it would help."

—*Linus, twelve, Riverside, California*

Ten-year-olds Taylor Herber and Ian O'Gorman lived in San Marcos, California, and were best buddies. So it was little surprise that Taylor visited Ian when he was in the hospital about to undergo chemotherapy for cancer. Ian told his pal that he was concerned about what the kids at school would say. "You lose your hair when you have chemo," Ian said. "All the kids will make fun of me."

Taylor told his pal not to worry; he had a plan. He left the hospital and told the boys in his class to meet at the local barbershop to support their classmate. And the thirteen fifth graders jumped on the "Bald-wagon" by lining up to shave their heads for their friend, and even named themselves The Bald Eagles. Their teacher showed up to shave his head as well.

"We shaved our heads because we didn't want him to feel left out," explained classmate Erik Holzhaurer. And he added, "If they decide to do more chemotherapy, we'll shave our heads for another nine weeks."[29]

I've shared the story with hundreds of students worldwide, and it never fails to bring tears. *And hope.* The Bald Eagles touch kids' hearts and help them recognize that they can do something to help friends who are hurting. New York University professor Jonathan Haidt calls that warm, uplifting glow we feel when we see unexpected acts of human goodness "elevation."[30] Such feelings can inspire kids to help others, find optimism, and even become better people. Uplifting stories like those of The Bald Eagles also help kids recognize that they can be agents of their destiny: optimists in the making! Here are tips to help kids learn to see the good in life.

Symbols designate recommended age suitability for each activity: Y = Young children, toddlers, and preschoolers; S = School age; T = Tweens and older; A = All ages

- **Share good news.** Look for uplifting stories of everyday helpers and kindhearted good guys like the fifth-grade Bald Eagles to help kids focus on the good in life instead of the negative. A mom told me her family texts links of inspiring stories to each other. "It helps my kids have hope about the world," she said. Heartwarming stories are in newspapers, websites, magazines, and your community.

    Set a Google alert for "inspiring stories" at goggle.com/alerts. **S, T**

    Glue articles on cards and put them into a basket on your dining table to review. **A**

    Start a good news family scrapbook of favorite stories. **A**

    Post inspiring articles on your refrigerator or bulletin board. **S, T**

    During the pandemic, filmmaker John Krasinski started the web series *Some Good News,* narrating viral clips demonstrating humanity's resilience and goodness. One episode featured the cast of *Hamilton* performing for a young girl whose long-awaited tickets to the Broadway show were canceled due to the coronavirus. Garden City High School (at students' request) added a video monitor to their front hall to display inspiring news stories and quotes to reduce pessimism and fears about the world. Share the good news to inspire optimism. **A**

- **Encourage good deeds.** Emily Roe, a mom from Minnetonka, started a goodness ritual by chance. Her five- and three-year-olds used to beg for Altoids when they got in her car. "To stop their bickering, I said that they were Goodness Mints and they're only given when someone talks about something good they did that day," she told me. "Then one day my five-year-old jumped in our car and said, 'I helped Beatrice clean up today,' and took a mint; all on her own volition! Sharing good deeds is now routine. The mints began an easy conversation starter to talk about goodness and appreciate each other in a natural way." Find easy rituals to help your kids talk about the good parts of life. **Y, S**

- **Watch good films.** Movies can elevate kids' hearts and offer hope. Younger kids: *Happy Feet, Charlotte's Web, Pete's Dragon, Pollyanna.* Older kids: *Patch Adams, The Pursuit of Happyness, Forrest Gump, A Wrinkle in Time.* Teens: *Pay It Forward, The Blind Side, Dunkirk.* Discuss how the characters depicted optimism despite adversity. **A**

- **Be a good turner.** Pessimistic thinking can easily become a habit and impact how your child responds to life. A second-grade teacher in Kansas uses a class "thumbs down" signal to help students catch their pessimism. The signal means "That's stinking thinking talk." The signaler then turns his thumb up to remind his classmate to say a "put up" or positive statement to replace it. "It's taken a while but kids are now tuning in to their words and using more optimistic messages," the teacher told me. Try it with your kids. **Y**

- **Hold goodness reviews.** Institute a nightly review of the simple good parts about each person's day like: "Sally asked me to play with her." "My teacher said I improved in math." "I didn't burn the cookies!" It's a precious way to spend the last waking hours and help your kids look on the bright side of life. **Y, S**

- **Be a good finder.** Encourage your kids to be "good finders" by watching for good things they see others do. Then have them report findings at a family meeting, dinner, or before going to sleep. "Kevin helped a boy fix his broken bike." "A man picked up all the groceries a woman spilled." "Sally walked a boy to the office because he was sick." Help your child realize that seeing goodness can improve your mood. Ask: "How did it make you feel? What can you learn from that?" A San Diego school keeps a "goodness jar" for students to write good findings about each other. The principal pins the findings on a hall bulletin board for kids to review, and it inspires others to do more good deeds. **S**

- **Read good books.** I was in Kohler, Wisconsin, interviewing teens for this book, but one was hesitant. When I asked why, his response said it all, "I'm reading this book and I can't put it down." He showed me *All the Light We Cannot See.* I smiled and told him, "Go read!" Other books that inspire kids: *Most People* by Michael Leannah; *I Walk with Vanessa,* by Kerascoët; *One* by Kathryn Otoshi; *The Power of One* by Trudy Ludwig; *Rain Brings Frogs: A Little Book of Hope* by Maryann Cocca-Leffler; *Good People Everywhere* by Lynea Gillen; *Come With Me* by Holly M. McGhee; *Last Stop on Market Street* by Matt de la Peña. **Y** *Miss Rumphius* by Barbara Cooney; *Out of My Mind,* by Sharon M. Draber; *Wonder* by R. J, Palacio; *Good News, Bad News* by Jeff Mack; *Most People,* by Michael Leannah **S**; *The Lions of Little Rock,* by Kristin Levine; *All We Have Left,* by Wendy Mill; *Pay It Forward* by Catherine Ryan Hyde; *The Fault in Our Stars* by John Green; *Rising Out of Hatred* by Eli Saslow. **T** Remind kids that though there are mean, scary events, there are also countless examples of goodness.

- **Turn bad into good.** Teens tell me their heroes are the Parkland High School students advocating for gun control and Greta Thunberg, the Swedish teen raising global awareness about climate change. "Their stories give us hope," they said. Share stories about ordinary children who are making extraordinary differences to better the world and encourage your kids to find more. Then talk about them as a family to help you discover your children's concerns as well as ways they want to make a difference. A

  Tainted drinking water: Gitanjali Rao, age eleven, from Flint, Michigan, invented a device that detects lead in drinking water as part of her science fair project.[31]

  Poverty: While Adam Braun, age sixteen, was traveling, he met a boy begging on the streets of India. Adam asked what he wanted most in the world and he answered, "A pencil." Adam has built more than 250 schools around the world. Encourage your teen to read Adam's book: *The Promise of a Pencil.*

  Homelessness: Jahkil Jackson, age eight, founded Project I Am to help the homeless in his Chicago hometown and distributed more than three thousand Blessing Bags filled with toiletry items, a towel, socks, and light snacks in a year.[32]

- **Find good quotes.** Help your child search for quotes that inspire him to see the good. A Palm Springs mom told me that her family writes inspirational quotes on index cards and puts them in a basket on their dining table. They draw one each night at their family meal and discuss. Her two teens are now posting their favorites on their screen savers! **S, T**

⇒ "If you think you are too small to make a difference, you haven't spent the night with a mosquito." —African proverb

⇒ "Try to be a rainbow in someone's cloud." —Maya Angelou

⇒ "You must be the change you wish to see in the world." —Mahatma Gandhi

⇒ "It always seems impossible until it is done." —Nelson Mandela

Trudy Esrey, a Los Gatos mom, said that her daughter Kelly's favorite quote was from Winnie-the-Pooh telling his little friend Piglet: "You're braver than you believe, stronger than you seem, and smarter than you think." (A. A. Milne) Kelly painted the quote above her bed while recovering from brain surgery. "That quote gave Kelly such hope and inspiration," Trudy said. "She saw it first thing in the morning and last thing before going to sleep. It reminded her that she could overcome her ordeal, and indeed, helped her make it through!" Find an inspiring quote that resonates with your child. **A**

- **Acknowledge good thinking.** Change is hard—especially when you are trying to alter an attitude that is a well-used habit. So do be on the alert for those times your child does utter optimism and acknowledge it. "I know how difficult your math tests have been. But saying you think you'll do better was being so optimistic. I'm sure you'll do better because you've been studying so hard." "It pleases me that you said you'll try your best to tie your shoes by yourself. Way to be positive!" **A**

- **Start a goodness box.** As tragedies increase, our brains can go into overload mode and feel there's "nothing I can do." Helplessness sets in. Tell kids to "focus on the few or one we can help," not the masses we can't help. "Lots of people lost their homes, but we can give used books to this family." "Hundreds need food, but let's bring clothes to the kids at the shelter." Keep a goodness box by your door and encourage your family to add gently used toys, clothes, books, and games. Each time it is filled deliver it as a family to a shelter, church, American Red Cross, or family. "I gave our goodness box to a boy who lost his home in a fire," Kevin, age ten, told me. "He smiled and said, 'thank you.' I told my mom we *have* to keep filling this box!" Hope! **S, T**

TOP FIVE TAKEAWAYS

1. Kids who remain upbeat about life despite uncertain times have parents who model optimism. Be the model you want your kids to copy.
2. Ungrounded pessimistic thinking erodes hope, sets kids up for failure, and shortchanges their thriving abilities, but optimism can be taught.
3. Seeing repeated violent images exacerbates anxiety, increases fear, and decreases optimism, which is why we

must monitor kids' news intake during disasters or
tragedies.

4. Parents who raise grateful kids expect them to be appreciative.

5. Every kid makes negative comments; be concerned when
pessimism becomes your child's typical operating mode.

ONE LAST LESSON

Beth Simmons, a high school teacher, requires service learning and
told me that she is convinced that the right project helps kids gain
hope, develop optimistic mind-sets, and be more appreciative about
life. But one fifteen-year-old was a challenge because he was constantly
in trouble for bullying and always expected the worst in every situation: "Everything goes bad. Why should this be any different?"

The teacher knew she had to prove him wrong to boost his optimism and hopefully change his behavior. And so, she assigned him to
tutor five-year-old Noah, who was struggling with his letters and numbers. Instead of buying into Justin's "It won't work" and "He won't like
me" pessimistic comments, she pressed: "What can you do to succeed?" They brainstormed ways he *could* connect and *could* help the
kindergartner. After each tutoring session, Justin journaled one thing
that worked with the boy so he focused on the positive, not the negative.

Things weren't always smooth, but the teacher knew that Justin has
been pessimistic most of his life. "I had to give him time," she said. But
about three weeks later, the moment came: Justin and Noah bonded.
The teen saw himself for the first time in a positive light. "I never knew
I could help someone," he told his teacher. And his bullying ceased.

Most remarkable was what the five-year-old told his teacher. "I knew Justin could do it," Noah whispered. "It just took him a while to figure it out. You can't give up on kids, ya know."

I told the story of Justin and Noah in my book, *UnSelfie,* but so many readers told me that they appreciated the message that I thought it important to mention again. Optimism is the last Character Strength that helps kids thrive. Teaching lessons of hope and instilling optimistic mindsets in our children is how we will build a generation of strong, independent, caring Thrivers who have the Character Advantage. But to do so we must heed Noah's advice. "Don't *ever* give up on a kid!"

Epilogue

WRITING THIS BOOK BEGAN WITH a question I've sought to answer for over forty years. And it all started one day when I was a college student visiting my parents and found my usually calm father pacing in our living room with a magazine in hand. He saw me, and held it up. "It says in here that the first three years make or break a child's chances to succeed. Don't believe it," he said. "I'd be dead if it was true." I couldn't grasp what he was saying. His parents died before I was born, so I never met my grandparents or heard much about his childhood. That day he finally opened up about his early life, and I understood why he was so upset about the article.

His parents came to America from Italy over a century ago in search of a better life. They spoke no English, were penniless, and illiterate. My grandfather somehow found a job as a manual laborer, and then died of the Spanish flu pandemic when Dad was two. His mother was forced to put Dad in an orphanage for several years until she could find a way to support him. Dad lived an impoverished life, but somehow he overcame. He earned a college scholarship, survived the Great

Depression, earned degrees from University of California at Berkeley and Stanford, fought in World War II, became a school superintendent, published books, married and was a loving father, and lived to be one hundred years of age.

In short, Dad was a Thriver. How?

I continued to ask my father about his childhood and slowly found answers. I learned that Dad had not just a loving mom but also caring adults in his community who helped him learn what I now have identified as the seven Character Strengths, all of which helped him triumph over adversity and the troubling early years of his life.

A caring nun in the orphanage made him feel safe and accepted, nurturing his **empathy**.

A librarian gave him books that helped him learn English, igniting his **curiosity**.

A teacher recognized his writing strengths and tutored him, building his **self-confidence** and showing the power of **self-control** in mastering new tasks.

A priest taught him to pray, keeping his hope alive and modeling **optimism** even in his darkest days.

A neighbor gave him a job that instilled in him **perseverance** and **integrity**.

For the next forty years of my career I would, in some way or another, seek to answer the question: why do some kids struggle while others shine? My quest for the answer to that query took me into the classroom, into academia, and into conversation with families all across the world. I learned so much along the way . . . not realizing of course that my very first teacher—my father—had so many of the answers himself. He'd lived it, after all, along with the remarkable adults who recognized my father's needs and became his guides.

They identified his Core Assets, and taught him crucial Character

Strengths that gave him the Character Advantage. Though each individual trait was important, their impact dramatically increased when Dad used the Character Strengths together:

Self-Confidence + Perseverance

Curiosity + Self-Control

Integrity + Empathy + Optimism

That Multiplier Effect—the combined power of Character Strengths nurtured by a community of caring adults—is why my dad was able to overcome and thrive.

The Multiplier Effect is what Thrivers use (and Strivers lack). Instilling those abilities depends on the intentional efforts of empathetic adults who know that the Character Advantage is not optional but essential. The challenges kids face at the beginning of the twenty-first century are very different than those my father faced in the beginning of the twentieth century. But no matter what life throws at them, these same Character Strengths will serve as the protective buffers and resilience builders to help kids be ready and able to take on an uncertain future, overcome adversity, ultimately triumph and be masters of their own destinies.

7 ESSENTIAL CHARACTER STRENGTHS TO HELP KIDS THRIVE

CHARACTER STRENGTH DESCRIPTION	ABILITIES TO TEACH	OUTCOMES
NURTURING A CARING HEART		
1. Self-Confidence: Healthy identity, self-awareness, using personal strengths to build self-assuredness and find purpose and meaning.		
	Self-Awareness	Healthy Sense of Self
	Strength Awareness	Positive Self-Identity
	Finding Purpose	Service and Meaning
2. Empathy: Understanding & sharing another's feelings, relating, acting compassionately to nurture healthy relationships and encourage equity and social justice.		
	Emotion Literacy	Reading & Sharing Emotions
	Perspective Taking	Understanding Other Views
	Empathic Concern	Compassionate Action
DEVELOPING A STRONG MIND		
3. Self-Control: Managing stress and strong emotions, delaying gratification, and stretching focus to develop mental strength and improve mental health.		
	Attentive Focus	Delayed Gratification
	Self-Management	Coping & Regulation
	Healthy Decision-Making	Self-Discipline/ Mental Strength

CHARACTER STRENGTH DESCRIPTION	ABILITIES TO TEACH	OUTCOMES
DEVELOPING A STRONG MIND		
4. Integrity: Valuing and adhering to strong moral code and values, ethical thinking, practicing honesty to lead a good, moral life.		
	Moral Awareness	Valuing Virtue
	Moral Identity	Strong Moral Compass
	Ethical Thinking	Ethical Decision Making
5. Curiosity: Having an open-mindedness to new experiences and thinking, the willingness to try new ideas, take risks to learn, innovate and expand creative horizons.		
	Curious Mind-Set	Creativity
	Creative Problem-Solving	Generating Alternatives
	Divergent Thinking	Innovation
CULTIVATING A DETERMINED WILL		
6. Perseverance: Exhibiting fortitude, tenacity, and the resolve to endure, so as to bounce back from failure, increase resolve to endure and develop personal agency.		
	Growth Mind-Set	Determination and Drive
	Goal-Setting	Self-Mastery & Agency
	Learning from Failure	Self-Sufficiency
7. Optimism: Displaying positivity and gratitude, learning self-advocacy, keeping unrealistic pessimism in check to reduce despondency and encourage a hopeful outlook and believe that life has meaning.		
	Optimistic Thinking	Positive Attitude
	Assertive Communication	Self-Advocacy
	Hope	Hopeful Life Outlook

Acknowledgments

There's a wonderful Chinese proverb that says, "A child's life is like a piece of paper on which every person leaves a mark." I've been enormously blessed because I've had so many people leave significant marks on my life. And each has helped shape my writing and the scope of my work. I express my heartfelt thanks:

To the stellar publishing team at G. P. Putnam's Sons, thank you for the honor. Working with them is truly a privilege. Special thanks to Michelle Howry, my editor, for so many things. She is a wise, kind, wonderful woman, exemplary wordsmith, and an absolute joy to work with. I would never have written this book unless she was at the helm to guide me. Every edit was gold.

To Joëlle Delbourgo, my agent extraordinaire, who has always been my champion. Thank you for your steadfast belief in me as well as your patience, friendship, and wise advice.

To the hundreds of teachers, counselors, and parents who have attended my seminars throughout the years. I am grateful to each and every one of them for so honestly sharing their concerns and successes with me. This book would not have come to fruition without their practical wisdom on how best to teach children these strengths.

To the dozens of teachers, counselors, and administrators who allowed me the privilege of conducting research at their school sites to analyze the effectiveness of implementing these ideas with their students. And for setting up focus groups as well as sessions with individual teens to hear their voices on what it is like growing up in today's world. In particular I thank Barbie Monty, Ingrid Grenci, Jonathan Hiett, Mick Davis, Gilda Ross, Lauren Schrero Levy, Krista Diamond, Diana Cashion, Tacy L. Duncan, Byron Williams, Kim Yeyna, Derenda Schubert, Lisa Stevenson, Krista Promnitz, Michelle Carr, Susan Seltzer, General T.S. Jones, Nancy O'Connell, Jessica Tlumacki, Martha Mack, Kate Berg, Lisa Ockerman, Audrey Holsten, Matthew Liberatore, Catherine Wang, Greg Minter, Derenda Schubert, Sawsan Yaseen, Nadine Alaeddine Jurdi, Mahmoud Hashem, Rawan Khatib, Victoria Olivadoti, Lisa Steenson, and Alicia Boggio-Hair.

To the hundreds of children and teens I interviewed for this book, I thank each and every one of you for your honesty and willingness to share your valuable insights about growing up in today's uncertain world. You give me hope for our future.

To extraordinary friends who have been my personal cheering squad. My parenting writer group: Madeline Levine, Phyllis Fagell, Catherine Steiner-Adair, Katie Hurley, Jessica Lahey, Julie Lythcott-Haims, Christine Carter, Tina Payne-Bryson, Audrey Monke, Katherine Reynolds Lewis, Debbie Reber, Devorah Heitner and Ned Johnson. Fellow writer supporters: Ellen Galinsky, Lisa Damour, Amy Morin, Barbara Gruener, Trudy Ludwig, Marilyn Price-Mitchell, Kari Kampakis, Diana Graber, and Susan Newman. Special women allies: Alice Wilder, Jaynie Neveras, Laura Obermann, Charlene Moran, Rasha Attar, Yasmin Agha. And my male research "team" who emailed news about the kid scene: Bob Fey, Jim Dunn, and Steve Kanold. But most especially, my rock and entourage, Sue Scheff, who is always there, always positive, forever appreciated, and kept me going (#MBWY).

To the numerous people whose work has contributed enormously to my thinking about the development of thriving over the years. These include Bruce Perry, William Damon, Anne Colby, Thomas Lickona, Ann Masten, Richard Weissbourd, Loris Malaguzzi, Emmy Werner, Angela Duckworth, Carol Dweck, Deborah Leong, Tamar Chansky, Norman Garmezy, Michael Rutter, Samuel Oliner, Harold Stevenson, Martin Seligman, Jean Twenge, and Aaron Beck. Your collective work has been a godsend to children: I only hope I've done it justice.

And finally, to my family, who have left the largest and most enduring mark in my life: they are my "rock." To my husband and best friend, Craig, for his unending support, encouragement, and love through every phase of this book. To the joys of my life: my sons, Jason, Adam, and Zach, and daughter-in-law, Erin, for the constant love and fun they have brought to my life. And Charlie and Hazel, who light our hearts, give us hope, and make life pure joy.

Notes

INTRODUCTION

1. Jean Twenge, *iGen: Why Today's Super-Connected Kids Are Growing Up Less Rebellious, More Tolerant, Less Happy—and Completely Unprepared for Adulthood.* New York: Atria Books, 2017.

2. Stav Ziv, "After Rash of Teen Suicides in Palo Alto, the CDC Sends Team to Investigate," *Newsweek*, February 16, 2016, https://www.newsweek.com/after-rash-teen-suicides-palo-alto-cdc-sends-team-investigate-427383.

3. Melissa Healy, "Suicide Rates for U.S. Teens and Young Adults Are the Highest on Record," *Los Angeles Times*, June 18, 2019.

4. Rick Nauert, "Survey: 1 in 5 College Students Stressed, Considers Suicide," *PsychCentral*, https://psychcentral.com/news/2018/09/11/survey-1-in-5-college-students-stressed-considers-suicide/138516.html. Retrieved November 9, 2018.

5. Connie Matthiessen, "Why Are So Many College Students Returning Home?" Greatschools.org, March 21, 2017, https://www.greatschools.org/gk/articles/dropping-out-of-college-record-numbers/.

6. Terri Williams, "Freshmen Students Are the Most Likely to Drop Out of College," Good-Call, https://www.goodcall.com/news/why-freshman-are-the-most-likely-to-drop-out-of-college-01421/. Retrieved November 24, 2019.

7. Suniya S. Luthar, "The Culture of Affluence: Psychological Costs of Material Wealth," *Child Dev.* 74(6) (2003): 1581–1593.

8. Martin Evans, "Children of Rich Parents Suffering Increased Mental Health Problems," *Telegraph*, November 10, 2013, http://www.telegraph.co.uk/education/10439196/Children-of-rich-parents-suffering-increased-mental-health-problems.html.

9. Emmy Werner, "Resilience and Recovery: Findings from the Kauai Longitudinal Study," *Focal Point: Research, Policy and Practice in Children's Mental Health* Summer 2005, vol. 19, no. 1, pp. 11–14; Emmy E. Werner and Ruth S. Smith, *Vulnerable but Invincible: A Longitudinal Study of Resilient Children and Youth.* New York: McGraw Hill, 1982; Emily E. Werner and Ruth S. Smith, *Overcoming the Odds: High-Risk Children from Birth to Adulthood.* Ithaca, NY: Cornell University Press, 1992; Emily E. Werner and Ruth S. Smith, *Journeys from Childhood to Midlife: Risk, Resilience and Recovery.* Ithaca, NY: Cornell University Press, 2001.

10. E. James Anthony and Bertram J. Cohler, eds, *The Invulnerable Child.* New York: The Guilford Press, 1987; Howard S. Friedman and Leslie R. Martin, *The Longevity Project.* New

York: Plume, 2011; M. Rutter, B. Maughan, P. Mortimore, and J. Ouston, *Fifteen Thousand Hours: Secondary Schools and Their Effects on Children.* Cambridge, Mass.: Harvard University Press, 1979; Lois Murphy and A. Moriarty, *Vulnerability, Coping and Growth from Infancy to Adolescence.* New Haven: Yale University Press, 1976; N.S. Watt, E. J. Anthony, L. C. Wynne and J. E. Rolf, eds, *Children at Risk for Schizophrenia: A Longitudinal Perspective.* London and New York: Cambridge University Press, 1984.

11. Ann Masten, *Ordinary Magic: Resilience in Development.* New York: Guilford Press, 2014, pp. 3, 7, 22.

12. Norman Garmezy, "Stress-Resistant Children: The Search for Protective Factors." In J. E. Stevenson (ed.), *Recent Research in Developmental Psychopathology: Journal of Child Psychology and Psychiatry Book Supplement no. 4* (1985): 213–233.

13. Masten, *Ordinary Magic*, pp. 3, 22.

14. Emmy E. Warner, "Children of the Garden Island," *Scientific American* 260, no. 4 (April 1989): 106–11.

15. Paul Tough, *How Children Succeed: Grit, Curiosity and the Hidden Power of Character.* New York: Houghton Mifflin Harcourt, 2012, p. xv.

CHAPTER 1

1. L. Follari, *Foundations and Best Practices in Early Childhood Education, 3rd ed.* USA: Pearson, 2015, chapter 9.

2. Wolfgang Achtner, "Obituary: Loris Malaguzzi," *Independent,* April 1994, https://www .independent.co.uk/news/people/obituary-loris-malaguzzi-1367204.html.

3. "The Ten Best Schools in the World and What We Can Learn from Them," *Newsweek,* December 2, 1991, 50–59.

4. M.E.P. Seligman, "Positive Education and Classroom Interventions," *Oxford Review of Education* 35, no. 3 (2009): 293–311; A. Shoshani, S. Steinmetz, and Y. Kanat-Maymom, "Effects of the Maytiv Positive Psychology School Program on Early Adolescents' Well-Being, Engagement and Achievement," *Journal of School Psychology* 57 (2016): 73–92.

5. A. Shoshani and M. Slone, "The Resilience Function of Character Strengths in the Face of War and Protracted Conflict," *Frontiers in Psychology* 6 (2016): doi: 10.3389/fpsyg.2015/02006.

6. Tasha Eurich, "What Self-Awareness Really Is (and How to Cultivate It)," *Self-Awareness: HBR Emotional Intelligence Series.* Boston, MA: Harvard Business Review Press, 2019, pp. 11–35.

7. Paul J. Silvia and Maureen O'Brien, "Self-Awareness and Constructive Function: Revisiting 'the Human Dilemma,'" *Journal of Social and Clinical Psychology* 23, no. 4 (August 2004): 475–489.

8. D. Scott Ridley, Paul A. Schutz, Robert S. Glanz, and Claire E. Weinstein, "Self-Regulated Learning: The Interactive Influence of Metacognitive Awareness and Goal-Setting," *Journal of Experimental Education* 60, no. 4 (Summer 1992): 293–306; Clive Fletcher and Caroline Bailey, "Assessing Self-Awareness: Some Issues and Methods," *Journal of Managerial Psychology* 18, no. 5 (2003): 395–404; Anna Sutton, Helen M. Williams, and Christopher W. Allinson, "A Longitudinal, Mixed Method Evaluation of Self-Awareness Training in the Workplace," *European Journal of Training and Development* 39, no. 7 (2015): 610–627.

9. M.E.P. Seligman et al., "Positive Psychology Progress: Empirical Validation of Interventions," *American Psychologist* 60, no. 5 (2005): 401–421; F. Gander et al., "Strengths-Based

Positive Interventions: Further Evidence for Their Potential in Enhancing Well-Being and Alleviating Depression," *Journal of Happiness Studies* 14, no. 4 (2013): 1241–1259.

10. Martin Seligman, *Authentic Happiness*. New York: Free Press, 2004, p. xi.

11. Benamin Bloom, *Developing Talent in Young People*. New York: Ballantine Books, 1985.

12. Jean Twenge, *Generation Me*. New York: Free Press, 2006.

13. Roy Baumeister, "Rethinking Self-Esteem: Why Nonprofits Should Stop Pushing Self-Esteem and Start Endorsing Self-Control," *Stanford Social Innovation Review, Graduate School of Business*, Winter 2005.

14. M. A. Scheirer, and R. E. Kraut, "Increased Educational Achievement Via Self-Concept Change," *Review of Educational Research*, vol. 49, no. 1 (1979): 131–150.

15. G. Maruyama, R. A. Rubin, and G. G. Kingsbury, "Self-Esteem and Educational Achievement: Independent Constructs with a Common Cause?" *Journal of Personality and Social Psychology* 40 (1981): 962–975.

16. C. I. Diener and C. S. Dweck, "An Analysis of Learned Helplessness II: The Processing of Success," *Journal of Personality and Social Psychology* 39 (1980): 940–952.

17. "One in Four Children Worry About Their Appearance, Poll Shows," *Independent*, July 10, 2018, https://www.independent.co.uk/extras/lifestyle/children-body-image-mental-health -under-16-physical-appearance-sleep-a8439896.html.

18. Rachel Williams, "Researchers Track Lives of 19,000 British Children," *Guardian*, February 17, 2010, https://www.theguardian.com/society/2010/feb/17/researchers-track-19000 -british-children.

19. Beth Chee, "Today's Teens: More Materialistic, Less Willing to Work," *SDSC News Center*, May 1, 2013, https://newscenter.sdsu.edu/sdsu_newscenter/news_story.aspx?sid=74179.

20. Elizabeth Chang, *Washington Post*, January 9, 2011.

21. Paul Tullis, "Poor Little Tiger Cub," *Slate*, May 8, 2013, http://slate.com/human-interest/2013/ 05/tiger-mom-study-shows-the-parenting-method-doesn't-work.html .

22. L. Marshall, "Smart, Privileged, and At-Risk," *WebMD* 55, October 2017.

23. Suniya S. Luthar, Phillip J. Small, and Lucia Cecola, "Adolescents from Upper Middle-Class Communities: Substance Misuse and Addiction Across Early Adulthood," *Development and Psychopathology*, vol. 30, issue 1 (Feb 2018): 315–335, https://www.cambridge. org/core/journals/development-and-psychopathology/article/adolescents-from-upper -middle-class-communities-substance-misuse-and-addiction-across-early-adulthood/ FDB120DD01CC8CEE7A9FB3979306A57C.

24. W. R. Miller, J. C'de Baca, D. B. Matthews, and P. L. Wilbourne of the University of New Mexico, Personal Values Card Sort.

25. Personal Values Card Sort, M.E.P. Seligman, *Authentic Happiness*. C. Peterson, *A Primer in Positive Psychology*. New York: Oxford University Press, 2006.

26. Gallup and Tom Rath, *StrengthsFinder 2.0: Discover Your CliftonStrengths*. New York: Gallup Press, 2017.

27. Thomas Lickona, *Character Matters*. New York: Touchstone, February 2004.

28. Lea Waters, "How to Spot Your Child's Strengths (These 3 Indicators Can Help)," November 27, 2017, https://www.leawaters.com/blog/how-to-spot-your-childs-strengths-these-3 -indicators-can-help.

29. Christopher J. Bryan, Allison Master, and Gregory M. Walton, "'Helping,' Versus 'Being a Helper': Invoking the Self to Increase Helping in Young Children," *Child Development*, vol. 00, no. 0, pp. 1–7.

30. Mihaly Csikszentmihalyi, Kevin Rathunde, and Samuel Whalen, *Talented Teenagers: The Roots of Success & Failure.* New York: Cambridge University Press, 1993, p. 245.

31. Ibid., p. 16.

32. Gallup and Tom Rath: *StrengthsFinder 2.0: Discover Your CliftonStrengths.* New York: Gallup Press, 2017.

33. Aimee Picchi, "Young Adults Living With Their Parents Hits a 75-Year High," *CBS News,* December 21, 2016, https://www.cbsnews.com/news/percentage-of-young-americans-living-with-their-parents-is-40-percent-a-75-year-high/.

34. Jean Twenge, Associated Press. "The Mental Health Crisis Among America's Youth Is Real—and Staggering," *WTOP (Washington's Top News),* March 14, 2019, https://wtop.com/national/2019/03/the-mental-health-crisis-among-americas-youth-is-real-and-staggering/.

35. Clare Ansberry, "Why Teens Need a Sense of Purpose," *Wall Street Journal,* February 10, 2018, https://www.wsj.com/articles/why-teens-need-a-sense-of-purpose-1518264001.

36. Terry Lobdell, "Driven to Succeed: How We're Depriving Teens of a Sense of Purpose," *Palo Alto Weekly,* November 18, 2011, https://ed.stanford.edu/news/driven-succeed-how-were-depriving-teens-sense-purpose .

37. Mihaly Csikszentmihalyi, *Flow: The Psychology of Optimal Experience.* New York: Harper-Perennial, 1990.

38. Susan Cain quote cited by Phyllis Fagell, "7 Strategies to Help Prepare Your Child for the Rapidly Changing Work World," in "On Parenting," *Washington Post,* May 22, 2018.

39. Paul Wiseman, "Teens Don't Work Like They Used To," *TimesUnion,* June 23, 2017, https://www.timesunion.com/business/article/Teens-don-t-work-like-they-used-to-11243834.php.

40. Jim Abbott with Tim Brown, *Imperfect: An Improbable Life.* New York: Ballantine, 2012, p. 22.

41. *Ibid.,* p. 271.

42. Ibid., p. 225.

43. *Ibid.,* p. 29.

44. Victor and Mildred Goertzel, *Cradles of Eminence: Childhoods of More than 700 Famous Men and Women,* 2nd Edition. Tucson, AZ, Gifted Psychology Press, 2004.

45. J. Gregory Hixon and William B. Swann Jr., "When Does Introspection Bear Fruit? Self-Reflection, Self-Insight, and Interpersonal Choices," *Journal of Personality and Social Psychology* 64, no. 1 (January 1993): 3–43 as cited by Tasha Eurich in "What Self-Awareness Really Is (and How to Cultivate It), in *Self-Awareness.* Boston, MA: Harvard Business Review Press, 2019, pp. 29–30.

46. Emmy E. Werner and Ruth S. Smith, *Vulnerable, but Invincible: A Longitudinal Study of Resilient Children and Youth.* New York: McGraw Hill, 1982.

CHAPTER 2

1. Jamil Zaki, *The War for Kindness: Building Empathy in a Fractured World.* New York: Crown, 2019, pp. 178–182.

2. J. Block-Lerner, C. Adair, J. C. Plumb, D. L. Rhatigan, and S. M. Orsillo, "The Case for Mindfulness-Based Approaches in the Cultivation of Empathy: Does Nonjudgmental, Present-Moment Awareness Increase Capacity for Perspective-Taking and Empathic Concern?" *Journal of Marital and Family Therapy* 33, no. 4 (October 2007): 501–16; Myriam Mon-

grain, Jacqueline M. Chin, and Leah B. Shapira, "Practicing Compassion Increases Happiness and Self-Esteem," *Journal of Happiness Studies* 12, no. 6 (December 2011): 963–81.

3. Mary Gordon, "Roots of Empathy Program," *Journal of Happiness Studies* 12, no. 6 (December 2011): 963–81.

4. Gordon Allport, *The Nature of Prejudice* (New York: Perseus Books, 1979), p. 434; Andrew R. Todd, Galen V. Bodenhausen, Jennifer A. Richeson, and Adam D. Galinsky, "Perspective Taking Combats Automatic Expressions of Racial Bias," *Journal of Personality and Social Psychology* 100, no. 6 (June 2011): 1027–42; Samuel P. Oliner and Pearl M. Oliner, *The Altruistic Personality: Rescuers of Jews in Nazi Europe*. New York: Touchstone, 1992; Eva Fogelman, *Conscience and Courage: Rescuers of Jews During the Holocaust*. New York: Random House, 2011.

5. PRWeb.com Newswire, "New Research from Momentous Institute Shows Empathy Predicts Academic Performance," *Digital Journal*, October 13, 2014, http://www.digitaljournal.com/pr/2252070; Saga Briggs, "How Empathy Affects Learning, and How to Cultivate It in Your Students," *informED*, November 1, 2014, http://www.opencolleges.edu.au/informed/features/empathy-and-learning/, accessed Nov. 23, 2014.

6. Daniel Goleman, "What Makes a Leader?" *Harvard Business Review OnPoint*, Summer 2014, pp. 24–33.

7. Kathy A. Stephen and Amy Baernstein, "Educating for Empathy," *Journal of General Internal Medicine* 21, no. 5 (May 2006): 524–30.

8. Sara Konrath, Edward H. O'Brien, and Courtney Hsing, "Changes in Dispositional Empathy in American College Students Over Time: A Meta-Analysis," *Personality and Social Psychology Review, Inc* 15, 2 (2011): 180–98.

9. J. M. Twenge and W.K. Campbell, *The Narcissism Epidemic: Living in the Age of Entitlement*. New York: Free Press, 2009.

10. Kevin Eagan et al., *The American Freshman: National Norms Fall 2015*, Cooperative Institutional Research Program at the Higher Education Research Institute at UCLA, 2015, https://www.heri.ucla.edu/monographs/TheAmericanFreshman2015-Expanded.pdf .

11. *2018: CIGNA U.S. Loneliness Index: Survey of 20,000 Americans Examining Behaviors Driving Loneliness in the United States*, https://www.multivu.com/players/English/8294451-cigna-us-loneliness-survey/docs/IndexReport_1524069371598-173525450.pdf.

12. V. Warrier, R., Toro, B. Chakrabarti et al., "Genome-Wide Analyses of Self-Reported Empathy: Correlations with Autism, Schizophrenia, and Anorexia Nervosa.," *Transl Psychiatry* 8, 35 (2018), https://doi.org/10.1038/s41398-017-0082-6.

13. Brigit Katz, "If You're Empathetic, It Might Be Genetic," *Smithsonian Magazine*, March 13, 2018, https://www.smithsonianmag.com/smart-news/if-youre-empathetic-it-might-be-genetic-180968466/.

14. Sara Konrath, "Age and Gender Differences in Dispositional Empathy," *Psychology Today*, June 30, 2013, https://www.psychologytoday.com/us/blog/the-empathy-gap/201306/age-and-gender-differences-in-dispositional-empathy.

15. Jamil Zaki, "Empathy: A Motivated Account," *Psychological Bulletin* 140, no. 6 (2014): 1608–47.

16. Alfie Kohn, *The Brighter Side of Human Nature*, p. 94.

17. Alfie Kohn, "It's Hard to Get Left Out of a Pair," *Psychology Today*, October 1987, pp. 53–57.

18. Victoria Rideout and Michael B. Robb, Ph.D., Common Sense, "Social Media, Social Life: Teens Reveal Their Experiences, 2018," Commonsense.org survey of 1,141 teens ages 13 to

17, Common Sense Media, September 10, 2018, https://www.commonsensemedia.org/about-us/news/press-releases/common-sense-research-reveals-everything-you-need-to-know-about-teens.

19. Ibid.

20. Jean M. Twenge, "Put That Phone Away—Now" *The View, TIME,* August 1, 2019, pp. 19–20.

21. "Controversy of the Week" *The Weeks,* August 9, 2019, p. 6.

22. Research led by Sara H. Konrath of University of Michigan at Ann Arbor involved seventy-two studies of college students collected over the past thirty years and was published online in *Personality and Social Psychology Review.* "Empathy: College Students Don't Have as Much as They Used To, Study Finds," *ScienceDaily,* May 29, 2010.

23. Eddie Brummelman, Sander Thomaes, Stefanie A. Nelemans, Bram Orobio de Castro, Geertjan Overbeek, Brad J. Bushman, "Origins of Narcissism in Children," *Proceedings of the National Academy of Sciences,* 2015, 201420870 DOI: 10.1073/pnas.1420870112.

24. R. Weissbourd and S. Jones, "The Children We Mean to Raise: The Real Messages Adults Are Sending About Values," Making Caring Commons: The President and Fellows of Harvard College, 2014.

25. John Gottman, *Raising an Emotionally Intelligent Child.* New York: Simon & Schuster, August 1998.

26. J. M. Twenge, T. E. Joiner, M. L. Rogers, "Increases in Depressive Symptoms, Suicide-Related Outcomes, and Suicide Rates Among U.S. Adolescents After 2010 and Links to Increased New Media Screen Time," *Clinical Psychological Science,* vol. 6, issue 1, January 1, 2018, pp. 3–17, https://doi.org/10.1177/2167702617723376.

27. Michael Robb, "Tweens, Teens, and Phones: What Our 2019 Research Reveals," Common Sense Media, October 29, 2019, https://www.commonsensemedia.org/research/the-common-sense-census-media-use-by-tweens-and-teens-2019.

28. Thirty-five percent of 1,000 teens in a 2005 national survey gave poor grades for listening, cited in E. Portillo, "Teens Give Adults Low Grades on Ruling World," *Desert Sun,* June 18, 2005, p. A17.

29. F. J. Bernieri, "Interpersonal Sensitivity in Teaching Interactions," *Personality and Social Psychology Bulletin 17* (1991): 98–103; H. Gehlbach, "Social Perspective Taking: A Facilitating Aptitude for Conflict Resolution, Historical Empathy, and Social Studies Achievement," *Theory and Research in Social Education 32* (2004b): 39–55.

30. Inductive reasoning produces children who are better adjusted, based on research by Nancy Eisenberg, Richard Fabes, and Martin Hoffman, cited by Dacher Keltner (ed.), "The Compassionate Instinct," in *The Compassionate Instinct* by Dacher Keltner, Jason Marsh, and Jeremy Adam Smith, New York: W.W. Norton & Co., 2010, pp. 13–14.

31. Virginia Slaughter, Kana Imuta, Candida C. Peterson, and Julie D. Henry, "Meta-Analysis of Theory of Mind and Peer Popularity in the Preschool and Early School Years," *Child Development 86,* no. 4 (April 2015): 1159–74.

32. L. L. Verhofstadt, A. Buysse, W. Ickes, M. Davis, I. Devoldre, "Support Provision in Marriage: The Role of Emotional Similarity and Empathic Accuracy," *Emotion 8* (2008): 792–802.

33. P. L. Jackson, E. Brunet, A. N. Meltzoff, And J. Decety, "Empathy Examined Through the Neural Mechanism Involved in Imagining How I Feel Versus How You Would Feel Pain: An Event-Related fMRI Study," *Neuropsychologia 44,* pp. 752–761.

34. M. A. Barnett, L. M. King, and J.A. Howard, "Inducing Affect About Self or Other: Effects on Generosity in Children," *Developmental Psychology 15,* no. 2 (1979): 164–67; D. Ander-

man, S. S. Brehm, and L. B. Katz, "Empathic Observation of an Innocent Victim: The Just World Revisited," *Journal of Personality and Social Psychology* 29, no. 3 (1974): 342–47.

35. Julia Krevans and John C. Gibbs, "Parents' Use of Inductive Discipline: Relations to Children's Empathy and Prosocial Behavior," *Child Development 67* (1996): 3263–3277.

36. Norma Deitch Feshbach, "Empathy, Empathy Training and the Regulation of Aggression in Elementary School Children." In *Aggression in Children and Youth—1984*, edited by R. M. Kaplan, Vladimir J. Konecni, and Raymond W. Novaco, pp. 192–208; Norma Deitch Feshbach, "Empathy Training: A Field Study in Affective Education." In *Aggression and Behavior Change: Biological and Social Processes,* edited by Seymour Feshbach and Adam Fraczek. New York: Praeger, 1979; Norma Deitch Feshbach, "Learning to Care: A Positive Approach to Child Training and Discipline," *Journal of Clinical Child Psychology* 12 (1983): 266–71.

37. Research project on gratitude and thanksgiving required several hundred people in three different groups to keep daily diaries. The first group kept a diary of daily events; the second their unpleasant experiences; the third a daily list of things for which they were grateful. R. A. Emmons and M. E. McCullough, "Counting Blessings Versus Burdens: Experimental Studies of Gratitude and Subjective Well-Being in Daily Life," *Journal of Personality and Social Psychology* 84, pp. 377–389.

38. Research on benefits of gratitude described by Rick Hanson, *Resilient: How to Grow an Unshakable Core of Calm, Strength and Happiness.* New York: Harmony Books, 2018, p. 96.

39. Grace Hauck, "Gratitude Is Good for Heart Health," *USA Today,* November 29, 2019.

40. S. Konrath, E. O'Brien and C. Hsing, "Changes in Dispositional Empathy in American College Students over Time: A Meta-Analysis," *Personality and Social Psychology Review* 15 (2) (2011): 180–198.

41. Jonathan D. Haidt, "Wired to Be Inspired." In *The Compassionate Instinct,* edited by Dacher Keltner, Jason Marsh, and Jeremy Adam Smith, 86–93. New York: W.W. Norton & Company, 2010.

42. Damon E. Jones, Mark Greenberg, Max Crowley, "Early Social-Emotional Functioning and Public Health: The Relationship Between Kindergarten Social Competence and Future Wellness," *American Journal of Public Health* (2015), e1 DOI: 10.2105/AJPH.2015.302630.

43. Ervin Staub, *The Psychology of Good and Evil: Why Children, Adults and Groups Help and Harm Others.* Cambridge, England: Cambridge University Press, 2003.

44. Emily E. Werner and Ruth S. Smith, *Journeys from Childhood to Midlife: Risk, Resilience, and Recovery.* New York: Cornell University Press, 2001.

45. Elizabeth Smart with Chris Stewart, *My Story.* New York: Griffin, 2014.

46. Ibid., Elizabeth Smart, p. 61

47. Bruce D. Perry and Maia Szalavitz, *The Boy Who Was Raised as a Dog.* New York: Basic Books, 2017, p. 261.

48. Ibid., Elizabeth Smart, p. 281.

49. "Josh-Opening Doors and Hearts," WestJet Above and Beyond Stories, Dec. 22, 2014, https://www.youtube.com/watch?v=PIHtuKc3Gjg.

50. Leigh Weingus, "How Opening Doors Changed This Teen's Life," *The Huffington Post,* Jan. 22, 2015. http://www.huffingtonpost.com/2015/01/22/opening-doors-teen-bullying_n_6526220.html.

50. David Comer Kidd And Emanuele Castano, "Reading Literary Fiction Improves Theory of Mind," *Science,* October 2013.

51. Raymond A. Mar et al., "Exposure to Media and Theory-of-Mind Development in Preschoolers," *Cognitive Development* (2009), doi: 10.1016/j.cogdev.2009.11.002.

52. Katrina Schumann, Jamil Zaki, and Carol S. Dweck, "Addressing the Empathy Deficit: Beliefs About the Malleability of Empathy Predict Effortful Responses When Empathy Is Challenging," *Journal of Personality and Social Psychology* 107, no. 3 (2014): 475–93.

53. Ezra Stotland, "Exploratory Investigations of Empathy," in *Advances in Experimental Social Psychology*, vol. 4, edited by Leonard Berkowitz, 271–313. New York: Academic Press, 1969.

54. Amit Kumar and Nicholas Epley, "Undervaluing Gratitude: Expressers Misunderstand the Consequences of Showing Appreciation," *Psychological Science* (2018): 1–13, doi: 10.1177/0956797618772506.

55. Jamil Zaki, *The War for Kindness: Building Empathy in a Fractured World*. New York: Crown, 2019, p. 6.

56. Derrick Bryson Taylor and Neil Vigdor, "School Violence: Footage Shows Coach Disarming Student," *New York Times*, October 20, 2019.

CHAPTER 3

1. Adele Diamond and Kathleen Lee, "Interventions Show to Aid Executive Function Development in Children 4–12 Years Old," *Science* 333 (6045) (August 19, 2011): 959–964, doi: 10.1126/science.1204529.

2. Alissa J. Mrazek et al., "Expanding Minds: Growth Mindsets of Self-Regulation and the Influences on Effort and Perseverance," *Journal of Experimental Social Psychology*, vol.79 (November 2018): 164–180, https://www.cmhp.ucsb.edu/sites/default/files/2018-12/Mrazek%20et%20al.%20%282018%29%20Expanding%20Minds.pdf.

3. Jonah Lehrer, "Don't! The Secret of Self-Control," *New Yorker*, May 18, 2009.

4. Angela L. Duckworth and Martin E. P. Seligman, "Self-Discipline Outdoes IQ in Predicting Academic Performance of Adolescents," *Psychol Sci.* 16 (12) (December 2005): 939–44.

5. Terrie E. Moffitt et al., "A Gradient of Childhood Self-Control Predicts Health, Wealth, And Public Safety," *Proceedings of the National Academy of* Sciences 108 (7) (February 2011): 2693–2698, DOI:10.1073/pnas.1010076108.

6. Terrie E. Moffitt et al., "A Gradient of Childhood Self-Control Predicts Health, Wealth and Public Safety," Proceedings of the National Academy of Sciences USA, vol. 108 (2011): 2693–2698.

7. M. M. Martel et al., "Childhood and Adolescent Resiliency, Regulation, And Executive Functioning in Relation To Adolescent Problems and Competence In A High-Risk Sample," *Dev Psychopathol.* 19(2) (2007): 541–63; N. Eisenberg, T. L. Spinrad, and N.D. Eggum, "Emotion-Related Self-Regulation and Its Relation To Children's Maladjustment," *Annu Rev Clin Psychol.* 27 (6) (2010):495–525.

8. Kathleen Ries Merikangas et al., "Lifetime Prevalence of Mental Disorders in U.S. Adolescents: Results from the National Comorbidity Survey Replication-Adolescent Supplement (NCS-A)," *Journal of the American Academy of Child & Adolescent Psychiatriy*, vol. 49, issue 10, October 2010, pp. 980–989, http://doi.org/10/1016/j.jaac.2010.05.017.

9. American Psychological Association, "Stress in America: Generation Z," Stress in America Survey, October 2018.

10. Jean Twenge et. al., "Age, Period and Cohort Trends in Mood Disorder Indicators and

Suicide-Related Outcomes in a Nationally Representative Dataset, 2006–2017," *Journal of Abnormal Psychology* 128, no. 3 (April 2019): 185–199, doi: 10.1037/abn0000410. Epub 2019 Mar 14.

11. Jonah Lehrer, "Don't!" The Secret of Self-Control," *New Yorker,* May 18, 2009 (Walter Mischel study).

12. Will Knight, "'Info-Mania' Dents IQ More Than Marijuana," *NewScientist,* April 22, 2005, https://www.newscientist.com/article/dn7298-info-mania-dents-iq-more-than-marijuana/.

13. Adam Gorlick, "Media Multitaskers Pay Mental Price, Stanford Study Shows," *Stanford News,* August 24, 2009, https://news.stanford.edu/2009/08/24/multitask-research-study-082409/.

14. Sofie Bates, "A Decade of Data Reveals That Heavy Multitaskers Have Reduced Memory, Stanford Psychologist Says," *Stanford News,* October 25, 2018, https://news.stanford.edu/2018/10/25/decade-data-reveals-heavy-multitaskers-reduced-memory-psychologist-says/.

15. Common Sense Media, "New Report Finds Teens Feel Addicted to Their Phones, Causing Tension at Home," May 3, 2016. Based on survey of 1,240 parents and kids from the same households (620 parents, 620 kids), https://www.commonsensemedia.org/about-us/news/press-releases/new-report-finds-teens-feel-addicted-to-their-phones-causing-tension-at.

16. Tim Elmore, "I'd Rather Lose My Ford or My Finger Than My Phone," *HuffPost,* May 4, 2014, https://www.huffpost.com/entry/id-rather-lose-my-ford-or-my-finger-than-my-phone_b_4896134?ec_carp=5438723550604748745.

17. Andrew Przybylski & Netta Weinstein, "Can You Connect with Me Now? How The Presence of Mobile Communication Technology Influences Face-To-Face Conversation Quality," *Journal of Social and Personal Relationships 30,* no. 3 (2012): 237–246.

18. *All Things Considered: 'The Shallows': This is Your Brain Online,* NPR, June 2, 2010, research from Nicholas Carr, author of *The Shallows.*

19. Pamela Paul, "Tutors for Toddlers," *TIME,* November 21, 2007, http://content.time.com/time/magazine/article/0,9171,1686826,00.html.

20. Peter Adamson, UNICEF Office of Research, "Child Well-Being in Rich Countries: A Comparative Overview," Innocenti Report Card 11, https://www.unicef-irc.org/publications/pdf/rc11_eng.pdf.

21. Thomas S. Dee and Hans Henrik Sievertsen, "The Gift of Time? School Starting Age and Mental Health," NBER Working Paper No. 21610, October 2015, JEL No. I1, I1, https://cepa.stanford.edu/sites/default/files/WP15-08.pdf.

22. Timothy J. Layton, "Attention-Deficit Hyperactivity Disorder and Month of School Enrollment," *New England Journal of Medicine* (2018) 2122–2130. DOI: 10.1056/NEJMoa1806828.

23. May Wong, "Study Finds Improved Self-Regulation in Kindergarteners Who Wait a Year to Enroll," Stanford Graduate School of Education, October 7, 2015, https://ed.stanford.edu/news/stanford-gse-research-finds-strong-evidence-mental-health-benefits-delaying-kindergarten.

24. Erika Christakis, "The New Preschool Is Crushing Kids," *Atlantic,* January/February 2016, https://www.theatlantic.com/magazine/archive/2016/01/the-new-preschool-is-crushing-kids/419139/.

25. William Doyle, "This is Why Finland Has the Best Schools," *Sydney Morning Herald,* March 26, 2016, https://www.smh.com.au/national/this-is-why-finland-has-the-best-schools-20160325-gnqv9l.html.

26. Olivia Goldhill, "Homework Around the World: How Much Is Too Much?" *Telegraph*, March 25, 2019, https://www.telegraph.co.uk/education/educationnews/11453912/Homework -around-the-world-how-much-is-too-much.html.

27. Elsie M. Taveras et al., "Prospective Study of Insufficient Sleep and Neurobehavioral Functioning Among School-Age Children," *Academic Pediatrics*, vol. 17, issue 6, pp. 625–632.

28. June J. Pilcher, Drew M. Morris, Janet Donnelly, and Hayley B. Feigl, "Interactions Between Sleep Habits and Self-Control," *Frontiers in Human Neuroscience* 11 (May 2015), https://doi.org/10.3389/fnhum.2015.00284.

29. Cari Gillen-O'Neel, Virginia W. Huynh, and Andrew J. Fuligni, "To Study or to Sleep? The Academic Costs of Extra Studying at the Expense of Sleep," *Child Development*, August 2012.

30. Michal Kahn, Shimrit Fridenson, Reut Lerer, Yair Bar-Haim, Avi Sadeh, "Effects of One Night of Induced Night-Wakings Versus Sleep Restriction On Sustained Attention and Mood: A Pilot Study," *Sleep Medicine* 15 (7) (2014): 825, DOI: 10.1016/j.sleep.2014.03.016.

31. Boston College: TIMSS & PRLS International Study Center "TIMSS 2011" *International Association for the Evaluation of Educational Achievement*, 2013.

32. Ruthann Richter, "Among Teens, Sleep Derivation an Epidemic," *Stanford Medicine*, October 8, 2015, https://med.stanford.edu/news/all-news/2015/10/among-teens-sleep-deprivation -an-epidemic.html.

33. Anne G. Wheaton, Sherry Everett Jones, Andina C. Cooper and Janet B. Croft, "Short Sleep Duration Among Middle School and High School Students-United States, 2015, Centers for Disease Control and Prevention, January 26, 2018/67 (3); 85-90, https://www.cdc.gov/ mmwr/volumes/67/wr/mm6703a1.htm?s_cid=mm6703a1_w.

34. Rhonda Clements, "An Investigation of the Status of Outdoor Play," *Contemporary Issues in Early Childhood* 5 (2004): 68–80.

35. Daniel Goleman, *Focus: The Hidden Driver of Excellence*. New York: HarperCollins, 2013, pp. 2–3.

36. Phone interview with Katherine Reynolds Lewis on August 7, 2019.

37. C. E. Kerr, "Effects of Mindfulness Meditation Training on Anticipatory Alpha Modulation in Primary Somatosensory Cortex," *Brain Research Bulletin* 85, nos. 3–4 (May 2011): 96–103.

38. A. Moore, T. Gruber, J. Derose, and P. Malinowki, "Regular, Brief Mindfulness Meditation Practice Improves Electrophysiological Markers of Attention Control," *Frontiers of Human Neuroscience* 6 (February 10, 2012): 18, DOI:10.3389/fnhum.2012.00018.

39. F. Zeidan, S. K. Johnson, B. J. Diamond, Z. David, and P. Gollkasian, "Mindfulness Meditation Improves Cognitive: Evidence of Brief Mental Training," *Consciousness and Cognition* 19, no. 2 (June 2010): 597–605.

40. Kimberly A. Schonert-Reichl et al., "Enhancing Cognitive and Social-Emotional Development Through a Simple-to-Administer Mindfulness-Based School Program for Elementary School Children: A Randomized Controlled Trial," *Developmental Psychology 51 (1)* (2015): 52, DOI: 10.1037/a0038454.

41. Walter Mischel, *The Marshmallow Test: Understanding Self-Control and How to Master It*. New York: Bantam Press, 2014.

42. Juliana Menasce Horowitz and Nikki Graf, "Most U.S. Teens See Anxiety and Depression as a Major Problem Among Their Peers," Pew Research Center, February 20, 2019.

43. Alan N. Simmons et al., "Altered Insula Activation in Anticipation Of Changing Emo-

tional States: Neural Mechanisms Underlying Cognitive Flexibility In Special Operations Forces Personnel," *Neuroreport 23* (4) (March 7, 2012): 234–9, DOI: 10.1097/WNR.0b013e3283503275.

44. "Boomerang Generation, Returning to the Nest," Ameritrade, May 2019, https://s2.q4cdn.com/437609071/files/doc_news/research/2019/Boomerang-Generation-Returning-to-the-Nest.pdf. Survey by The Harris Poll on behalf of TD Ameritrade from February 28 to March 14, 2019, among 3,054 U.S. adults and teens ages 15 and older.

45. Jean M. Twenge, *iGen: Why Today's Super-Connected Kids Are Growing Up Less Rebellious, More Tolerant, Less Happy—and Completely Unprepared for Adulthood.* New York: Atria Books, 2017, pp. 45–46.

46. M. Schulman and E. Mekler, *Bringing Up a Moral Child.* Reading, MA: Addison-Wesley, 1985, p. 20; "STAR" (Stop, Think, Act Right) developed by Michele Borba, *Building Moral Intelligence.* San Francisco: Jossey-Bass, 2004.

47. Phelps, *No Limits,* p. 133.

48. Ibid., p. 20.

49. Ibid., pp. 146–147.

50. Ibid., p. 135.

51. Margaret Loftus, "How a Gap Year Can Make Students Successful," *US News& World Report,* September 23, 2014, https://www.usnews.com/education/best-colleges/articles/2014/09/23/how-a-gap-year-can-make-students-successful.

52. Kirsten Weir, "The Power of Self-Control," *American Psychological Association, vol. 43, no. 1* (January 2012), https://www.apa.org/monitor/2012/01/self-control

CHAPTER 4

1. Description of the history day project from Jack Mayer, *Life in a Jar: The Irena Sendler Project.* Middlebury, Vermont: Long Trail Press, 2011, pp. 6–7, and personal interview with Megan Stewart Felt in Flint, Michigan.

2. Ibid, p. 6-7.

3. Ibid, p. 336.

4. Ibid, p. 350.

5. Ibid, p. 259.

6. Descriptions of how Irena Sendler parented from Tilar J. Mazzeo, *Irena's Children: The Extraordinary Story of the Woman Who Saved 2,500 Children from the Warsaw Ghetto.* New York: Gallery Books, 2016.

7. Thomas Lickona, *How to Raise Kind Kids: And Get Respect, Gratitude and a Happier Family in the Bargain.* New York, Penguin Books, p. 69.

8. Josephson Institute Center for Youth Ethics, "2012 Report Card on the Ethics of American Youth," Los Angeles, CA: Character Counts, 2012.

9. Rich Jarc, "The Ethics of American Youth: 2010," February 10, 2011; Josephson Institute Center for Youth Ethics, April 26, 2011, http://charactercounts.org/programs/reportcard/2010/installment02_report-card_honesty-integrity.html.

10. "Are today's kids more self-centered than those of past generations?" *MSNBC-Health 26* April 26, 2011, http://health.newsvine.com/_news/2009/05/05/2779662-are-todays-kids-more-self-centered-than-those-of-past-generations.

11. Justin Patchin, "School Bullying Rates Increased by 35% from 2016 to 2019"; Cyberbullying

Research Center, May 29, 2019, https://cyberbullying.org/school-bullying-rates-increase -by-35-from-2016-to-2019.

12. Josephson Institute Center for Youth Ethics: "2012 Report Card on the Ethics of American Youth," Los Angeles, CA: Character Counts, 2012.

13. "Post-Election Survey of Youth," Human Rights Campaign, Washington, D.C., 2017, www .hrc.org., https://assets2.hrc.org/files/assets/resources/HRC_PostElectionSurveyofYouth.pdf

14. "American Teens Lie, Steal, Cheat at 'Alarming' Rates: Study," Breitbart, December 1, 2010 and April 26, 2011, http://www.breitbart.com/article.php?id=081201214432.rjut4n2u

15. Justin McCarthy, "About Half of Americans Say U.S. Moral Values Are 'Poor,'" *Gallup News,* June 1, 2018, https://news.gallup.com/poll/235211/half-americans-say-moral-values -poor.aspx.

16. Julie Bosman, Serge F. Kovaleski, and Jose A. Del Real, "A College Scam Built With Swagger, and Secrets," *New York Times,* March 18, 2019.

17. Jen Doll, "The Moral Decline in the Words We Use," *Atlantic,* August 24. 2012, https:// www.theatlantic.com/entertainment/archive/2012/08/moral-decline-words-we-use/ 324319/; Pelin Kesebir and Selin Kesebir, "The Cultural Salience of Moral Character and Virtue Declined in Twentieth Century America," *Journal of Positive Psychology* (2012), https://ssrn.com/abstract=2120724.

18. David Brooks, *The Road to Character.* New York: Random House, 2016, p. 233.

19. William Damon, "The Moral Development of Children," *Scientific American,* August 1999.

20. Christian Smith, Kari Christoffersen, Hilary Davison and Patricia Snell Herzog, *Lost in Transition: The Dark Side of Emerging Adulthood.* New York: Oxford University Press, 2011.

21. Maurice J. Elias, "Helping Your Students Identify Their Values," *Edutopia,* July 3, 2017, https://www.edutopia.org/blog/helping-your-students-identify-their-values-maurice -elias.

22. Malala Yousafzai, *I Am Malala: How One Girl Stood Up for Education and Changed the World.* New York: Little, Brown and Company, 2010, p. 210.

23. S. P. Oliner and P. M. Oliner, *The Altruistic Personality: Rescuers of Jews in Nazi Europe.* New York: Free Press, 1988, pp. 164–68.

24. Malala Yousafzai with Christina Lamb, *I Am Malala: The Girl Who Stood Up for Education and Was Shot by the Taliban.* New York: Back Bay Books, 2015, p. 7.

25. Transcript of Margaret Warner's Interview of Malala Yousafzai, "Malala Says Assassination Threats Can't Weaken Her Cause," PBS, October 11, 2013, https://www.pbs.org/news hour/education/malala-says-assassination-threats-cant-weaken-her-cause.

26. Hailey Reissman, "Why Is My Daughter Strong? I Didn't Clip Her Wings: Ziauddin Yousafzai at TED2014, *TEDBlog,* March 17, 2014, https://blog.ted.com/why-is-my-daughter -strong-because-i-didnt-clip-her-wings-ziauddin-yousafzai-at-ted2014/.

27. Alamo Heights ISD "Cambridge Rocks Kindness" personal visit to the school and discussion with Diana Cashion, Cambridge Elementary counselor.

28. "Teenagers Most Influenced by Celebrities," *Telegraph,* August 12, 2019, https://www.tele-graph.co.uk/news/uknews/6012322/Teenagers-most-influenced-by-celebrities.html.

29. Linda Lyons, "No Heroes in the Beltway," *Gallup News,* July 30, 2002, https://news.gallup. com/poll/6487/heroes-beltway.aspx.

30. Donald McCabe and Linda Klebe Trevino, "Honesty and Honor Codes," *Academic* 88, no. 1 (January/February 2002): 37; Donald McCabe, "Toward a Culture of Academic Integ-

rity," *Chronicle of Higher Education* 15 (October 1999): B7; Linda Klebe Trevino and Donald McCabe, "Academic Integrity in Honor Code and Non-Honor Code Environments," *Journal of Higher Education* 70 (1999): 211–35.

31. Alexander W. Astin, Lori J. Vogelgesang, Elaine K. Ikeda, Jennifer A. Yess, "How Service Learning Affects Students," Higher Education, Paper 144 (2000), http://digitalcommons. unomaha.edu/slcehighered/144.

32. Anne Colby and William Damon, *Some Do Care: Contemporary Lives of Moral Commitment.* New York: Free Press, 1992.

33. Account of the massacre and Thompson's actions: P. Block, "The Choices Made: Lessons from My Lai on Drawing the Line," *Seattle Times,* March 20, 2002, http://seattletimes .nwsource.com/pacificnw/2002/0310/cover.html.

34. H. Thompson, Jr.: "Moral Courage in Combat: The My Lai Story," a lecture by Hugh Thompson, Jr. at the U.S. Naval Academy, Center for the Study of Professional Military Ethics, Annapolis, MD, 2003; Trent Angers, *The Forgotten Hero of My Lai: The Hugh Thompson Story.* Lafayette, LA: Acadian House Publishing, 1999.

CHAPTER 5

1. "'Youngest Inventor' Patents Broom," *BBC News,* April 16, 2008, http://news.bbc.co.uk/2/ hi/uk_news/7350341.stm.

2. "Alissa Chavez's Hot Seat Alarm Aims to Prevent Child Hot Car Deaths," *CBC News,* July 29, 2014, https://www.cbc.ca/news/technology/alissa-chavez-s-hot-seat-alarm-aims -to-prevent-child-hot-car-deaths-1.2721351.

3. Shay Maunz, "Inventing the Future," *TIME,* February 3, 2020, p. 49.

4. Frank Moss, *The Sorcerers and their Apprentices.* New York: Crown Business, 2011.

5. Mihaly Csikszentmihalyi, "The Secret to Happiness," *TED2004,* https://www.ted.com/ talks/mihaly_csikszentmihalyi_on_flow; M. Csikszentmihalyi, *Flow: The Psychology of Optimal Experience.* New York: HarperCollins, 2009.

6. IU New Room, Indiana University, "Latest HSSSE Results Show Familiar Theme: Bored, Disconnected Students Want More from Schools," June 8, 2010, http://newsinfo.iu.edu/ news-archive/14593.html; Research by Ethan Yazzie-Mintz, "Charting the Path from Engagement to Achievement: A Report on the 2009 High School Survey of Student Engagement."

7. David Shernoff, Mihaly Csikszentmihalyi, Barbara Schneider, and Elisa Shernoff, "Student Engagement in High School Classrooms from the Perspective of Flow Theory," *School Psychology Quarterly* 18 (2003): 158–176, 10.1521/scpq.18.2.158.21860.

8. John Roach, "Students, Prompted by Massacre, Design Emergency Lock to Thwart Shooters," NBC News, October 24, 2013, https://www.nbcnews.com/sciencemain/students -prompted-massacre-design-emergency-lock-thwart-shooters-8C11451971.

9. Hoai-Tran Bui, "D.C. Students Invent Emergency Door Lock to Stop Shooters," *NBC Washington,* October 29, 2013, https://www.nbcwashington.com/news/local/DC-Students -Invent-Emergency-Door-Lock-to-Stop-Shooters-229201391.html.

10. Chase Purdy, "American School Shootings Are So Common Teens Are Inventing Tools to Stay Safe," *Quartz,* February 20, 2018, https://qz.com/1211304/us-school-shootings-are-so -common-teens-are-inventing-tools-to-stay-safe/.

11. Frank Moss, "The Power of Creative Freedom: Lessons from the MIT Media Lab," from

Innovation: Perspectives for the 21st Century. *BBVA Openmind,* https://www.bbvaopen mind.com/en/articles/the-power-of-creative-freedom-lessons-from-the-mit-media-lab/.

12. Katie Reilly, "When Schools Get Creative," *The Science of Creativity,* TIME Special Education, May 2019, p. 85.

13. Todd B. Kashdan and Paul J. Silvia, "Curiosity and Interest: The Benefits of Thriving on Novelty and Challenge," in *Handbook of Positive Psychology.* New York: Oxford University Press, 2009, pp. 367–375.

14. Jenny Soffel, "What Are the 21st-Century Skills Every Student Needs?" World Economic Forum. March 10, 2016, https://www.weforum.org/agenda/2016/03/21st-century-skills -future-jobs-students/. Accessed Jun 26, 2019.

15. Pew Research Center, "The State of American Jobs," October 6, 2016, https://www.pew socialtrends.org/2016/10/06/the-state-of-american-jobs/.

16. Darin J. Eich, "Innovation Skills for the Future: Insights from Research Reports," *Innovation Training,* 2018. Retrieved June 19, 2019, https://www.innovationtraining.org/ innovation-skills-for-the-future/ /. Francesca Levy and Christopher Cannon, "The Bloomberg Job Skills Report 2016: What Recruiters Want," *Bloomberg,* https://www.bloomberg. com/graphics/2016-job-skills-report/; American Management Association (AMA) Critical Skills Survey (complex problem solving, critical thinking, creativity, collaboration and team building, December 2010.

17. S. Hidi and D. Berndorff, "Situational Interest and Learning." In L. Hoffman, A. Krapp, K. A. Renninger, and J. Baumert (eds.), *Interest and Learning.* Kiel, Germany: IPN, pp. 74–90. U. Schiefele, A. Krapp, and A. Winteler. (1992). "Interest as a Predictor of Academic Achievement: A Meta-Analysis of Research." In K. A. Renninger, S. Hidi, and A. Krapp (eds.), *The Role of Interest in Learning and Development.* Hillsdale, NJ: Erlbaum, pp. 183–212.

18. Association for Psychological Science, "Curiosity is Critical to Academic Performance," ScienceDaily, www.sciencedaily.com/releases/2011/10/111027150211.htm (accessed July 3, 2019).

19. F. D. Naylor, "A State-Trait Curiosity Inventory," *Australian Psychologist,* 16 (1981): 172–183; N. Park, C. Peterson, M.E.P. Seligman, "Strengths of Character and Well-Being," *Journal of Social and Clinical Psychology,* 23 (2004): 603–619; J. Vitterso, "Flow Versus Life satisfaction: A Projective Use of Cartoons to Illustrate the Difference Between the Evaluation Approach and the Intrinsic Motivation Approach to subjective Quality of Life," *Journal of Happiness Studies* 4 (2003): 141–167.

20. S. Engel, "Children's Need to Know: Curiosity in School," *Harvard Educational Review* 81 (4), pp. 625–645, Doi: 10.17763/haer.81.4.h054131316473115; T. B. Kashdan, R. A. Sherman, L. Yarbro, and D. C. Funder, "How are curious people viewed and how do they behave in social situations? From the perspectives of self, friends, parents, and unacquainted observers," *Journal of Personality 81* (2) (2013): 142–154, doi: 10.1111/j.1467- 6494.2012.00796.x.

21. George Land and Beth Jarman, *Breaking Point and Beyond.* San Francisco: HarperBusiness, 1993.

22. Po Bronson and Ashley Merryman, "The Creativity Crisis," *Newsweek,* July 10, 2010, https://www.newsweek.com/creativity-crisis-74665.

23. "100 years of research prove that rewards only result in temporary obedience": Interview with Alfie Kohn and D. J. Heiss, "Rewards Can Be as Bad as Punishments," *Redlands Daily Facts,* November 15, 2007.

24. Jeremy Dean, "Do Big Money Bonuses Really Increase Job Performance? *PsyBlog,* archived June 26, 2019, https://www.spring.org.uk/2008/04/do-big-money-bonuses-really-increase .php.

25. M. R. Lepper, D. Greene, and R. E. Nisbett, "Undermining children's intrinsic interest with extrinsic reward: A test of the 'overjustification' hypothesis," *Journal of Personality and Social Psychology 28* (1),(1973):129–137, http://dx.doi.org/10.1037/h0035519.

26. Ruth Butler, "Task-Involving and Ego-Involving Properties of Evaluation Effects of Different Feedback Conditions on Motivational Perceptions, Interest, and Performance," *Journal of Educational Psychology* 79 (1987): 474–82.

27. Ruth Butler and Mordecai Nisan, "Effects of No Feedback, Task-Related Comments, and Grades on Intrinsic Motivation and Performance," *Journal of Educational Psychology* 78 (1986): 210–216, 10.1037/0022-0663.78.3.210.

28. Alfie Kohn, *Hooked on Rewards,* p. 67.

29. Raina Kelley, "Getting Away with It," *Newsweek,* April 30, 2008, online exclusive: http: www/newsweek.com/id/134920/output/print.

30. R. Dobson, "Why First-Born Children Have Higher IQs," *The Times,* April 11, 2008.

31. Joseph Price, economics professor at Brigham Young University, analyzed data on over 21,000 people and found that our youngest children are hugely shortchanged on one-on-one talking time with parents: J. Price, "Parent-Child Quality Time: Does Birth Order Matter?" *Journal of Human Resources* 43 (1) (Winter 2008): 240–265.

32. John S. Dacey, "Discriminating Characteristics of the Families of Highly Creative Adolescents," *Journal of Creative Behavior,* vol. 23, no. 4 (1989): 263–71, https://doi.org/10 .1002/j.2162-6057.1989.tb00700.x.

33. Scott Barry Kaufman and Carolyn Gregoire, *Wired to Create: Unraveling the Mysteries of the Creative Mind.* New York: Penguin Random House, 2015, p. 47.

34. Benjamin Baird, Jonathan Smallwood, Michael D. Mrazek, Julia W. Y. Kam, Michael S. Franklin, and Jonathan W. Schooler, "Inspired by Distraction: Mind Wandering Facilitates Creative Incubation." *Psychological Science* 23, no. 10 (October 2012): 1117–22, doi:10.1177/0956797612446024.

35. Stephanie Pappas, "Busy Kids: Overscheduled Worriers Overstated," *LiveScience,* April 10, 2011, https://www.livescience.com/13642-kids-overscheduled-extracurricular-activities. html.

36. David McCullough, *The Wright Brothers.* New York: Simon & Schuster, May 3, 2016.

37. Aly Weisman, "Meet Steven Spielberg's Parents in This Revealing '60 Minutes' Profile," *Business Insider,* October 22, 2012, https://www.businessinsider.com/meet-steven-spielbergs -parents-in-this-revealing-60-minutes-profile-2012-10.

38. Nancy Carlsson-Paige, "How to Raise a Grounded, Creative Child," *CNN,* January 30, 2014, https://www.cnn.com/2014/01/30/opinion/carlsson-paige-raising-children/index. html Accessed Jun 22, 2017.

39. Myrna B. Shure and George Spivack, "Interpersonal Problem Solving as a Mediator of Behavioral Adjustment In Preschool and Kindergarten Children," *Journal of Applied Developmental Psychology,* vol. 1, issue 1 (Winter 1980): 29–44, https://www.sciencedirect.com/ science/article/pii/019339738090060X.

40. Odyssey of the Mind, Creative Competitions, Inc., 2020, https://www.odysseyofthemind.com

41. "Sex and Drugs? Today's Teens a 'Cautious Generation," CBS News, June 9, 2016, https:// www.cbsnews.com/news/teen-survey-sex-drugs-smoking-trends/ Archived June 30, 2019.

42. William Deresiewicz, *Excellent Sheep: The Miseducation of the American Elite and the Way to a Meaningful Life*. New York: Free Press, 2015, p. 2.

43. Jean Twenge, *iGen, Why Today's Super-Connected Kids Are Growing Up Less Rebellious, More Tolerant, Less Happy—and Completely Unprepared for Adulthood*. New York: Atria Books, 2017, p. 154.

44. Greg Lukianoff and Jonathan Haidt, *The Coddling of the American Mind: How Good Intentions and Bad Ideas are Setting Up a Generation for Failure*. New York: Penguin Press, 2018, p. 48.

45. Jamaal Abdul-Alim, "Experts Tell Congress Free Speech on Campus 'Essential,'" DiverseEducation.com, October 26, 2017, https://diverseeducation.com/article/103956/.

46. Adam Grant, "Kids, Would You Please Start Fighting?" *New York Times,* November 4, 2017, https://www.nytimes.com/2017/11/04/opinion/sunday/kids-would-you-please-start-fighting.html?_r=0.

47. ARE acronym credited to Kate Shuster, executive director of the Middle School Public Debate Program, cited by Marge Scherer, "Teaching Students to Think!" *Educational Leadership,* vol. 65, no. 5 (February 2008), http://www.ascd.org/publications/educational-leadership/feb08/vol65/num05/toc.aspx.

48. Einstein's childhood from Walter Isaacson, "20 Things You Need to Know About Einstein," *TIME,* April 5, 2007, http://content.time.com/time/specials/packages/article/0,28804,1936731_1936743_1936745,00.html; Walter Isaacson, *His Life and Universe*. New York: Simon & Schuster, 2007; John Shepler, "Einstein's Compass," JohnShepler.com, November 2018, https://www.johnshepler.com/articles/einstein.html.

49. Tom Head, "Six Interesting Musical Facts About Albert Einstein," *CMUSE,* April 29, 2015, https://www.cmuse.org/interesting-musical-facts-about-albert-einstein/.

50. Erik L. Westby and V. L. Dawson, "Creativity: Asset or Burden in the Classroom?" *Creativity Research Journal* 8 (1) (1995): 1–10, DOI: 10.1207/s15326934crj0801_1.

51. Nick Bilton, "Steve Jobs Was a Low-Tech Parent," *New York Times,* September 10, 2014, https://www.nytimes.com/2014/09/11/fashion/steve-jobs-apple-was-a-low-tech-parent.html?_r=0 Accessed Jun 22, 2019.

52. Chris Weller, "Bill Gates and Steve Jobs Raised Their Kids Tech-Free-and It Should've Been a Red Flag," *Business Insider,* January 10, 2018, https://www.businessinsider.com/screen-time-limits-bill-gates-steve-jobs-red-flag-2017-10. Accessed Jun 22, 2019.

53. Emma Elsworthy, "Curious Children Ask 73 Questions Each Day—Many of Which Parents Can't Answer, Says Study," *Independent,* December 3, 2017, https://www.independent.co.uk/news/uk/home-news/curious-children-questions-parenting-mum-dad-google-answers-inquisitive-argos-toddlers-chad-valley-a8089821.html.

54. Personal interview with Adam El Rafey and his parents, Soha and Mohie El Rafey, at the Global Educational Supplies and Solutions (GESS) conference in Dubai, February 26, 2019.

CHAPTER 6

1. Research on grit all from Angela Duckworth, *Grit: The Power of Passion and Perseverance*. New York: Scribner, 2016.

2. Ibid., p. 56.

3. Geoff Colvin, *Talent Is Overrated: What Really Separates World-Class Performers from Everybody Else*. New York: Penguin Books, 2008, pp. 3, 51.

4. Mihaly Csikszentmihalyi, Kevin Rathunde and Samuel Whalen, *Talented Teenagers: The Roots of Success & Failure.* New York: Cambridge University Press, 1993, p. 10.

5. Greg Toppo, "Rethinking What Spurs Success," *USA Today,* October 4, 2012, 3A/.

6. Mark D. Seery, E. Alison Holman, and Roxane Cohen Silver, "Whatever Does Not Kill Us: Cumulative Lifetime Adversity, Vulnerability and Resilience," *Journal of Personality and Social Psychology,* 99 (6) (2010): 2012–1041 http://dx.doi.org/10.1037/a0021344.

7. Carol S. Dweck, "The Secret to Raising Smart Kids," *Scientific American Mind,* Summer 2016, pp. 11–17.

8. Carol S. Dweck, *Mindset: The New Psychology of Success.* New York: Ballantine Books, 2006, p. 6.

9. Emphasize effort: L. S. Blackwell, C. S. Dweck, K. H. Trzesniewki, "Implicit Theories of Intelligence Predict Achievement Across an Adolescent Transition: A Longitudinal Study and an Intervention," *Child Development,* vol. 78, issue 1 (February 7, 2007).

10. David Paunesku, "Scaled-Up Social Psychology: Intervening Wisely And Broadly In Education" (doctoral dissertation, Stanford University, August 2013), https://web.stanford.edu/~paunesku/paunesku_2013.pdf; Thomas Toch and Susan Headden, "How to Motivate Students to Work Harder," *Atlantic,* September 3, 2014.

11. Joel N. Shurkin, *Terman's Kids: The Groundbreaking Study of How the Gifted Grow Up.* Boston: Little Brown and Company, 1992.

12. Ibid., p. 294.

13. Michael Phelps, *No Limits: The Will to Succeed.* New York: Free Press, 2009, p. 14.

14. Amy Morin, *13 Things Mentally Strong People Don't Do.* New York: William Morrow, 2014, p. 149.

15. Michael Jordan and Mark Vancil, *Driven from Within.* New York: Atria Books, p. 16.

16. Ibid., p. 75.

17. Ibid., p. 18.

18. Ibid., p. 87.

19. Ibid., p. 145.

20. Ibid., p. 126.

21. Ibid., p. 154.

22. H. W. Stevenson and J. W. Stigler, *The Learning Gap.* New York: Simon & Schuster, 1992, University of Michigan research on Asian vs. American children's perseverance.

23. Angela Duckworth, *Grit: The Power of Passion and Perseverance.* New York: Scribner, 2016.

CHAPTER 7

1. Jasmin Malik Chua, "No Kidding, One in Three Children Fear Earth Apocalypse," *Treehugger,* April 20, 2009, https://www.treehugger.com/culture/no-kidding-one-in-three-children-fear-earth-apocalypse.html; Telephone survey polled a national sample of 500 American preteens: 250 boys and 250 girls. Commissioned by Habitat Heroes and conducted by Opinion Research.

2. Tamar E. Chansky, *Freeing Your Child from Anxiety.* New York: Harmony Books, 2014, p. 105.

3. William Stixrud and Ned Johnson, *The Self-Driven Child: The Science and Sense of Giving Your Kids More Control Over Their Lives.* New York: Penguin Books, 2018, p. 2.

4. Martin E.P. Seligman, *The Optimistic Child: A Proven Program to Safeguard Children*

Against Depression and Build Lifelong Resilience. New York: Houghton Mifflin Company, 1995, p. 53.

5. Amy Novotney, "Resilient Kids Learn Better," *American Psychological Association, vol. 40, no. 9* (October 2009), https://www.apa.org/monitor/2009/10/resilient.

6. Sonja Haller, "Bullet-Resistant Backpack Sales on the Rise," *USA Today,* August 14, 2019, p. 3D.

7. Martin Seligman, *The Optimistic Child,* p. 98.

8. Statistic from the Anxiety and Depression Association of America, 2018, https://adaa.org/about-adaa/press-room/facts-statistics.

9. Jean M. Twenge, "The Age of Anxiety? Birth Cohort Change in Anxiety and Neuroticism, 1952–1993," *Journal of Personality and Social Psychology 79,* no. 6 (2000): 1007–1021.

10. Pat Eaton-Robb, "Teacher Unions: Children Terrified by Active Shooter Drills," *ABC News,* February 11, 2020, https://abcnews.go.com/US/wireStory/teachers-unions-express -opposition-active-shooter-drills-68916676.

11. Zusha Elinson, "Shooter Study Raises Doubts on Readiness," *Wall Street Journal,* November 14, 2019.

12. "When Is It OK for Parents to Let Their Kids Watch Violent Movies?" *HealthDay,* June 13, 2018, https://www.health24.com/Parenting/News/when-is-it-ok-for-parents-to-let-their -kids-watch-violent-movies-20180613-3.

13. George C. Patton, M.D., professor, adolescent health research, Centre for Adolescent Health, Royal Children's Hospital, Melbourne, Australia; Hilary Tindle, M.D., M.P.H., researcher, Center for Research on Health Care, Division of General Internal Medicine, University of Pittsburgh, February 2011; *Pediatrics* online, January 10, 2011.

14. Interview with Michael Morgan and George Gerbner, "The Mean World Syndrome, Media Violence and the Cultivation of Fear," Media Education Foundation, 2010, www.mediaed .org.

15. "Boys and Girls Clubs of America: National 'You Report': By Teens, About Teens," NPR, https://www.npr.org/templates/story/story.php?storyId=5350682 April 16, 20016.

16. Statistics: National Center for Education Statistics, https://nces.ed.gov/fastfacts/display. asp?id=719.

17. Martin E. P. Seligman, *The Optimistic Child.* New York: Houghton Mifflin Company, 1995, p. 7

18. Benjamin Wagner, "Mister Rogers: 'Look for the Helpers' in Times of Disaster," Mister Rogers & Me, December 18, 2012, http://www.misterrogersandme.com/2012/12/18/mister -rogers-quote/.

19. E. C. Chang, "Hope, Problem-Solving Ability, and Coping in a College Student Population: Some Implications for Theory and Practice," *Journal of Clinical Psychology 54,* no. 7 (November 1998): 953–62.

20. Rich Gilman, Jameika Dooley, and Dan Florell, "Relative Levels of Hope and their Relationship with Academic and Psychological Indicators Among Adolescents," *Journal of Social and Clinical Psychology,* vol. 25, issue 2 (February 2006), https://guilfordjournals.com/doi/ abs/10.1521/jscp.2006.25.2.166.

21. C. R. Snyder, Diane McDermott, William Cook, and Michael A. Rapoff, *Hope for the Journey: Helping Children Through Good Times and Bad.* Clinton Corners, NY: Percheron Press/Eliot Werner Publications, 2002.

22. Ruby Bridges, *Through My Eyes.* New York: Scholastic Inc., 1999, p. 22.

23. Ibid., p. 56

24. Ibid., p. 9.

25. Robert Coles, *The Story of Ruby Bridges*. New York: Scholastic Inc., 1995.

26. Many resilient individuals were found to rely on faith and prayer as an important source of support in times of difficulties: Emmy E. Werner and Ruth S. Smith, *Overcoming the Odds: High Risk Children from Birth to Adulthood*. Ithaca, New York: Cornell University Press, 1992, p. 71.

27. Ruby Bridges, *Through My Eyes*. New York: Scholastic Inc., 1999, pp. 40–41.

28. Ibid., p. 49.

29. People Staff, "Kindest Cut," *People*, April 11, 1994, https://people.com/archive/kindest -cut-vol-41-no-13/; Brigitte Greenberg, "Fifth Grade Boys Shave Heads to Save Classmate's Face: Cancer: Fellow Students Didn't Want Friend to Feel Out of Place When Chemotherapy Causes Hair to Fall Out," *Los Angeles Times*, March 20, 1994, http://articles.latimes.com/1994-03-20/local/me-36274_1_cancer-head-shave.

30. Jonathan Haidt, "Wired to Be Inspired." In *The Compassionate Instinct*, edited by Dacher Keltner, Jason Marsh, and Jeremy Adam Smith, 86. New York: W.W. Norton & Company, 2010.

31. Laurel Wamsley, "Troubled by Flint Water Crisis, 11-Year-Old Girl Invents Lead-Detecting Device" *NPR*, October 20, 2017, https://www.npr.org/sections/thetwo-way/2017/10/20/559071028/troubled-by-flint-water-crisis-11-year-old-girl-invents-lead-detecting-device.

32. Project I Am, https://www.iamnaeem.com.

Index

Abbott, Jim, 54–56, 61, 219
academic performance
    of Asian students, 217–18
    and empathy, 69
    impact of multitasking on, 111
    and optimism, 228
    and pushing kids, 112–13
    and self-confidence, 30
    and self-control, 107, 108
    and self-discipline, 200
    and self-esteem, 34
achievement, pressure for, 11
ACT (Assess Stress; Calm Down; Talk
    Positively), 120–25
adaptability, 41
adults as advocates in kids' lives, 13, 58
adversity
    faced by Elizabeth Smart, 91–92
    and optimism, 228
    and Outdoor Odyssey, 197, 199
    and protective factors, 90
    and self-confidence, 30
affective empathy, 68–69
affluent communities, 11, 36
agency of kids, 204
alcoholic parents, 58
alienation, 36
alone, time spent, 172–73, 177–78
altruism, 72, 154
American Academy of Child & Adolescent
    Psychiatry, 109
American Academy of Pediatrics, 113
American Community School (ACS) in
    Beirut, Lebanon, 28–29
American Federation of Teachers, 231
American Psychological Association, 109

Anderson, Chris, 189
Angelou, Maya, 254
Antrom, Deonté, 164
anxiety
    in affluent families, 11
    and gratitude, 86
    hiding from parents, 4
    and play deprivation, 114
    rising rates of, 50, 109
appearance, cultural focus on, 34–35
apps
    for cultivating mindfulness, 118–19
    for cultivating self-control, 134
    for limiting technology, 189
ARE acronym, 186
arguments, encouraging constructive, 185–86
Asian students, 217–18
assisting others, 90
Association of American Medical Colleges,
    69
attention, 39, 116
attention deficit hyperactivity disorder
    (ADHD), 112, 129–30

Bald Eagles, 249, 250
balloon ride, imaginary, 97
Battle Hymn of the Tiger Mother (Chua), 35
Baumeister, Roy F., 135
Beck, Aaron, 227
behavioral empathy, 68, 69
behavioral issues, 13
beliefs, asserting, 153
Bloom, Benjamin, 31
bodily kinesthetic/physical abilities, 42
Bodrova, Elena, 106
body language, 241

Boniwell, Ilona, 58–59
book resources
    for cultivating curiosity, 188–89
    for cultivating empathy, 85, 94
    for cultivating integrity, 157, 158–60
    for cultivating mindfulness, 133
    for cultivating optimism, 245, 252
    for cultivating perseverance, 218, 219
    for cultivating personal strength, 61
"bouncing back," 215, 219–20
Boys & Girls Clubs of America, 239
brag boards, 61
brainstorming, 180, 191–92
Braun, Adam, 253
breathing practices, 98–99, 122–24, 135
Bridges, Ruby, 219, 247–48
Brooks, David, 144
Brown, Deb, 159
Bucks, Christian, 66
bullying, 69, 141, 239, 256–57
burnout
    and ambitions for cognitive development, 11
    and declining empathy levels, 70
    and gratitude, 86
    overwhelm as symptom of, 110
    rising rates of, 8
    role of stress in, 18

caffeinated/energy drinks, 116
Cain, Susan, 53
Calley, William, 160–61
CALM acronym, 239–42
Cambridge Elementary School in San
    Antonio, 155
CARE acronym, 87–90
caring, demonstrations of, 87–90, 201
Carr, Nicholas, 111
Carrollwood Day School, 65–67
Cashion, Diana, 155
catastrophizing problems, 219
challenging kids, 189–90, 208
Chansky, Tamar, 225
character, 5–6
Character Strengths, 16–17
    assessment tool for, 21–23
    benchmarks of, 15
    benefits of instilling, 15
    and depletion factor, 18
    inner foundation built by, 20
    Multiplier Effect for, 17–18
    and "Three Little Pigs" fable, 19–20
Chavez, Alissa, 162

cheating, rates of, 141
chess club in refugee camp, 64
choices, allowing, 128
Chua, Amy, 35
chunking tasks into smaller pieces, 220
circles of concern, widening, 96
cognitive abilities
    pressure to optimize, 11–12
    and sleep deprivation, 113
Cognitive Behavior Therapy (CBT), 227–28
cognitive empathy, 68–69
collages displaying strengths, 60–61
college admissions
    as all-consuming goal, 9
    and ethically challenged adults, 143
    and pressure felt by families, 11–12
    and risk avoidance of students, 165, 181
college students
    decision making abilities of, 125–26
    declining empathy among, 70, 87
    difficulties with transition to adulthood,
        125–26
    and dropout rate for freshmen, 9
    emotional safety demanded by, 182
    gap years taken by, 134–35
    "maturity fears" experienced by, 126
    mental health issues of, 70
    narcissism among, 75
    overwhelm experienced by, 9
    and pandemic of 2020, 125
    See also college admissions
comebacks, 240
comfort zones, stretching, 183
common ground, finding, 96–97
communication abilities, 31
comparisons, making, 4, 35, 207
compassion, 68
competition, 72–73
Conard, Norm, 137–38, 139, 157
confidence, 15
conflict, making space for, 134
"Connect 4" approach to making friends,
    94–95
consoling others, 90
control, sense of, 225–26
Coons, Sabrina, 138
Core Assets
    acknowledging, 47
    advantages of understanding, 63
    and father of author, 260
    hand talks for enumerating, 59
    identifying, 37–39, 44–45

six common characteristics of, 39
survey, 40–43
coronavirus/Covid-19. *See* pandemic of 2020
creativity, 16, 31, 41
critical thinking skills, 69, 168
Csikszentmihalyi, Mihaly, 51, 163–64, 203
curiosity, 162–94
about, 16, 167
age-by-age ideas for instilling, 188–92
benefits of, 15, 168–69
challenges of teaching, 169–73
and Core Assets, 41
declining levels of, 170
and father of author, 260
and flow state, 163–64
importance of, 111, 168
at MIT's Media Lab, 163–67, 179
Multiplier Effect for, 17, 18, 169
outcomes associated with, 263
and perseverance, 201
risks of low levels of, 5–6
and self-control, 261
as superpower, 187–88
teaching, 173–86
unlearning, 170

Damon, Matt, 174
Damon, William, 51, 53, 149
daydreaming, 177
debating, 185
decision-making abilities, 31, 125–29
demanding parents, 217
Denmark, 112
depression
in affluent families, 11
and digital media use, 79
and gratitude, 86
optimism's ability to thwart, 17
and pessimism, 228, 229
and play deprivation, 114
rising rates of, 2, 8, 32, 34, 50, 109
social media's link to, 35
and Tiger parenting style, 36
Deresiewicz, William, 182
digital devices. *See* technology
disabilities, overcoming discomfort with, 98
disagreement, allowing for, 151–52
disappointment, parental statements of,
84–85
disciplining kids, 144–45
Disney, Walt, 220
disputes, encouraging, 184–85

dissension, 185
distance learning, 74
dogs, 77
"don't give up" phrases, 221
Duckworth, Angela, 108, 199–200, 203, 205,
221–22
Dweck, Carol, 205–6, 208

eagerness, 39
Edison, Thomas, 219
education
and cooperative learning, 72
and distance learning, 74
and elimination of recess, 173
and grades, 8–9, 28–29, 72–73, 75, 228
preschool, 12, 103–7, 112
private schools, 204
and rates of cheating, 141
and Reggio Emilia educational philosophy,
27–29, 64
and risk avoidance of students, 181
school shootings and drills, 4, 99–100, 164,
224, 231–32, 234
and self-directed learning, 28
and Tools of the Mind curriculum, 104–7
See also academic performance; college
students
effort, praising, 49, 208
Einstein, Albert, 187–88, 219
"either-or" decisions, 128
Elias, Maurice, 152
emotions
and affective empathy, 68–69
emotional agility, 15
emotional literacy, 75, 76–78
emotional safety demanded by students, 182
identifying, 99
imaging, in others, 95–96
labeling, 77, 82
managing, 16, 120–25
nonverbal cues of, 77
recognizing, in others, 75, 76–78
sharing, 78
See also empathy
empathy, 65–100
about, 16, 67–68
age-by-age ideas for instilling, 93–94
and age of child, 71
benefits of, 15, 69, 88
challenges of teaching, 70–75
and competition, 72–73
and Core Assets, 40

empathy (*cont.*)
  and curiosity, 169
  declining levels of, 66, 69–70, 87
  and face-to-face connection, 87, 88
  and father of author, 260
  and gender, 71
  and gratitude, 86
  and integrity, 261
  modeling, 81–82, 99
  Multiplier Effect for, 17, 18, 76
  outcomes associated with, 262
  and perseverance, 201
  and perspective taking, 75, 82–84, 85–86
  putting into action, 87–90
  and recognizing others' emotions, 75, 76–78
  risks of low levels of, 5–6
  setting expectations of, 84–85, 99
  as superpower, 90–92
  teaching, 75–90
  technology's impact on, 73–74
  three types of, 67–69
employment, 54
emptiness, feelings of
  in affluent families, 11
  and competition, 72
  and excessive praise, 75
  rising rates of, 71
  and Tiger parenting style, 36
entrepreneurial spirit, cultivating, 54
Ericsson, Anders, 202
Esrey, Trudy, 254
ethical values, 16. *See also* integrity
expectations
  difficulties managing, 9, 11
  setting the right, 220–21
  setting the wrong, 203–4
  and strengthening focusing abilities, 116
extracurricular activities, 173
eye contact, 81

Facebook, 35
FaceTime, 80
face-to-face connection
  decreasing levels of, 4
  and empathy, 87, 88
  encouraging, 78–81
  technology enabling, 80–81
Fagell, Phyllis, 97
failure
  avoidance of, 33
  and building self-confidence, 34
  fear of, 4, 208

  learning from, 16
  and moral development, 145
  and permission to fail, 214
  and reframing mistakes, 212–15
  rescuing kids from, 204–5
  setting expectations for, 165–66, 183
failure to launch, 50
families
  and digital media use, 79, 80
  family chats about strengths, 61
  family meetings, 183–84
  goal-setting sessions in, 212
  and gratitude prayer, 86
  and mealtimes, 79
  and unconditional love, 91–92
  and vacations, 53
Fantastic Failures (Reynolds), 219
fear
  gender differences in, 224
  and pandemic, 230, 232
  prevalence of, 224, 229–30
"Feeling Thermometer," 76
Ferrell, Trevor, 66
Feshbach, Norma, 85
50 American Heroes Every Kid Should Meet
    (Denenberg), 157
Finland, 112–13
fixed mind-sets, 205, 206, 208
flow state, 163–64
Floyd, George, 232–33
Focus (Goleman), 115–16
focusing on what matters, 115–20
Fox, Paula, 32–33
Freeing Your Child from Anxiety (Chansky),
    225
free time, 45–46
Freeze Tag, 118
future, hopefulness for, 242–47

gains, redefining success as, 207
Gandhi, Mohandas, 254
gap years, 134–35
Gates, Bill, 189
Geisel, Theodor, 220
Generation Z, 2
Genius Hour, 166–67
Gerbner, George, 233
gifted kids, 36, 209
Giraffe Heroes Project, 157
goal setting, 209–12
Goertzel, Victor and Mildred, 58
Golden Rule, 156–57, 161

Goleman, Daniel, 115–16
good deeds/rituals, encouraging, 250–52
goodness boxes, 255
good news, sharing, 250
good thinking, acknowledging, 254–55
grades
    emphasis on, 75
    feeling overwhelmed by, 228
    as poor indicator of success, 8–9
    and report card alternative, 28–29
    and risk avoidance of students, 181
Grant, Adam, 47–48, 186
gratitude
    benefits of, 86
    and breathing practices, 98–99
    strategies for boosting, 86
    and thank-you notes, 97–98
Great Britain in World War II, 234
grit
    about, 200
    and Core Assets, 41
    and Outdoor Odyssey, 197, 199
    as predictor of success, 200, 217
    See also perseverance
Grit (Duckworth), 203
growth mind-set, cultivating, 205–8

Haidt, Jonathan, 87, 249
handicaps, overcoming, 54–56, 58
hand problem solver, 191
happiness
    and digital media use, 73
    and empathy, 88
    in Finland, 113
    and self-confidence, 31
    and self-control, 108
    and self-esteem, 34
    strivers' struggles with, 5
"hard thing rule," 221–22
Harry Potter (Rowling), 219
Harvard Business Review, 69
Harvey, Anjreyev, 164
Hashem, Mahmoud, 64
helicoptering parenting, 9, 145
"hello," saying, 93–94
helplessness, feelings of, 204
Henry, Barbara, 247–48
Herber, Taylor, 249
hero box, creating, 157
heroes, 157–58
history, studying, 137–40, 234
Hixon, J. Gregory, 59–60

hobbies, 46, 62
Holocaust, 137–40, 154
Holocaust Memorial Museum, US, 83–84
Holzhaurer, Erik, 249
honor code, 159
hope/hopelessness, 41, 50
hostility, 134
Houghton, Sam, 162
human connection, 73–74
hyperactivity, 112

identity, cultivating a sense of, 47–49
"if-then" plans, 119–20
"I messages," 240
inadequacy, feelings of, 4, 8
inquisitiveness, stretching, 176
Instagram, 35
integrity, 137–61
    about, 16, 140–41
    age-by-age ideas for instilling, 155–60
    benefits of, 15
    challenges of teaching, 142–45
    and Core Assets, 40–41
    and curiosity, 169
    declining levels of, 141
    and empathy, 261
    and father of author, 260
    Multiplier Effect for, 17, 18
    and optimism, 261
    outcomes associated with, 263
    and perseverance, 201
    as superpower, 153–55
    and TEACH acronym, 147–48
    teaching, 145–53
    and Three As, 151–53
intelligence and IQs
    and academic achievement, 108, 168
    and curiosity, 168
    and fear of failure, 208
    and goal setting, 209
    and grit's prediction of achievement, 200
    and mind-set theory, 206, 208
    parents' emphasis on, 11
    and self-control, 107, 108, 115
interests, awareness of, 32
"I will + what + when" formula for goals, 211
"I wonder?" exercise, 176

Jackson, Jahkil, 253
Jobs, Steve, 174, 176, 189, 220
Jones, T. S. (Tom), 197, 199
Jordan, Michael, 215–17, 219

Karumanchi, Riya, 162
Kim, Kyung Hee, 170
kinder-cramming, 112
kindergarten, delaying, 112
Knitt, Gus, 12
Knots on a Counting Rope (Martin), 223
Kohn, Alfie, 72, 171
Konrath, Sara, 71, 87
Krasinski, John, 250

Land, George, 170
learning
    as characteristic of Core Assets, 39
    cooperatively, 72
    learning difficulties, 58
    self-directed, 28
    and Socratic process, 150–51
Lebanon, Shatila refugee camp in, 63–64
Leong, Deborah, 104, 106
Lewis, Katherine Reynolds, 117
linguistic strengths, 41
listening, empathetic, 81–82
lockdown drills and school shootings,
    4, 99–100, 164, 224, 231–32,
    234
logical/thinking strengths, 42
loneliness
    in affluent families, 11
    and competition, 72
    and gratitude, 86
    high levels of, 2
    rising rates of, 9
    self-reports of, 4
love, unconditional, 91–92
Lowe, Keanon, 100
Luthar, Suniya, 11
lying, 141

Malaguzzi, Loris, 27
Mandela, Nelson, 254
marshmallow experiment, 108, 119
materialism, 86
"maturity fears," 126
mealtimes, family, 79
meaning and purpose
    helping kids find, 49–51, 63
    lack of, 51
    Multiplier Effect for, 51
    and self-confidence, 31
"mean world syndrome," 233
media, frightening images in, 232–33
mental health

on college campuses, 9
and digital media use, 73
and gratitude, 86
and long-term impacts of trauma, 13
and pandemic of 2020, 4, 50
rising rates of problems with, 8, 9, 36, 109
and self-confidence, 31
mental toughness, 15
mentors, 53–54
micromanaging kids, 171–72
Middle School Matters (Fagell), 97
Milne, A. A., 254
Milton Hershey School in Pennsylvania,
    121
mindfulness, 118–20, 133, 134
mind-set theory, 205–8
Mischel, Walter, 108, 119
mistakes
    and hand problem solver, 191
    learning from, 16
    modeling, 213
    as problems to be solved, 212–15
Mistakes That Worked (Jones), 219
Mister Rogers' Neighborhood (series),
    243–44
MIT's Media Lab, 163–67, 179–80
mobile devices, 110–11. *See also* technology
mobiles displaying strengths, 60
Monty, Barbie, 65–67
morality
    and Character Strengths, 15
    and Core Assets survey, 40–41
    developing moral identity, 148–50
    Four Rs of, 149–50
    modeling moral awareness, 145–48
    See also integrity
Morin, Amy, 214–15
Moss, Frank, 165
Mother May I, 118
motivation and self-confidence, 31
mottos, 246
movies
    cultivating optimism, 251
    curious minds depicted in, 190–91
    divergent thinking illustrated in, 185
    promoting empathy with, 94
    self-control illustrated in, 132
    violence portrayed in, 232
Multiplier Effect, 17–18, 261
    with curiosity, 17, 18, 169
    with empathy, 17, 18, 76
    with integrity, 17, 18

with meaning/purpose, 51
with optimism, 18
with perseverance, 17, 18, 201
with self-control, 17, 116
multitasking, 110–11
musical strengths, 42
music for cultivating optimism, 246
My Lai massacre, 160–61

Nagorno-Karabakh, schools of, 230
narcissism, 34, 70, 75
National Education Association, 231
nature strengths, 42
Navy SEALS, 124, 215
networks, 159–60
news consumption, 244–45
New Zealand, 60
"no," saying, 240
No Contest: The Case Against Competition
    (Kohn), 72
noncognitive skills, 14. See also character
nouns used in praise, 47–48

Odyssey of the Mind, 178–80
O'Gorman, Ian, 249
Oliner, Samuel and Pearl, 154
open-ended play and learning, 175–76, 192
optimism, 224–57
    about, 16–17, 227
    age-by-age ideas for instilling, 248–55
    benefits of, 15, 228–29
    and CALM acronym, 239–42
    challenges of teaching, 229–33
    and Core Assets, 41
    and father of author, 260
    and gratitude, 86
    and hopefulness for future, 242–47
    and integrity, 261
    Multiplier Effect for, 18
    outcomes associated with, 263
    and perseverance, 200
    risks of low levels of, 5–6
    and sense of control, 225–26
    as superpower, 247–48
    teaching, 233–47
Optimistic Child, The (Seligman), 239
Originals (Grant), 186
Outdoor Odyssey Leadership Academy, 197–99
out-of-box thinking, 165
overprotection of children, 182–83
overscheduled kids, 48, 116, 202
overwhelm, 110, 220. See also burnout

pandemic of 2020
    and concerns for emotional/physical safety,
        182
    and culture of fear, 230, 232
    and digital media use, 79
    and face-to-face connection, 80–81
    and lack of human connection, 73–74
    and mental health issues, 4, 50
    and young adults moving home, 125
parents
    demanding + supportive parenting style,
        217
    emphasis on intelligence/IQs, 11
    ethically challenged behavior of, 143
    fixation on weaknesses, 49
    helicoptering parenting, 9, 145
    inability to let go, 126
    micromanaging kids, 171–72
    modeling empathy, 81–82, 99
    modeling moral awareness, 145–48
    modeling optimism, 233–35
    modeling perseverance, 218
    modeling self-control, 131–32, 136
    parenting styles of, 127, 144–45
    performance expectations of, 32
    poor sportsmanship of, 97
    statements of disappointment, 84–85
    struggles to recognize strengths, 35–36,
        38, 39
    Tiger parenting style, 35–36
participation awards, 33, 34
passion, 4, 200
peer pressure, 239
performance, parental expectations for, 32
perseverance, 197–223
    about, 16, 199–200
    age-by-age ideas for instilling, 217–22
    benefits of instilling, 15
    challenges of teaching, 201–5
    and Core Assets, 41
    and curiosity, 169
    and father of author, 260
    grit compared to, 200
    importance of, 201
    Multiplier Effect for, 17, 18, 201
    outcomes associated with, 263
    risks of low levels of, 5–6
    and self-confidence, 261
    as superpower, 215–17
    teaching, 205–15
personality traits, 14
perspective taking, 69, 75, 82–84, 85–86

pessimism
   of adults, 230, 234–35
   and Cognitive Behavior Therapy, 227–28
   as common theme of youth, 225, 228, 229
   impact of, 225, 228
   strategies for mitigating, 226, 235–38
Peterson, Jillian, 232
Phelps, Michael, 129–30, 211, 219
Picasso, Pablo, 169
planning abilities, 105
play deprivation, 114–15
portfolios of strengths, 60
practicing
   deliberate practice, 202–3, 219, 222
   and "hard thing rule," 221–22
   improving self-control, 135
   making practice fun, 48–49
   making time for, 202–3
praise
   for caring, 89
   in earshot, 47
   for effort, 49, 208
   excessive, 74–75
   for teamwork, 97
   using nouns rather than verbs in, 47–48
preschools, 12, 103–7, 112
private schools, 204
problematic behavior in children, 105–6
problem solving, 15, 168, 171, 178–81, 191
Psychology of Good and Evil, The (Staub), 88
Punished by Rewards (Kohn), 171
puppets, 85
purpose. See meaning and purpose

questions, asking, 152–53, 191
Quiet (Cain), 53
quitting, rules for, 222
quotes that inspire optimism, 253–54

racism, 141
Rafey, Adam El, 193–94
Randolph, Dominic, 204
Rao, Gitanjali, 253
reading for pleasure, 46
Real Heroes (Reed), 157
reassuring others, 90
recess, disappearance of, 173
Red Light, Green Light, 117–18
Reggio Emilia educational philosophy, 27–29, 64
relationships and relational skills
   and Core Assets, 40
   and empathy, 16, 88

encouraging real time, 80
healthy, 15
and self-confidence, 31
rescuing kids, pervasive problem of, 204–5
resilience
   and empathy, 88
   and gratitude, 86
   impact of helping others on, 88
   increasing, 15
   and optimism, 228, 229
   and self-confidence, 30
   and self-control, 136
Resnick, Mitchel, 166
rewards, overreliance on, 170–71
risk taking, 165, 181–86
Road to Character, The (Brooks), 144
Roe, Emily, 250–51
Rogers, Fred, 243–44
role models depicting strengths, 61
role playing, 85
Rowling, J. K., 219

Sandy Hook school massacre, 164
school shootings, 164, 231–32, 234
school shootings and drills, 4, 99–100, 164,
   224, 231–32, 234
Seery, Mark, 204
self-absorption, 75
self-advocacy, 239–42
self-awareness
   as benefit of Character Strengths, 15
   declining levels of, 31
   and recognizing strengths/weaknesses, 28,
   30, 31
   and sense of meaning, 51
   and what-type questions, 59–60
self-centeredness, 72, 86, 141
self-confidence, 27–64
   about, 16, 29–30
   age-by-age ideas for instilling, 56–62
   benefits of, 15, 30–31
   challenges of teaching, 32–36, 110–15
   and Core Assets, 40
   and cultivating a sense of "who," 47–49
   and curiosity, 169
   and excessive praise, 75
   and father of author, 260
   and finding a kid's purpose, 49–54, 63
   and identifying Core Assets of kids, 37–39,
   44–45, 63
   outcomes associated with, 262
   and perseverance, 261

and recognizing strengths/weaknesses, 28, 30
and Reggio Emilia educational philosophy, 27–29, 64
self-esteem vs., 33–34
sources of, 34
as superpower, 54–56
teaching, 37–39, 44–45
self-control, 103–36
about, 16, 107–8
age-by-age ideas for instilling, 131–35
benefits of, 15
and Core Assets, 41
and curiosity, 261
declining levels of, 109
and father of author, 260
importance of, 107–10
modeling, 131–32, 136
Multiplier Effect for, 17, 116
outcomes associated with, 262
and perseverance, 200
as superpower, 129–31
teaching, 115–29
and Tools of the Mind curriculum, 104–7
self-discipline, 200. *See also* perseverance
self-esteem, 33–34
self-harm, 109
self-medication, 109
self-reliance, 13
self-respect, 40
self-talk, positive, 124–25
Seligman, Martin E. P., 31, 108, 229, 239
Sendler, Irena, 137–40, 157, 161
service projects, 159
setbacks of successful people, 219–20
Shallows, The (Carr), 111
Shatila refugee camp in Lebanon, 63–64
Shure, Myrna, 178
Siegel, Dylan, 66
Simmons, Beth, 256–57
Simon Says, 117–18
Sitting Still Like a Frog (Snel), 122
Skype, 80–81
sleep
and digital media use, 116
recommended hours of, 2
sleep deprivation, 2, 113, 116
Smart, Elizabeth, 91–92, 219
Smith, Christian, 150
Snel, Eline, 122
social competence, 15. *See also* relationships and relational skills

social media
addiction to, 111
depression linked to, 35
and discovering kids' strengths, 44
and empathy, 73
and self-reports of loneliness, 4
See also technology
Socratic process, 150–51
solution game, 191–92
Some Good News (web series), 250
Songy, Sally, 158
SPARK acronym, 180–81
speaking out, 150–53
Spielberg, Steven, 174
Spivack, George, 178
sportsmanship of parents, poor, 97
standing up for oneself, 239–42
Staub, Ervin, 88
stealing, 141
Stevenson, Harold, 217–18
Stone-Faced Boy (Fox), 32–33
"Stop, Think, Act Right" (STAR), 128–29
strengths
and book resources, 61
declines in ability to recognize, 31
discovering, 39, 44–45
and identifying Core Assets of kids, 37
methods for helping kids recognize, 56–62
parents' struggles to recognize, 35–36, 38, 39
and Reggio Emilia educational philosophy, 28
and self-confidence, 16, 56, 58–62
stress
ability to manage, 30
and ACT (Assess Stress; Calm Down; Talk Positively), 120–25
in affluent families, 11
and burnout, 18
and declining empathy levels, 70
and dropout rate for college freshmen, 9
high and rising rates of, 2, 109, 120, 230
impact of helping others on, 88
long-term impacts of, 12–13
and pandemic of 2020, 50
from peer pressure, 239
recognizing signs of, 121
resistance to, 13
self-reports of, 4
triggers of, 121–22
strivers, 3–10, 12, 19, 204, 261
student focus groups, 3–5

substance abuse
    in affluent families, 11
    and gifted kids, 36
    and long-term impacts of trauma, 13
sugar, foods high in, 116
suicidal thoughts and suicides
    and digital media use, 79
    rising rates of, 2, 7–8, 109
summer jobs, 54
superficiality, cultural focus on, 34–35
Swann, William, 59–60

Taipei American School, 159
talent, 35–36
TALENT acronym, 39
TEACH acronym, 147–48
teamwork, praising, 97
technology
    addiction to mobile devices, 111
    apps for cultivating mindfulness, 118–19
    apps for cultivating self-control, 134
    apps for limiting access to, 189
    average usage of, 79
    and cultivating curiosity, 189
    and declining rates of self-control, 110–11
    for face-to-face peer interaction, 80–81
    impact on human connection, 73–74, 78–79
    interruptions from mobile devices, 110–11
    setting clear limits for, 79–80
    and sleep hygiene, 116
    See also social media
temptations, managing, 119
tenacity, 39
Terman, Lewis, 209
terrorism, 232
texting, 73
thank-you notes, 97–98
13 Things Mentally Strong People Don't Do
    (Morin), 214–15
Thompson, Hugh, Jr., 157, 160–61
"Three Little Pigs" fable, 19–20
Thunberg, Greta, 253
Tiger parenting style, 35–36
tinkering spaces, creating, 176–77
tone of voice, 39
Tools of the Mind curriculum, 104–7
trauma, 12–13, 91
triumph logs, 212
troubled childhoods, 58

Tutu, Desmond, 185
Twenge, Jean, 73, 182, 230

UNICEF, 112
United States Holocaust Memorial Museum,
    83–84
Unselfie (Borba), 65
unstructured time, 45–46, 172–73, 176
upper-middle-class families, 11

vacations, family, 53
variety of experiences, offering, 53, 62
verbs used in praise, 47–48
victory logs, 61–62
violence, physical, 141, 232–33
virtues, 14, 147–48, 158. See also character
visual strengths, 43
voice and vocal patterns, 39, 242
volunteering, 54, 246–47

waiting games, 117–18
wait time, stretching, 116–17
weaknesses
    and identifying Core Assets of kids, 37
    parents' fixation on, 49
    recognizing and accepting, 16, 28
well-being, 31
well-rounded kids, 36
Werner, Emmy, 12–13, 90
"What if?" exercise, 157
WhatsApp, 35
what-type questions, 59–60
Williams, Byron, 179
Willpower (Baumeister), 135
Winfrey, Oprah, 220
Woods, Tiger, 61
World War II, 234
Wright, Orville, 173–74

Yandt, Josh, 93–94
Yaseen, Sawsan, 28, 29
"yet" responses to negative self-assessments,
    207
yoga, 134
Yousafzai, Malala, 61, 153–55, 157, 161, 219

Zaki, Jamil, 68
Zimmer, Robert, 184–85
Zoom, 80–81

Book Discussion Guide

HOW TO START AND FACILITATE A THRIVERS BOOK CLUB

- Identify parents or educators interested in forming a book club to discuss *Thrivers*.
- Determine the specific days, times, places, and frequency for your group meeting. There are several ways to divide your discussion content. Here are three possibilities, but choose the number of total book sessions based on group consensus and needs. 1. Seven meetings discussing one chapter per month. Most book clubs meet once a month. 2. Traditional book club: one meeting total. Meet just once and discuss issues participants find most relevant. 3. Two chapters per meeting; four meetings total. You might divide *Thrivers* into four sections and discuss the Introduction and first chapter at the first meeting and then two chapters at each additional meeting.
- Assign a discussion leader or rotate the role at each discussion.

- Use the questions provided to facilitate discussion. Some groups ask each participant to develop one question for each meeting. The key is to make your meetings meaningful for participants.

BOOK DISCUSSION QUESTIONS

1. Why did you or your group choose to read *Thrivers?* What preconceptions about resilience and thriving did you have before you began reading? Which of your views were challenge or changed by your reading?

2. Do you think raising children who can thrive today is easier, no different, or more difficult than when your parents raised you? Why?

3. Many people feel there is a mental health crisis in today's children. Do you? Which other (if any) concerns do you have about today's children? What factors may be preventing children from developing their thriving capacities?

4. The book shared many quotes by children the authored interviewed. Did any quote concern or resonate with you? If so, which quote and why?

5. A major theme of the book is that thriving abilities are learned and that parents do make an enormous difference in influencing their children's thriving potential. How much influence do you think parents actually have? How did your parents influence your character development? At what age do you think parents start losing their influence? Do you think that the ability to influence kids comes back? If so, at what age? What influences children's character and thriving development most: peers, media, education, parents, pop culture, or something else?

6. The book describes seven Character Strengths essential to achieve peak performance and thrive. Which trait do you feel is most essential for children today? Which do you consider most difficult to nurture? Which trait do you emphasize most in your family? Least? Which would you like to emphasize more? What could you do to help your child acquire the virtue? If you were to rank the seven Character Strengths by importance to children's abilities to thrive, what would your list be? Why?

7. *Thrivers* states that Character Strengths are teachable. Do you agree? Which of the seven Character Strengths do you think are more difficult to teach to children today? Why?

8. The book emphasizes that one of the best ways our kids learn Character Strengths is by watching us. How would your child describe your behavior? Which of the seven Character Strengths best exemplify your character? Which Character Strength would you like to increase in yourself, and how would you do so?

9. What kind of person do you want your child to become? How will you help your child become that person?

10. The book stresses that one reason for the character void is our obsession with grades, scores, and rank? Do you agree? If you asked your child what matters most to you, his character or his grades, how do you think (or hope) he would respond?

11. The first Character Strength is self-confidence that emanates from children's awareness of themselves and their strengths and interests. How would you describe your child to someone? And how would your child describe himself? What strengths or interests do you see in your child that could help him gain accurate self-knowledge? What did you

identify as his or her Core Assets in the Core Assets Survey? What are you doing to help your child develop those assets and strengths?

12. The book emphasizes that children are born with the potential for empathy, but unless it is purposely nurtured it will remain dormant. In fact, studies show that empathy in teens has decreased 40 percent in thirty years. What outside factors are hindering the development of this second Character Strength? What are you doing to enhance empathy in your child? What could you do to enhance this critical trait even more?

13. What are some of the sayings, proverbs, or experiences you recall from your childhood that helped you define your values? How are you passing on your moral beliefs to your child to help her develop integrity? What have you done with your child recently to reinforce your moral beliefs so she sees herself as a moral being?

14. How was discipline handled in your family as you were growing up? How did it affect your integrity or self-control? What is the most common method you use to discipline your child? How effective is it in enhancing her knowledge of right and wrong and willingness to adhere to those values?

15. Research shows that self-control is a better predictor of adult wealth, health, and happiness than grades or IQ. Do you agree or disagree and why? Are today's children being raised to have self-control? Are you noticing a change in children's (and adults') ability to regulate their self-control? If so, to what do you attribute the increase? How well do your children manage emotions? The book describes several

approaches (like mindfulness, yoga, meditation, and stress management) to nurture children's self-control. Do any interest you? Are there ways you might join other parents (playgroups, scouting, playdates) to teach stress management and self-control practices to your children together?

16. The chapter on perseverance stresses the need for parents to praise their children for their effort, not the grade or end product. What type of praise do you typically give your child? Do you think it helps to instill a growth mind-set? After reading Carol Dweck's research on the power mind-set has on grit, did you consider changing how you praise or help your child handle mistakes or failures? If so, how?

17. How important is it to you to have an optimistic child? What impact do you think events such as the pandemic, racial injustice, climate change, or school shootings have on children's views? Do you think it's harder to raise a child with hope and optimism about the world? What are ways that you and your community could help children see the "good" in their world?

18. What would you like your greatest legacy to be for your child? What will you do to ensure that your child attains that legacy?

How to Contact Dr. Michele Borba

Here's how to connect with Michele to give children the Character Advantage in your home, school, or community to help children thrive.

- To watch videos of Michele's latest talks and media appearances and to read her blog, where she discusses the latest in cultivating the seven Character Strengths of thrivers, visit her website: www.micheleborba.com or subscribe to her YouTube channel at Dr. Michele Borba.
- Bring Michele as a guest speaker to your school, conference, or company event and hear her practical, evidence-based ways to help kids thrive. Learn more at www.micheleborba.com or contact the American Program Bureau to invite Michele to speak to your parents, teachers, students, or community: https://www.apbspeakers.com/speaker/michele-borba/ or contact her speaking agent, Laura Obermann, lobermann@apbspeakers.com.

- Follow Michele's musings and photo posts about character building, and her visits to schools across the United States and around the world on Twitter: www.twitter.com/micheleborba.
- Join Michele to chat with other parents and educators about thriving-building strategies: Instagram: @drmicheleborba, Facebook: www.facebook.com/drmicheleborba or LinkedIn: Dr. Michele Borba.
- Contact Michele to arrange a virtual book club meeting via Skype or to contact her directly: http://micheleborba.com.